A verit   D1337591   y and practice of the Lord's Supper   ch will be of interest to the entire church. Maclean's handling of the subject is comprehensive and sure-footed, delving into practical areas of frequency and observance as much as the theological principles which underpin the Communion Service. A timely and important book that will aid in the rediscovery of importance and function of the sacrament of the Lord's Supper in the life of the church.

Derek W. H. Thomas,
Reformed Theological Seminary,
Jackson, Mississippi

Few things are more precious in the ordinary life and experience of the church than the sacramental meal instituted by Christ. Yet few things are more poorly understood and appreciated by his people. Round the Lord's Table we not only meet with Christ and hear his voice – which is true on every occasion his people gather in his name – but we also commune with him. In the language of the Book of Common Prayer: here his people 'feed upon him by faith in their hearts with thanksgiving.'

Malcolm Maclean has done the church of the 21st Century an enormous service by providing a resource that opens up the meaning of the Supper so helpfully. He not only unpacks its significance as he explores its theology, but by looking at the past he also makes us think again about the practicalities of how it should be celebrated. All who long to benefit more fully from the Lord's Supper will do well to read these pages.

Mark Johnston,
Grove Chapel, London

Malcolm Maclean's study of the biblical basis, historical development and practical administration of the Lord's Supper in our churches is a rich blend of scholarly analysis and pastoral insight. The question of what Jesus is doing in the Lord's Supper rather than what we are doing challenges the subjectivism that drives much of our practice, and restores a much needed emphasis on the Supper as a means of grace. This study is highly recommended.

Iain D. Campbell,
Free Church of Scotland,
Back, Isle of Lewis

The Lord's Supper

Malcolm Maclean

MENTOR

Malcolm Maclean is a minister of the Free Church of Scotland. Prior to studying for the ministry he was Managing Editor of Christian Focus Publications.

Copyright © Malcolm Maclean 2009

ISBN 978-1-84500-428-1

Published in 2009 in the
Mentor Imprint
by
Christian Focus Publications, Geanies House,
Fearn, Ross-shire, IV20 1TW, Scotland.

www.christianfocus.com

Cover design by Alister MacInnes
(www.moose77.com)

Printed and bound by
Bell & Bain, Glasgow

Contents

To
Katie

Foreword

It is my pleasure to write this foreword for my long-time friend, Malcolm Maclean, both out of high esteem for him and his ministry, and also out of excitement over this much-needed volume on the meaning and practice of the Lord's Supper.

Over my many years as a theology professor, I have longed for a clearly written volume of modest size on the subject of the Lord's Supper. My desires have been that it would start off with fair-minded Biblical exegesis of crucial passages; that it would look honestly (while avoiding bitterness or exaggeration) at the different (and competing) understandings of the presence of Christ in the Lord's Supper among the major Christian traditions; and that finally it would state attractively, but humbly (with awareness of conceptual limitations of any viewpoint), the insights of John Calvin on the spiritual presence of Christ in the Lord's Supper.

I have wished for something like this, not only as a professor, but also as an ordinary church-goer. For at times, I am disappointed at being told at communion services what is wrong with the non-Presbyterian views, and then there is a 'full stop' before the elements are passed out. I wonder, do these ministers have no idea what Scripture actually teaches about how the risen Christ is using the Lord's Supper to strengthen the bonds of union with himself? I will be surprised if Malcolm Maclean's new book does not greatly help them get beyond the mere negative critique of defective views, into something beautifully positive and full of life for the congregation of believers, as well as seekers.

All of these long-desired things, I have – to my great pleasure and gratitude – been given in this work of Malcolm Maclean. I normally do not like preparing forewords to books. But this one was an exception: I could barely put it down! While it is fairly and soberly written with academic care, somehow it is beautifully and intriguingly written, so that it keeps you wanting more, and will simply not let you go until you have finished it.

Malcolm Maclean adds something in addition to the points I had for years desired in a book on communion, and I am glad he did so. He 'earths' the theology and practice of the sacramental life that is based upon faith in the presence of Christ in the Lord's Supper, in the experience of the Reformed Churches in Scotland for the last 500 years. His account of sacramental Calvinism in Scotland does not pass through rose-tinted glasses. It combines appreciation with necessary, realistic critique. But somehow, it all comes alive, and leaves one hopeful for the future of local churches, who are determined to minister fruitfully Word and sacrament in their own generation and culture.

This book will become a required text in the course I teach each year on 'Church and Sacraments' at Reformed Theological Seminary in Charlotte.

Douglas F. Kelly
Professor of Systematic Theology
Reformed Theological Seminary,
Charlotte, North Carolina, USA.

Preface

This book is an expression of my search for my spiritual roots, or at least an important aspect of them – the Lord's Supper, and of the benefits I should be receiving from it. I can still recall the sense of reverence for God and the awareness of his presence that characterised the occasions when the Lord's Supper was held in the congregation that my parents attended when I was young. The congregation was a Protestant, Presbyterian and evangelical one, it met in Inverness in the Scottish Highlands, and its method of celebrating the Lord's Supper was in line with the traditional practices associated with Scottish Highland communion seasons. These practices were an expression of the spirituality and discipleship that had been found in Scottish Highland Christianity for over three centuries. The main features of the communion season, in addition to the Supper itself, were the centrality of the preaching of the Bible and the warmth of the fellowship that was displayed among the people.

Inevitably, with the passing of years, I became aware that other evangelical Christian groups had different ways of expressing their spirituality as far as the Lord's Supper was concerned. Although I was brought up within a Presbyterian church, I became a Christian through the witness of believers who belonged to a Christian Brethren Assembly, and eventually became a member of their fellowship. Immediately I was aware of several differences between their practices and what I had seen in my parents' church, and one of the striking differences was the way in which the Breaking of Bread service happened. It was held weekly, was not led by a clergyman, and did not involve a sermon (although there were several devotional comments made on biblical passages by a number of individuals). Nevertheless, the sense of reverence and awareness of God's presence was as real there as it had been in the congregation in which I grew up.

I am now a pastor in a Free Church of Scotland congregation

in the Scottish Highlands. One of my pastoral duties is the administration of the Lord's Supper, both in my own congregation and in other congregations. Over the years, I had wanted to understand, in some measure, what takes place at the Lord's Supper and this desire continues to increase as I serve Christ in full-time Christian work. The opportunity arose to study the topic, which I did in three areas: the Lord's Supper in the New Testament; the Lord's Supper in Scottish Reformed Theology as it affected my denominational background; and the Lord's Supper in my current experience. The results of the study are presented in this book. I am grateful for the guidance and insights that I received from Dr. Derek Thomas of Reformed Theological Seminary, Jackson, Mississippi, and from Rev. Hector Morrison of the Highland Theological College, Dingwall, Scotland.

I am also grateful to my friend, Professor Douglas F. Kelly, for his generous foreword, and to another friend, Dr. Iain D. Campbell, for reading the manuscript and making helpful observations.

I am very thankful for my spiritual roots and for the heritage I have received. If there is one feature of the Lord's Supper that has been written on my heart as a result of this study it is that we should be more focussed on what the Lord Jesus, as the Head of his church, is doing at each celebration of the Lord's Supper. I suspect that many believers, including myself, are more concerned with what *we* are doing. Obviously, our state of heart is very important, but sometimes we can be so occupied with ourselves that we fail to observe the activities of Jesus. Thankfully, his activities are not dependant on our observation.

It will become clear that the person to whom I am most indebted regarding my understanding of the Lord's Supper is John Calvin. If this book encourages any to read what that profound and humble theologian wrote on this subject, then its publication will be worthwhile.

This book is dedicated to my dear wife, Katie, who has shared so much of my spiritual journey.

Malcolm Maclean
September, 2008

The Lord's Supper
in the New Testament

1

The Lord's Supper in the Gospels

An account of the origin of the Lord's Supper is found in each of the Synoptic Gospels (Matthew, Mark and Luke). Each account places the event during the Passover period of the last year of Christ's life on earth, in the same week as his death. The occasion, but not the actual institution of the Supper, is referred to in the Gospel of John (13:1).

Some scholars argue that Jesus' teaching in John 6:52-56, concerning eating his flesh and drinking his blood, is a reference to the Lord's Supper.[1] The passage has to do with Jesus presenting himself as the true bread as against the manna that God gave to the Israelites as they travelled from Egypt to Canaan. Jesus interpreted the true bread as both a reference to him as coming from God (vv. 33, 50) and as giving himself for the world (v. 51), and the eating of this bread along with the drinking of his blood is essential for possessing eternal life (vv. 51-53). The main argument for this view is the similarity of language used by Jesus in that incident and in his later inauguration of the Lord's Supper.

Leon Morris outlines four arguments against such an interpretation.[2] First, Jesus is speaking to a mixed audience that includes opponents and lukewarm disciples; second, the words in John 6 are strong, pointing to the necessity of eating Christ's flesh and drinking his blood in order to receive salvation, and it is impossible to think that Jesus regarded partaking in the Lord's Supper as being the way of salvation; third, the eating and the drinking are the consequences[3] of believing in Christ; fourth, the metaphor of eating and drinking was common among the Jews, pointing to a taking within one's innermost being. These arguments would indicate that Jesus was not predicting the Lord's Supper nor was John using the incident as a kind of hidden allusion to the Lord's Supper.

If the eating and drinking here do not refer to the Lord's Supper, to what do they refer? A suitable answer is that they refer to spiritual interaction with Christ. Ridderbos points out that the passage itself indicates that Jesus meant a mutual 'remaining in' one another between himself and his people. The eating and drinking are a repeated activity of faith by Christ's people, a lasting fellowship between Christ and those who believe in him – 'on their part as a continual centering on him who gave himself for them, on his part as his indwelling in them with all his gifts and power'.[4]

While the interpretations of Morris and Ridderbos are valid, it does not mean that there is not a connection between the incident in John 6 and the inauguration of the Lord's Supper. Guthrie comments that 'The words must have posed a riddle to all who heard them, until the twelve sat with Jesus in the upper room. It would have been strange indeed if Jesus had provided no previous preparation for the meaning of the words of institution.'[5]

There is disagreement also as to whether or not the meal during which the Supper originated was the Passover meal. For example, Anderson writes that

> there is nothing in the account of the Passover itself that demands it be understood as a Passover meal ([Mark] 14:17-25).... Certain features are consistent with a Passover meal [the hymn at the end, the late hour of the night, the reclining posture of the guests, the use of wine].... But these features, with the probable exception of the hymn-singing which in fact stands outside of the report of the Supper, are not inconsistent with a specially solemn religious fellowship (*haburah*) meal, which could take place at any time. Moreover there is no mention of the lamb that figured very prominently in the Passover ritual, nor of the bitter herbs nor of the traditional lengthy explanation of the meaning of the bread and the lamb that preceded the serving of the meal in the Jewish context, nor of the first part of the Hallel (Pss. 113-114) that was always recited.

Anderson mentions other difficulties with regard to the Supper as a Passover meal:

(1) if the Last Supper had been known to be a Passover, we might have expected the Church to celebrate the Eucharist only annually instead of weekly; (2) on the Synoptic dating it is hard to imagine (though the possibility is not excluded) the wholesale desecration of a sabbatical feast-day involved in the arrest in Gethsemane, trial, and execution of Jesus.[6]

Yet the three Synoptic accounts give the impression that it was a Passover meal, that the Supper took place on the evening after the day of unleavened bread (the Jewish liturgical day began with the evening).

The Gospel of John, however, suggests that Christ was arrested, tried, put to death and taken down from the cross before the Passover meal was held (John 18:28; 19:14). The timetable according to this interpretation would be as follows: The time when the two disciples prepared the meal was the afternoon of Thursday 13th Nisan. The day of unleavened bread was 14th Nisan, beginning at evening (Thursday evening and Friday), which was when the meal attended by Jesus and his disciples took place; later that evening he was arrested; the trials and execution occurred throughout the night and morning, with the crucifixion of Jesus occurring on the afternoon of 14th Nisan, at the same time as the Passover Lamb was slain. On the evening of 15th Nisan (Friday evening) the official Passover meal would have been held.[7]

Various suggestions are made regarding this situation. Redaction criticism suggests that John rewrote his account for a typological reason, to emphasise that Jesus was the true Paschal lamb. 'Yet it is remarkable that if the Evangelist had intended to highlight this typology of Jesus in the moment of his death, he does so only by means of two chronological allusions, without even hinting at their significance.'[8]

Another suggestion is the possibility of two calendars, with Jesus following an unofficial date used by the Pharisees and the Essenes, who held the Passover meal on the day previous to the official day kept by the temple authorities, the Sadducees. The synoptists followed the unofficial calendar and John the official calendar.[9] This suggestion requires that the lamb of the meal would have been slain separately from the official slaying.[10] It is possible that lamb was not on the menu at the Last Supper.[11] Motyer sees significance in this, suggesting that Jesus arranged this in order to identify himself as the true Lamb.[12] Stanton, in commenting on the lack of mention of a lamb, says: 'it can be claimed that the earliest Christians who transmitted the accounts of the last meal were primarily interested in the words of Jesus over the bread and the cup; hence reference to the Passover lamb may have dropped out of the tradition concerning the meal itself and been retained only in the accounts of the preparations for the meal.'[13] No evidence has been discovered that indicates there were two different days for slaying the lambs (one for the Pharisees, the other for the Sadducees). The Gospels continually present Jesus as keeping the Jewish feasts according to the Temple schedule, with the Gospel of John, which is supposed to suggest that Jesus used a different calendar, detailing that Jesus kept the Feasts of Passover (2:13) and Tabernacles (2:7), as well as the Feast of Dedication (10:22), although the last of these was not authorised in the Old Testament.

A third suggestion is that it was unlikely for the Jews to have wanted to execute a person on the feast day. However, Hamilton mentions that the Mishnah teaches that a rebellious teacher should be put to death on a feast day, and that the execution should be delayed until the feast if he was condemned prior to it.[14]

It is possible, however, to fit John's details into the Synoptic account, and to interpret the evidence as indicating that Jesus arranged for the usual Passover meal to be held. These theories can be elaborate, but the nature of the difficulty requires them to be. Carson provides such an explanation, in which the difficult references in John's Gospel are explained.

John 18:28: 'Then the Jews led Jesus from Caiaphas to the palace of the Roman governor. By now it was early morning, and to avoid ceremonial uncleanness the Jews did not enter the palace; they wanted to be able to eat the Passover.' Carson suggests that their desire 'to eat the Passover' is not just a reference to the

Passover meal, but to the continuing feast.[15]

John 19:13-14: 'When Pilate heard this, he brought Jesus out and sat down on the judge's seat at a place known as the Stone Pavement (which in Aramaic is Gabbatha). It was the day of Preparation of Passover Week, about the sixth hour. "Here is your king," Pilate said to the Jews.' Carson notes that 'There is strong evidence to suggest that *paraskeuē* ("Preparation Day") had already become a technical name for Friday, since Friday was normally the Day on which one prepared for the Sabbath (Saturday); and we have no evidence that the term was used in the evangelist's time to refer to the eve of any festal day other than the Sabbath.... Thus John 19:14 most probably means "Friday in Passover Week".'[16]

John 19:31: 'Now it was the day of Preparation, and the next day was to be a special Sabbath.' According to Carson, the 'next day' does not refer to the day of the Passover meal. The weekly Sabbath was special that week 'not only because it fell during the Passover Feast, but because on the second paschal day, in this case a Sabbath (Saturday), the very important sheaf offering fell.'[17]

Therefore, it is possible to harmonise the details of the Synoptics and of John and recognize that the Last Supper was inaugurated by Jesus during the regular Passover meal. The timetable is this:

Thursday afternoon	14 Nisan	two disciples prepare for the Passover
Thursday evening	15 Nisan	Jesus and his disciples eat the Passover
Thursday evening	15 Nisan	Jesus arrested, tried
Friday	15 Nisan	Jesus crucified

The Passover could not be eaten until sunset, and the meal had to be taken within the city limits of Jerusalem, which explains why Jesus remained in the city instead of going out to Bethany as he had on the previous evenings.

The four accounts of the Supper (Matthew, Mark, Luke and Paul) differ slightly, yet because Matthew and Mark are so similar it is possible to regard the four accounts as three. Marshall's comment is wise: 'It must be emphasised that there is no good reason for supposing that any one of the three versions must be necessarily closer to the original form of the account than any of the others.'[18] Carson also asks why we must limit ourselves to one account when there were at least eleven eyewitnesses.[19]

According to Stanton, the Passover meal contained four parts:

1. The Preliminary Course:
Blessing (*Kiddush*) spoken over the first cup of wine
Dish of green herbs, bitter herbs, and fruit sauce
Serving of the meal and mixing of the second cup of wine

2. The Passover Liturgy
The Passover narrative (*haggadah*, based on Exodus 12), was recited by the head of the household, in response to the youngest son's question, 'Why is this night different from all other nights?'
Drinking of the second cup of wine
Singing of Psalm 113

3. The Main Meal:
Grace spoken over the unleavened bread, bitter herbs (Exodus 12:8)
Meal of lamb, unleavened bread, bitter herbs
Grace over the third cup of wine

4. Conclusion:
Singing of Psalms 114—118 (the great *hallel*)
Praise over the fourth cup of wine.[20]

Taking the Synoptic accounts together we can summarise the significance of the words and actions by Jesus at this meal. This occasion had been earnestly desired by Jesus (Luke 22:15). If the meal followed a Passover meal pattern, Jesus began the meal with the cup that followed the prayer of blessing (Luke 22:17-18). The next detail mentioned is the meal; usually it involved eating unleavened bread and lamb. The Synoptics mention the bread and how Jesus took it, gave thanks, broke it, passed it to his disciples and told them this action was going to be repeated as an act of remembrance of him by them. The third action of Jesus was to take a cup (the third cup of the ritual) and refer to its contents as symbolic of his blood that would be poured out on behalf of his disciples and would ratify the new covenant. After the meal, they sang a psalm (Matt. 26:30; Mark 14:26), probably from the great Hallel (Psalms 114–118) which were usually sung at this stage in the Passover. Concerning the bread, Jesus said, 'This is my body.' His words were accompanied by his action of breaking the bread and handing it to his disciples to eat. The *haggadah* did include explanations of the various parts of the meal, but it was unusual for the host to speak during the distribution of the bread and the wine.[21] Jesus' action and words in this regard are significant, because they suggest he was teaching that what was going to be recalled was not the deliverance from Egypt but his voluntary sacrifice on their behalf. His words and actions indicate that he intended bread and a cup of wine to be means of future communal remembrance of his voluntary offering of his body and blood.

The significance of the instruction, 'remember'
The remembrance mentioned by Jesus is one that acknowledges his authority to institute a meal, the celebration of which was binding on his followers. It is evident that the early church obeyed this requirement – we have a record of it being done in Troas (Acts 20:7) and in Corinth (1 Cor. 11:17-34) as well as in Jerusalem (Acts 2:42) – which indicates that there was submission on the part of Christians concerning the practice.

When Jesus instructed his disciples to remember him by means of the Lord's Supper he was not asking them to shut their eyes and engage in mental imagination in order to recall his death (which is a common response today at the Lord's Table). Rather he asked them to use the symbols of bread and wine as signs pointing to his death. In doing so, he arranged for the Lord's Supper to be a visual, as well as a verbal, reminder[22] in a way similar to how the Passover was a visible reminder to Israelites. The Passover had unleavened bread, a roast lamb and bitter herbs, as well as other elements. The Lord's Supper has bread and wine. The Lord's Supper is not only about eating the bread and drinking the wine; it also involves watching the breaking of the bread and the pouring out of the wine into the cup.[23]

Eugene Merrill has pointed out that remembering was a crucial feature of Old Testament worship. Israel remembered the activities of God as Creator (the Sabbath requirement) and Redeemer (the Passover institution). Merrill notes in particular the response of the exiles in Babylon, as recorded in Psalm 137:

> A poignant and powerful illustration of the centrality of memory to proper worship is the plight of the exilic community as related in Psalm 137. There in Babylon, the poet says, "we sat and wept when we remembered Zion" (v. 1). This is more than homesickness, for when the captors request the Jews to sing songs of Zion, they reply that this cannot be done outside the sacred precincts (v. 4). Then the psalmist, reflecting on the need to remember the holy city and its temple as the locus of community worship, cries out in imprecation.... ("if I forget you, Jerusalem, may my right [hand] forget"; v. 5). And he goes on to say, "may my tongue cling to my palate if I do not remember you".... Praise is impossible when Jerusalem and all it signifies is forgotten. This forgetting is more than mental lapse. It is failing to recognize the significance of special times and places for legitimate worship (v. 6).[24]

When Jesus gave the requirement to his disciples that memory be involved in the Lord's Supper, he was giving it with the meaning as understood in the worship of Israel in the past. Merrill further comments on use of the memory in New Testament worship:

> Remembrance as a constituent of NT worship is, not surprisingly, associated with (and limited to) the Lord's Supper, for the Lord's Supper was instituted as a New Covenant expression of the Passover-Unleavened Bread ceremony of the OT (Luke 22:7–8; cf. Matt 26:17–19; Mark 14:12–15). Just as that festival was to be celebrated as a memorial to the exodus redemption (Exod 13:14–16), so the Lord's Supper was to be a perpetual reminder of the new and greater exodus by which all sinners could find release from sin's bondage and deliverance into new and everlasting life.
>
> At its inauguration Jesus, having taken the bread and wine and blessed them, said, "This is my body given for you; do this in

remembrance of me" (Luke 22:19). The word translated "remembrance" (*anamnēsis*) is regularly used in LXX to render Hebrew *'azkārä*, a nominal from *zkr*, "remember." The Hebrew vocable occurs only seven times, all but once in Leviticus (2:2, 9, 16; 5:12; 6:8 [15]; 24:7; cf. Num 5:26). The NIV consistently translates it "memorial portion," the idea being that the offerings so described drew attention to Yahweh, that is, brought him and his saving works to mind (cf. *TDOT* 4:80).

This is at least the point in the Lord's Supper observation—it is to be done in his remembrance. Paul reinforces this interpretation in 1 Corinthians, where he presents the authoritative theological interpretation of the Eucharist. Both the eating of the bread and drinking of the cup are in remembrance (*anamnēsis*) of Christ (1 Cor. 11:24, 25). Whenever these are done properly, Paul says, "you proclaim the Lord's death until he comes" (v. 26). The symbolism or reenactment of the death of our Lord is a proclamation without words of the fundamental work of human redemption. It is ritual and drama that eloquently calls to mind the meaning of the gospel.[25]

Jesus and the new covenant

In each record of the institution of the Supper, reference is made to the covenant (Matt. 26:7-8; Mark 14:24; Luke 22:20; 1 Cor. 11:25). The Passover was connected to the old covenant given through Moses by God, when Moses ratified the covenant by the sprinkling of the blood of a sacrificed animal (Exod. 24:8). Jeremiah had predicted that the old covenant would be replaced by a new covenant (Jer. 31:31-34) in which three salvation benefits would be given. Firstly, God's laws would be written on the minds and hearts of believers; secondly, all believers would know God by having a personal relationship with him; and thirdly God would forgive them their sins. Kevan notes that Jeremiah's prophecy is incomplete, in that he does not mention the ratifying blood which Jesus himself mentioned.[26] Because of his ratification, the Lord's Supper is a source of assurance to Christians that the blessings predicted by Jeremiah will continue to be given to them.

The cup was a sign of Jesus' shed blood that would ratify the new covenant and result in forgiveness of sins for those in this covenant. Other covenants that God made with his people had signs reminding them of his commitment to them: while the rainbow was primarily a sign for God to remember his promise, it was also a sign to Noah that God was keeping his promise (Gen. 9:12-17); Abraham had the sign of circumcision; the Israelites had the details of the Passover and other feasts. In a similar way, Christians have the symbols of bread and wine to remind them of God's commitment to them in Christ.

Stibbs suggests that Jesus' action in separating the taking of the bread from the taking of the cup pointed to the same feature as did the pieces of a slain animal that were divided during the making of a covenant – it pointed to the violent death of the covenant maker.[27] What believers receive, when taking the bread and the wine, are separate pledges of the same covenant. They are pledges of each believer's security, even at those occasions when they are guilty of backsliding. The failures of a particular believer do not remove him or her from Christ, because he suffered their penalty.

Those who were to receive the consequences of Christ's covenant action are described as 'the many'. In Matthew 26:28, 'for many' is the translation of *peri pollōn*; in Mark 14:24 'for many' is the translation of *huper pollōn*; and Luke 22:19-20, 'for you' is the translation of *huper humōn*. Since it is likely that Jesus spoke in Aramaic, the appearance of two Greek prepositions (*peri* and *huper*) is accounted for by variety of translation. The idea conveyed is that Jesus was giving himself as the representative of others, a representation that would be understood as similar to that of the Passover lamb whose death protected the Israelites from divine judgment. But who are 'the many'?

It is possible that Jesus had in mind Isaiah's language concerning the death of the Servant of the Lord as recorded in Isaiah 53, particularly verse 12.[28] In Isaiah 53:11-12, the prophet predicts that the Servant will justify the many and make intercession for the many, with both these benefits linked to his bearing their iniquities and sins. It seems clear that 'the many' are the people of

God because it is only believers who can be described as justified. Johnston argues from this point that 'the many' is limited to the elect and does not include every person.[29] Whether or not the passage is an evidence of a particular atonement rather than a universal one, the benefits of Christ's giving is limited to those who believe in him, who have 'experienced the remission of their sins in and through Jesus' sacrifice and so are enabled to participate in the salvation provided under the new covenant'.[30]

The disciples' eating of the bread and drinking from the cup was also symbolic of their communal involvement in the benefits coming from the death of Christ. Jesus' actions raised for his disciples the question of their *identity*. This is seen in two ways.

Firstly, the Passover was a time of remembrance of God's rescuing Israel as a nation from Egypt; Jesus, in telling his disciples to remember him, was requiring that they now get their identity from being his people, and no longer as the descendants of those liberated from Egypt. Instead of recalling what had happened on the night of the Exodus they were to recall what had happened to Jesus when he laid down his life.

Secondly, Jesus' celebrating his meal with his followers rather than with his family points to a new relationship. The Passover was usually a family occasion, but here the disciples are reminded that their connection to Jesus has priority over earthly relationships.

Furthermore, there is a solemn and serious aspect to joining with Jesus in the newly inaugurated ritual. 'The wine contained in the cup represents the blood which is the seal of the covenant. The statement here suggests that to drink the cup is to enter into the covenant established in the blood of Christ. This indicates a seriousness in the participation in the Lord's Supper that is rarely stressed. To partake is to recognize that one is professing a covenantal relationship with God.'[31]

Jesus' actions also raised for his disciples a further dimension as to the question of their *loyalty*. In a real sense, they had now come to the dividing line between their previous loyalties and their future dedication. Up until then it had been possible for them to be disciples of Jesus and still remain within the Jewish system; indeed Jesus himself had encouraged such participation. But here was a new test. Right at the onset of the Passover, probably the meal that indicated most clearly why they were Israelites called to serve God, Jesus initiated a replacement meal that would take priority over their connection to Israel.

The contexts in which the Gospels' authors locate the original Lord's Supper are useful for locating suitable themes that sermons on the Supper can address. Each of the Synoptics refers to Judas' betrayal of Jesus, Peter's denial of Jesus, and Jesus' prediction that all of his disciples would be scattered. Luke also informs his readers that the conversation in which the disciples were engrossed was that of leadership, not the leadership of Jesus, but their desire for prominence in the new kingdom they imagined was about to come into being (Luke 22:24-30). These negative attitudes and practices can be addressed at the Supper: it is not a place for those who apostatise from the faith but it is the place for believers even though they may be cowardly and self-centred. Remembrance of and fellowship with the Saviour at the Supper strengthens believers to be true to Christ and informs them that service of Christ should be their ambition.

The institution of the Supper by Jesus stresses several matters that should be noted:

- The various actions of the Lord's Supper point to Jesus, particularly to his death. While it is the disciples who break the bread and drink the cup, they do these actions as symbolic of his voluntary death. Their action could also point to their responsibility in the sense of causing Jesus to have to die for their sins.

- The Lord's Supper depicts a substitutionary death by Jesus, in which he used language reminiscent of the Suffering Servant described in Isaiah 53.

- The Lord's Supper is a reminder of the new and permanent relationship believers have with God through the inauguration of the prophesied new covenant.

- The Lord's Supper is a memorial. This is clear from Jesus' command to his disciples that they remember him.

- The Lord's Supper is a communal act. It is not an action for individuals to engage in so as to have fellowship with Jesus, as Bible reading or prayer can be. The Supper stresses the togetherness of those who are Christ's disciples. Does this mean that a housegroup of believers or Christians living in the same street should have celebrations of the Lord's Supper? The Gospel accounts don't answer this question, but, as I will argue in the next section, the example of the church in Jerusalem in Acts 2 could indicate that it is appropriate for a large community of believers to have celebrations of the Lord's Supper at which only a proportion of the believers are present.

- The Lord's Supper has a future aspect to it. This is brought out by Jesus' statement that the kingdom of God is yet to come. As believers look back and remember Jesus through the symbols of bread and cup, they look ahead to what is also signified, the marriage supper of the Lamb (Rev. 19:9).

- The Lord's Supper is a simple ritual, in that the occasion of its inauguration did not involve a great number or detail of rituals.

- There was a time gap between the eating of the bread and the drinking of the cup.

- The Lord's Supper is associated with a meal (either the Passover or another meal) but distinct from it.

Chapter 2

The Lord's Supper in Acts

It is possible to see a reference to the Lord's Supper in Acts 2:42, where Luke gives a fourfold description of the practices of the church in Jerusalem: apostles' doctrine, fellowship, breaking of bread and prayers, with 'breaking of bread' referring to the Lord's Supper. The other use of the term 'breaking of bread' is in Acts 20, where it is a clear reference to an event that involved the Lord's Supper.

Some dispute that the phrase 'breaking of bread' refers to the Lord's Supper. For example, James Dunn comments that the term may indicate shared meals 'presumably in continuance in some degree at least of the meals characteristic of Jesus' earlier ministry',[1] although he allows that on some occasions the meal would have included a shared commemoration of the Lord's Supper.

Witherington, however, notes that the 'phrase "the breaking of bread" could refer to an ordinary meal, especially in view of the fact that this was the act which opened a Jewish meal, though the phrase was not a technical term in Judaism for such a meal.' Yet 'texts like Acts 2:42, 46 and 20:7, 11 all suggest that this sort of breaking of bread was part of an act of worship that involved eating, praying, teaching, and singing in homes, to mention but a few elements of the service. On the whole, then, the phrase "the breaking of bread" seems to be a primitive way of alluding to the Lord's Supper, though it cannot be ruled out that the reference is to an ordinary meal.'[2]

Kistemaker admits that the question as to whether the breaking of bread was a communion service or an ordinary meal is difficult to answer, but argues that the context, where the breaking of bread appears within a sequence of teaching, fellowship and prayers of a worship service, points to it being an early description of Holy Communion.[3] He also refers to Alford's remark that the interpretation of it as referring to the 'celebration of the Lord's Supper has been, both in ancient and modern times, the prevalent one'.

Marshall agrees that Acts 2:42 records 'the four elements which characterised a Christian gathering in the early church', which points to 'breaking of bread' being an early Palestinian name for the Lord's Supper.[4]

The context in Acts 2 indicates that the 'breaking of bread' occurred in private homes rather than in the temple courts (2:46). (Teaching and prayer would have taken place in the temple area[5] where there were courtyards large enough to accommodate the large number of disciples.) This passage in Acts 2 suggests several possibilities:

- The reference in 2:42, where breaking of bread is linked with teaching, fellowship and prayers, suggests the breaking of bread was an act with religious connotations. It seems to be a reference to celebrations of the Lord's Supper.

- The use of private homes for the breaking of bread points to the Lord's Supper being part of a communal meal in which the family fed guests. Its being part of a communal meal is a continuation of the original occasion when the Supper was instituted by Jesus.

- The celebration of the Lord's Supper in this way points to participation by those who were not official leaders of the church. While it is likely that the apostles would lead the occasion in the home in which they were located, they could not be in every home. It is plausible to argue that the head of the house may have led the event in some way. Acts 2:42 stresses what the converts did more than what the apostles did.

- It could indicate hospitality shown by local believers to converts who had been visiting Jerusalem for the feasts. It is reasonable to assume that some of those converted on the Day of Pentecost stayed on for a few weeks in order to learn from the apostles before returning home.

• These occasions were marked by the joy and gladness of the Christians.

The other reference in Acts to the breaking of bread is in Acts 20:6-12. Paul and his companions were in Troas and attended the communal worship of the Christians there. This occasion gives further insight into how the early church worshipped.

• The first day of the week is mentioned as the day when they gathered. This day was chosen no doubt because it was the day on which Jesus rose from the dead. A further reason may have been their desire to distinguish between the Christian gathering and the Jewish gatherings that met on the seventh day of the week in synagogues.

• The church in Troas met in the evening. Evening was suitable, for it allowed most of the members, who were servants or slaves, to meet after their day's work was over.[6]

• The meeting was held in a private house.

• The breaking of bread was preceded by teaching from Paul. Luke does not indicate at what time Paul began to teach, but he was still teaching at midnight. The impression given is that the meeting lasted several hours. This points to a connection between the preached word and the celebration of the Supper.

• Local leaders allowed him to preach, no doubt because he was an apostle. He was also a visiting teacher and probably the church followed the custom of the synagogue in inviting visiting teachers to address the gathering.

• In Troas, 'the breaking of bread was probably a fellowship meal in the course of which the Eucharist was celebrated.'[7]

29

- The preaching was not a monologue. Luke uses the term *dialegomai*, which suggests interaction, perhaps in the form of questions and answers.[8]

- After the Supper was taken, Paul talked informally with the congregation, having fellowship with them, probably over a meal.[9]

- The only item mentioned in Acts 2:42 that is not mentioned in Acts 20:6-12 is prayer. It is certain, however, that prayer would have been part of the worship.

The two accounts of the Lord's Supper in Acts indicate similarities and differences in the way the Supper was celebrated. Similarities include the need for teaching to accompany the Supper and that the Supper was usually part of a meal. Differences include frequency of meeting and whether all Christians in one locality should meet together to participate. While this points to the necessity of certain elements and flexibility and innovation regarding others, it also indicates that the situation in Acts 2 belonged to an unusual situation connected to the onset of the Christian church when the followers of Jesus were found mainly in Jerusalem and includes practices, such as taking the Lord's Supper during household meals, that were not to be expected once local congregations had developed.

Chapter 3

The Lord's Supper in the Epistles

Outside the writings of Paul, there are not many references to the Lord's Supper in the epistles. Jude refers to love feasts, which presumably included the Lord's Supper, in connection with false teachers (Jude 12). There may be a reference to the love feast or to the Supper in Revelation 3:20: 'Behold, I stand at the door and knock. If anyone hears my voice and opens the door, I will come in to him and eat with him, and he with me.' It is not clear that the risen Christ does have the Lord's Supper in mind; although he is addressing a church, his focus in the verse seems to be on an individual rather than a corporate meal.

What is not often realised is that Paul's description in 1 Corinthians 11 of the Lord's Supper is the oldest account of its institution, since 1 Corinthians predated the earliest Gospel by about a decade.[1] First Corinthians is also the only letter in the Pauline correspondence that refers to the Lord's Supper. Nevertheless, it is likely that Paul gave instructions concerning the Supper in each of the churches founded by him. His letters to specific churches are responses to problems in local situations, and the absence of reference to the Lord's Supper in his other letters is evidence that perhaps abuse of the Supper did not occur in the other churches to which he wrote. Paul's two references to the Supper in 1 Corinthians 10 and 11 indicate that participation in the Supper has consequences regarding involvement in certain non-Christian social activities and in how rich and poor Christians behave towards each another.

1 Corinthians 10
In this chapter Paul responds to the practice of some Christians in Corinth attending meals connected to pagan temple worship.

He begins by mentioning the divine judgment that fell on the Israelites in the desert after they participated in pagan feasts, emphasising his point by noting that the Israelites had previously undergone a baptism into Moses and shared in divinely provided food and drink. The parallel between the Israelites and the Corinthians is obvious: the latter had been baptised into Christ and had been given spiritual food and drink in the Lord's Supper, but because of their involvement with pagan religious meals they were in danger of divine judgment. Possibly the Corinthians imagined that baptism and the Lord's Supper had magical qualities of protection that secured them from any dangers arising from attendance at the pagan temples.[2]

Concerning the dangerous situation facing the Corinthian believers, and also believers living in other locations near to pagan temples, Ralph Martin has written:

> The custom of taking a meal in a shrine dedicated to a cult deity, or of receiving wine which had been formally offered as a libation to a cult god, was a very popular one in the ancient Greco-Roman world. An Oxyrhynchus papyrus dated in the second century AD may be cited as a striking parallel to such an invitation as we have recorded in 1 Corinthians x, 27.... 'Chaeremon invites you to dinner at the table of our lord Serapis (the cult god) in the Serapeum tomorrow the 15th at nine o'clock.' Such an invitation to a meal, whether in the temple or in a private house, would be commonplace in the social life of the city of Corinth. For converted men – and perhaps, at times more acutely, for converted women – there was a problem posed by this custom. Should a Christian join in these feasts (many of them, the Corinthian Church told Paul, were harmless – they were on a par with the lunch engagements of the modern business-man), or may a Christian housewife buy in the market meat which had been left over from the sacrifice?[3]

Paul makes it clear that sharing in these temple meals involved communion with the pagan gods (or the demonic powers behind these gods), which was similar, in a way, to the communion believers had with Christ at the Supper. Paul's response was that it was incompatible for a person who had fellowship with Christ also to have fellowship with the demons behind the worship of the false god. This passage indicates that there is a real fellowship between Christ and his people at the Supper. Taking the bread and drinking the cup are acts of communion with Christ (10:16). 'Paul assumed a similar spiritual effect also took place between the demons and the worshippers in the idols' temples, and he forbade participation in pagan ceremonies as a result.'[4]

Therefore, the Lord's Supper was a separating ordinance. It not only gave identity to who or what Christians were, but it also required that they not identify with a group that would compromise what they had in Christ.

1 Corinthians 11:17-34

This is the only occasion in the Bible where the meal is referred to as 'the Lord's Supper'. The expression can suggest a number of meanings, for example, 'the Supper belonging to the Lord,' 'the Supper hosted by the Lord,' 'the Supper which the Lord ordained,' 'the Supper at which the Lord's body and blood are shared.'[5] Paul's description of the practice in Corinth reveals that the Lord's Supper was connected to a meal. His description also reveals that the entire church, particularly the poorer members, did not share in this meal. But what did Paul say the purpose and the meaning of the Supper are?

The Lord's Supper is a *sacrificial* meal, not in the sense that the participators are offering a sacrifice, but in the sense that they, in eating and drinking the elements of the bread and wine, participate in the benefits that Christ gives to them because of his sacrifice.[6] This aspect of a sacrificial meal is evident from Paul's contrasting the Supper with the pagan sacrificial meals associated with the temples in Corinth (1 Cor. 10:21). A parallel connection is Jesus' relating the Supper to the Passover, which also involved a sacrificial meal.

The Lord's Supper is a *communal* meal. It is a meal that expresses the unity of the congregation. This emphasis is found in both of the 1 Corinthian passages, 10:14-22 and 11:18-34. In 1 Corinthians 10 Paul uses the bread not only as a symbol of Christ's physical body but also as a symbol of Christ's figurative body, the church. His argument is that the solidarity that the Supper brings to the unity of the congregation means it is not appropriate to engage in a meal associated with a false religion. Every believer is a partaker in the Lord's body, that is, the church, and cannot therefore belong to a group that is linked to an alternative religion.[7] The implications from this aspect of the communal meal are similar to those of the Supper as a sacrificial meal.

In 1 Corinthians 11 the emphasis is slightly different, although Paul does use the imagery of a body again. On this occasion he uses the imagery to argue for behaviour appropriate to those within the body, whereas in 1 Corinthians 10 it was behaviour towards those outside the body. Usually, in the early church, the Lord's Supper was part of a longer meal, the *agape*. In Corinth the wealthy believers were using this *agape* meal as an opportunity for gluttony and drunkenness; poor believers, some of whom would have been slaves, were deprived of a share in the *agape* and were being humiliated. Instead of indicating unity the meal in Corinth highlighted social diversity.[8] Paul's response was to instruct the wealthy believers to eat their normal menu at home, a response that also suggests that the *agape* was not essential for the Lord's Supper to take place. He regarded the selfish behaviour of the wealthier believers in this regard as a great evil, for in abusing the poor they were despising the church of God. It is evident that Paul would not tolerate any activity connected to the Lord's Supper that denied the visible unity of believers.

The meal is also a *proclamation* that says something to those looking on. Macleod notes that it is probable the early Christians did not sit in silence at the Supper. An account of what happened to Jesus was narrated, either from recollection or from written accounts. He also notes that Jesus gave instructions during the first Lord's Supper. It was this combination of ritual (taking the bread and wine) and Word (reading the accounts) that Paul referred to by 'proclaim'.[9] Fee comments that 'the verb "to proclaim" does not mean that the meal in itself is the proclamation, but that during the meal there is a verbal proclamation of Christ's death.'

He supports this by noting that on every other occasion of its use in the New Testament *kataggellete* means to preach Christ or the gospel.[10]

Alan Stibbs, while affirming that partaking of the bread and wine was essential to the proclaiming, also suggests that there was a verbal confession of faith by the participants. He thinks that each believer, when taking the bread, 'proclaimed the Christian significance of his participation', by saying words such as, 'I take and eat this in remembrance that Christ died for me, and I feed on Him in my heart by faith with thanksgiving,' and then said something similar regarding the cup.[11]

This combination of word and action suggests that the Lord's Supper is an act of *prophetic symbolism*.[12] Old Testament prophets engaged in symbolic actions. Some actions were only illustrative of the accompanying message, such as when the prophet Ahijah tore a new garment into twelve pieces, and gave ten to Jeroboam, thus indicating that he would be king of the ten northern tribes (1 Kings 11:29-40). A different type of symbolic action is detailed in the interview between Joash and Elisha in 2 Kings 13:15-17, which resulted in Joash being rebuked for only striking the ground three times with the arrows. Joash was not acting by divine command when he struck the earth three times, yet he is criticised for limiting himself to three strikes. Other symbolic actions include Isaiah's walking naked and barefoot (Isa. 20:2-4), Ezekiel's lying on his side (Ezek. 4:4-6), and Hosea's marriage to Gomer (Hos. 1). The point of a symbolic action was to illustrate God's purpose for his people, and indicated his initiative in their situation, whether it was a response of judgement or one of restoration. Some of the actions were unexplained until the prophet was asked concerning his unusual behaviour: for example, Isaiah walking barefoot and naked for three years was 'a sign and portent against Egypt and Cush, so the king of Assyria will lead away the Egyptian captives and Cushite exiles' (Isa. 20:3f.).

It is possible that the disciples of Jesus, as they reflected on what he did in the Upper Room, would have concluded that Jesus there acted in a prophetic manner. His actions and words were typical of prophetic behaviour in that they were surprising and shocking (for example, when he washed the disciples' feet, and when he said that the some of the elements in the meal depicted his death), and yet powerful.[13] His actions with the bread and the cup, along with his words that accompanied them, were prophetic in the sense of the prophetic symbolism recorded in the Old Testament.

Jesus is not visibly present at the Lord's Supper. Yet the bread and wine are signs of his presence, speaking of and giving to us the blessings he obtained for his disciples through his death for them. Yet they have to be received by faith, otherwise nothing is given to them by Christ. The elements are prophetic signs promising pardon and fellowship to those who partake expectantly, believing that what is depicted will take place.

In the Messianic age, all believers are prophets, a feature stressed by Peter in his sermon on the Day of Pentecost (Acts 2:17-18). This general prophetic status exists alongside the particular spiritual gift of a prophet that Paul mentions in 1 Corinthians 12:28 and 14:1-40. The general prophetic activity can be described as witness to society by word and deed, with the aim of producing a response in which a person asks Christians to explain their actions. The Lord's Supper is one means of prophetic witness, although its nature means it is always a corporate witness. For example, their meeting together illustrates their reconciliation to God through the death of Christ and their reconciliation to one another in Christ. The failure of the church in Corinth to publicly display this unity by action meant that the accompanying word was not illustrated to observers, with the further effect that true prophetic symbolism was not performed. The unbelievers in Corinth would have asked why there were divisions at the Lord's table, an indication that the believers were not functioning in a truly prophetic capacity. Prophetic symbolism is a reminder that the teaching contained in God's Word must be lived out in the lives of his people.

The Lord's Supper is also a meal that *anticipates* another meal, the Messianic banquet that is to mark the coming of the Messianic age. There is a sense in which believers, because of the blessings of the new covenant, already enter partly into the blessings associated with this future age. But the fullness of that age will not be known until Jesus returns. The Bible often depicts that fullness by the image of a banquet (Luke 12:37; 22:29, 30; Rev. 19:9). Jesus indicated that he was anticipating this banquet when he said, as he instituted the Passover, that he would not drink again of the fruit of the vine until the kingdom of God would come (Luke 22:16-18). Matthew and Mark present Jesus as saying this after the taking of bread and wine, whereas Luke has him saying the words before they took the elements. This suggests that Jesus said this more than once during the evening meal[14] and points to the stress he laid on this aspect of the Supper. The anticipation of believers, as they share the Lord's Supper, should be one of joy.

Paul mentions two other aspects of participating in the Lord's Supper. First, he stresses the need for self-examination as part of the process of preparation for participating (1 Cor. 11:27-29). Second, he mentions the fact of divine judgment because of abuse of the Lord's table (1 Cor. 11:27-32).

Self-examination is a reminder that the Lord's table is holy and that the guests are still sinful (the Lord's Supper is an holy occasion because the Lord Jesus instituted it as an activity of his church and because he is present by the Holy Spirit). In a passage that has strong corporate emphases, Paul stresses this individual responsibility. Paul does warn against partaking of the Lord's Supper in an unthinking and irreverent manner. His warning enjoins 'seriousness and deliberation and at least that measure of hesitancy which regards preparation as indispensable'.[15] The initial reason for self-examination is the Corinthians' failure to discern the body, which may be a reference to the symbols of bread and wine or to the church as the body of Christ. Many manuscripts only say 'body' (as translated in the English Standard Version) and not 'the Lord's body' (as translated in the King James Version).[16] Blomberg suggests that the addition is a copyist's attempt to explain the meaning of 'body',[17] which also indicates that there was an acceptance in the early church that it referred to the symbols and not to the congregation. In further support of 'body' being a reference to the symbols of the bread and wine is its close proximity to the phrase 'body and blood of the Lord' in verse 28. Having said that, it is also the case that in previous references where Paul wishes to specifically use the term 'body' in connection to Christ or the symbols of bread and wine he uses the necessary qualifiers, either of action (*eat* the bread and *drink* the cup, vv. 26, 27, 28) or of description ('of the Lord', v. 27).[18] The context also lends support to 'body' being a reference to the believers; Fee suggests that Paul is referring back to his mention of 'body' in 10:17.[19] What Paul may have been doing here is using a term which pointed to both meanings. The Corinthians, in any case, failed in both these regards. With the former, they did not regard the meal as holy, and with regard to the latter, the affluent members mistreated the poorer members and so did not treat the body of Christians as should have been done.

Paul does not expect self-examination to result in a person not partaking. His comment is, 'Let a man examine himself, *and so let him eat*' (11:28). This expectation is noteworthy given the lax procedures tolerated in Corinth. Paul anticipated that 'any unworthy Christian would make the necessary amendments immediately'.[20]

Self-examination followed by appropriate behaviour will prevent divine chastisement. In Corinth, the chastisement involved illness and, in some cases, death (1 Cor. 11:30). There is a parallel between the judgment that fell on the Israelites who abused their spiritual food and drink and the judgment on the Corinthian Christians who abused the Lord's Supper. The Israelites can be regarded as failing to respect the blessings that God gave them and also of failing to recognise that they were all set apart to be the Lord's people, which made their sinful behaviour more serious. In the Lord's Supper, believers are open to both divine blessing and divine chastisement – blessing for those who partake in faith, and chastisement for those who engage in the Supper with sinful aims and actions.

Paul's account gives no hint that a particular person was in charge of the Lord's Supper. As Motyer notes, for Paul, 'the antidote to disorder is not *proper structures* — the right words, the right leadership — but *proper relationships*, rightly understanding the respective roles of men and women in worship'.[21]

Paul's relatively short treatment of the Lord's Supper highlights several crucial elements of it, which I detail below:

- the Supper is communion with Christ.
- the Supper is communion with and an expression of unity with all fellow believers, despite their various social standings.
- the Supper is a proclamation of Christ's death.
- the Supper is a separating ordinance.
- the Supper is an anticipation of the Messianic banquet.
- practices that may cause abuse, such as an accompanying meal, should cease if that is the only way to prevent the abuse.
- individual self-examination is essential preparation for sharing in the Supper.
- wrong partaking of the Supper will result in divine chastisement.

The Lord's Supper
in Scottish Church History

4

Reformed Understanding of the Lord's Supper

The Presbyterian church in the Highlands traces its descent from the Presbyterian churches of the Reformation. The principles of the Reformation were introduced early into Easter Ross, mainly through the seaports of Cromarty and Inverness, which at that time engaged in trade with the European continent. One incident which shows the influence of the Reformation in the Highlands is that in 1560, when the Scottish Parliament met, every commissioner north of the Grampians to the North Sea voted for the disestablishment of the Roman Catholic Church and the ratification of the Scots Confession.[1]

Timothy George writes that at the time of the Reformation the rite of the Lord's Supper had developed beyond recognition from the practice of the early church. The rite had become *clericalised*, in that the Mass was the function of the priest rather than the people, and *commercialised*, in the growth of private Masses offered for a wide variety of personal reasons, and which were purchased with money. The theology of the Sacrament was *scholastized* through the dogma of transubstantiation with its use of Aristotelian philosophy. The rite became an occasion of *spectator excitement*, particularly at the moment of the consecration of the bread, with parades and processions following the host through the streets.[2] It is not surprising that an attempt was made to reform the church.

At the Reformation, in response to the Roman Catholic teaching of transubstantiation, three views of the meaning of the Lord's Supper were found among the Reformers, and each of these views has become identified with a leading Reformer. Consubstantiation has been identified with Martin Luther; memorialism has been identified with Ulrich Zwingli; the real spiritual presence has been identified with John Calvin.

In this chapter I will consider the writings of leading Protestant theologians of the Reformation era and of the period that immediately followed it in Scotland. The reason for doing this is to see which of the views of the Lord's Supper espoused at the Reformation were accepted by the Reformed Church in Scotland. After considering the ideas of transubstantiation and consubstantiation, I will consider the views of Zwingli and Calvin.

Transubstantiation

Transubstantiation, which was prescribed by the Fourth Lateran Council in 1215,[3] is the teaching that the bread and wine actually become the body and blood of Christ. According to the *Catholic Encyclopedia*, the concept of transubstantiation was the contribution of the Latin theologians.[4] The term *transubstantiation* seems to have been first used by Hildebert of Tours (about 1079) and was used by several theologians before it was adopted by several ecumenical councils, including the Fourth Lateron Council (1215) and the Council of Trent.[5] The last mentioned Council 'not only accepted as an inheritance of faith the truth contained in the idea, but authoritatively confirmed the "aptitude of the term" to express most strikingly the legitimately developed doctrinal concept'. The *Catholic Encyclopedia* affirms that the fundamental notion of the concept of transubstantiation is the conversion of the bread and wine into the body and blood of Christ.

But how did the notion of transubstantiation develop? Robert Letham suggests two reasons.[6] First,

In the Western or Roman Catholic view, Aristotelian philosophy was used to explain what appears at first glance to be impossible. How can the bread and wine be changed into the actual physical body and blood of Christ when it is obvious to our eyes that they are still the same as they ever were? The Aristotelian distinction between *substance* and *accidents* was the means to resolve this conundrum. The substance of a thing is what that thing really is, its intrinsic nature. On the other hand, accidents refer to incidentals, features relating not to a thing's inner nature but more to what it may appear to be, or to something adventitious that could be withdrawn without altering the thing's substance. The works of Aristotle were rediscovered from around 1050 and so proved a fruitful resource for the church. Hence, the bread and wine were held to change into the body and blood of Christ according to substance (hence *trans* = change, *substantia* = of substance), according to what they really were intrinsically, while they remained bread and wine per *accidens*, in terms of accidents or appearances. Certainly they seemed to remain what they had been, while having undergone this change of inner essence. At root, this was not magic but a sacramental mystery. It occurred when the priest consecrated the elements.

Letham explains his second reason for the development of transubstantiation:

> Again, the position of the Roman church on the relationship between nature and grace also helped in the development of transubstantiation. According to Rome, grace perfects nature. Natural gifts and gifts from the Holy Spirit are effectively one and the same. In this sense the physical and the spiritual are so closely identified that in practice they merge into one. From this perspective, it is easy to see how the bread and wine can be said to be the body and blood of Christ and how spiritual grace can be conveyed more or less automatically by physical means.[7]

The acceptance of the doctrine of transubstantiation results in two inevitable consequences. First, since the bread has been changed into the body of Christ it becomes an object of worship, which occurs when the priest elevates it in the sight of the worshippers for them to adore. Second, since the bread that has become the body of Christ does not return to being bread and the wine that has become the blood of Christ does not return to being wine, it means that any of the sacramental elements that remain after the Supper cannot be discarded; the bread must be preserved and eaten at a subsequent sacrament and the wine drunk immediately by the priest.

A major response of the Roman Catholic Church to the teachings of the Reformers was the Council of Trent, where among other doctrinal matters, the official teaching of the Church concerning the Lord's Supper was clarified. Among its decisions are the following statements, which allow responses to be made to Roman Catholic teaching at the Reformation period:

> First of all, the holy council teaches and openly and plainly professes that after the consecration of bread and wine, our Lord Jesus Christ, true God and true man, is truly, really, and substantially contained in the august sacrament of the Holy Eucharist under the appearance of those sensible things (Thirteenth session, chapter 1).

> But since Christ our Redeemer declared that to be truly His own body which He offered under the form of bread, it has, therefore, always been a firm belief in the Church of God, and this holy council now declares it anew, that by the consecration of the bread and wine a change is brought about of the whole substance of the bread into the substance of the body of Christ, and of the whole substance of the wine into the substance of His blood. This change the holy Catholic Church properly and appropriately calls transubstantiation (Thirteenth session, chapter 4).

> If anyone denies that in the sacrament of the most holy Eucharist are contained truly, really, and substantially the body and blood together with the soul and divinity of our Lord Jesus Christ, and consequently the whole Christ, but says that He is in it only as in a sign, or figure or force, let him be anathema (Canon 1).

> If anyone says that in the sacred and holy sacrament of the Eucharist the substance of the bread and wine remains conjointly with the body and blood of our Lord Jesus Christ, and denies that wonderful and singular change of the whole substance of the bread into the body and the whole substance of the wine into the blood, the appearances only of bread and wine remaining, which change the Catholic Church most aptly calls transubstantiation, let him be anathema (Canon 2).

> If anyone says that after the consecration is completed, the body and blood of our Lord Jesus Christ are not in the admirable

sacrament of the Eucharist, but are there only *in usu*, while being taken and not before or after, and that in the hosts or consecrated particles which are reserved or which remain after communion, the true body of the Lord Jesus does not remain, let him be anathema (Canon 4).[8]

A first response is that the Council interpreted Jesus' words of institution literally and did not recognize that his words concerning the bread and the wine could be interpreted symbolically. Mathison notes that the Council ignored the original liturgical context of the statement of Jesus, where in the Passover ritual the words 'this is the bread of affliction which our ancestors ate when they came from the land of Egypt' were clearly symbolic.[9] There is no evidence in the New Testament that its writers, when referring to the elements of bread and wine in the Lord's Supper, believed that any change occurred to their substance. Consistently they are referred to as bread and wine. Letham comments that

> transubstantiation confuses the sign (bread and wine) with the reality (Christ's body and blood). In the sacraments, there are always these two distinct poles to consider. Christ is presented in the sacraments in the form of physical elements. These latter are signs. Like signposts, which direct us to a destination other than themselves, the sacramental signs point elsewhere. They direct us away from themselves to Christ. At the same time, there is a connection between sign and reality. The elements in the sacraments are appropriate to the reality they represent…as bread and wine sustain and nourish us physically, so in the eucharist we are nourished by Christ—we feed on him by faith to eternal life. In the case of Roman Catholic teaching, this connection is stressed at the expense of the distinction. By identifying the signs with the reality Rome has compressed the spiritual and the physical, nature and grace.[10]

Second, the Roman Catholic concept of the Mass does not accept the New Testament emphasis on the finality and completeness of Christ's atoning work on the cross. In contrast, the Council of Trent claims:

And inasmuch as in this divine sacrifice which is celebrated in the mass is contained and immolated in an unbloody manner the same Christ who once offered Himself in a bloody manner on the altar of the cross, the holy council teaches that this is truly propitiatory and has this effect, that if we, contrite and penitent, with sincere heart and upright faith, with fear and reverence, draw nigh to God, we obtain mercy and find grace in seasonable aid. For, appeased by this sacrifice, the Lord grants the grace and gift of penitence and pardons even the gravest crimes and sins. For the victim is one and the same, the same now offering by the ministry of priests who then offered Himself on the cross, the manner alone of offering being different. The fruits of that bloody sacrifice, it is well understood, are received most abundantly through this unbloody one, so far is the latter from derogating in any way from the former. Wherefore, according to the tradition of the Apostles, it is rightly offered not only for the sins, punishments, satisfactions and other necessities of the faithful who are living, but also for the departed in Christ but not yet fully purified (Twenty-second session, chapter 2).

Some Protestants have claimed that the Mass involves a repetition of Christ's atoning death. Mathison notes that this is not the position of the Council of Trent, which argues instead that Christ's actual death and the sacrifice in the Eucharist are one single sacrifice, which is how the 1994 Catechism of the Catholic Church understands what takes place ('the sacrifice of Christ and the sacrifice of the Eucharist are one single sacrifice').[11]

Nevertheless there are biblical arguments against the definition of Trent. First, the biblical accounts do not suggest that the last Supper was a sacrifice; rather it was a sacrificial meal of fellowship based on the sacrifice of Christ.

Second, the biblical writers argue that Christ's death is sufficient to deal with sin and does not require reenactment; for example, Hebrews 9:25-28: 'Nor did he enter heaven to offer himself again and again, the way the high priest enters the Most Holy Place every year with blood that is not his own. Then Christ would have had to suffer many times since the creation of the world. But now he has appeared once for all at the end of the ages to do away with sin by the sacrifice of himself. Just as man is destined to die once, and after that to face judgment, so Christ was sacrificed once to take away the sins of many people; and he will appear a second time, not to bear sin, but to bring salvation to those who are waiting for him.'

Third, there is no evidence in the biblical writings that the celebration of the Supper by the church on earth has any benefit for believers who have died and are in an unperfected state.

Consubstantiation

Advocates of consubstantiation insist that Christ's statement, 'This is my body,' must be understood in a literal sense. Martin Luther's teaching was that while the bread did not become the physical body of Christ, yet the body of Christ was present 'in, with and under' the bread.[12] Grudem gives an illustration of this idea: 'The example sometimes given is to say that Christ's body is present in the bread as water is present in a sponge – the water is not the sponge, but is present "in, with, and under" a sponge, and is present wherever the sponge is present.'[13]

In his *The Babylonian Captivity of the Church*, Luther disagrees with three practices of the Roman Catholic Church concerning the Lord's Supper. The first is withholding the cup from the laity, which he shows from Christ's institution recorded in the Gospels and from Paul's account in 1 Corinthians 11 to be different from the original practice which was to give both the bread and the cup to all who participated.[14] The second practice is transubstantiation, which Luther regarded as a lesser bondage than the first practice. Transubstantiation was based on a philosophical distinction between substance and accidents in the elements. Luther regarded transubstantiation as 'a monstrous word and a monstrous idea'.[15] He also asked why a 'transaccidentation' could not occur,[16] so that the body of Christ may be identified with the accidents. Rather than using philosophical concepts, he admitted:

> For my part, if I cannot fathom how the bread is the body of Christ, yet I will take my reason captive to the obedience of Christ [II Cor.

10:5], and clinging simply to his words, firmly believe not only that the body of Christ is in the bread, but that the bread is the body of Christ. My warrant for this is the words which say: "he took bread, and when he had given thanks, he broke it and said, 'Take, eat, this (that is, this bread, which he had taken and broken) is my body'" [I Cor. 11:23-24]. And Paul says: "The bread which we break, is it not a participation in the body of Christ?" [I Cor. 10:16]. He does not say "in the bread there is," but the bread itself is the participation in the body of Christ." What does it matter if philosophy cannot fathom this? The Holy Spirit is greater than Aristotle. Does philosophy fathom their transubstantiation?[17]

The third practice to which Luther objected was the sacrifice of the Mass, which he regarded as the most evil of the three.[18] For Luther, the Mass is not a good work by which a Christian gains merit.[19] Rather the Mass is Christ's testament or promise 'of the forgiveness of sins made to us by God, and such a promise as has been confirmed by the death of the Son of God'.[20] Since the Mass is a promise, the appropriate response is faith and not works. Alongside the word of promise, Christ gives the sign of his body and blood in the bread and wine.[21] The Mass is not a sacrifice offered to God.[22]

When it came to disputing with those who denied Christ's presence in the elements, Luther argued that in the Lord's Supper there are two things that should be known and proclaimed; the first is what a person should believe and the second is the use a person 'should make of that in which he believes'. 'The first lies outside the heart and is presented to our eyes externally, namely, the sacrament itself, concerning which we believe that Christ's body and blood are truly present in the bread and wine. The second is internal, within the heart, and cannot be externalized. It consists in the attitude which the heart should have toward the sacred sacrament.'[23]

In opposing the teaching that Christ was not present in the bread and wine, Luther likened it to a person removing the contents of an egg and leaving only the shell (Christ is the contents and the bread and wine is the shell). He accused these teachers of not being willing to accept the clear meaning of Christ's words when he said at the first Lord's Supper, 'This is my body' and 'This is my blood'. Luther dismissed their claims that the presence of Christ in the elements was neither fitting nor necessary.

Concerning the fitness of Christ's presence, Luther notes that Christ did many things that were not fitting for God, as evidenced in his incarnation and in his cruel death; therefore, it is not up to men to decide what is fitting or not for the Son of God. In attempting to prove the reality of Christ's presence in the elements, Luther resorts to subtle analogies; for example, (a) a person's soul is present at all times in all the members of his body; (b) a person can think and speak simultaneously, and see and feel as one does so, and at the same time can digest food; (c) a spoken word can influence many people at the same time. When Christ is preached, and by a bodily voice (the preacher) brought into a person's heart, Christ's presence is real; and this experience can be known by many people at the same time, with each person receiving a whole Christ. This does not mean that Christ has left heaven, rather he is still there and also in the heart of each believer. If one believes this, then it is not difficult to accept that Christ can also be in heaven and in the elements of bread and wine at the same time. What causes the elements to have the presence of Christ is the Word of divine authority indicating he is there. 'Just as he enters the heart without breaking a hole in it, but is comprehended only through the Word and hearing, so also he enters into the bread without needing to make any hole in it.'[24]

As far as the necessity of Christ's presence in the elements is concerned, Luther comments that it is not men but God who decides what is necessary. A person could just as well ask why God should feed us through the bread and wine when he could have done so by the Word itself. For Luther, such arguments were the devil's activities to cause people to measure God's will and work by human reason. Instead, believers should listen to God's Word and remain in it.[25]

Luther taught, against the Roman Catholic practice, that Christians should not use the sacrament as a means of meriting heaven. Instead they are to believe that Christ is given to them in the Lord's Supper. For Luther, this giving of Christ involved an awareness of the forgiveness of sins in particular, although it also included a sense of freedom from death and hell, of being a son of God and an heir of heaven.[26] Participating in the sacrament also included penitence for our shortcomings and the receiving of strength to amend our frailties. It is important to realize that complete sinlessness is unobtainable.[27]

The fruit of the sacrament is seen especially in love. Luther argues that this was Christ's intention, which he demonstrated by giving himself for the redemption of sinners, so they are to give themselves for their neighbours. But Christ also stressed love by giving the symbols of bread and wine, both of which consist of many individual things made into one. The bread is many kernels baked into one loaf and the wine is many grapes pressed together.[28]

Another practice that Luther linked to the Lord's Supper was confession, of which he identified three types, and which preceded partaking in the sacrament. The first type is lifelong confession of sins to God. The second type is twofold: there is mutual, public confession of sins, in which believers express their sorrow at failing to help their neighbours, and confession of any particular sins against an individual. The third type is private confession when a believer confesses his sins to another believer. The last type has particular benefits: the other party forgives as in the stead of God; it enables believers to practice what they have been taught; it allows another believer to give advice and consolation.[29]

In his *Confession Regarding Christ's Supper*, which Luther regarded as his last word on the subject, he attempted to explain how the human nature of Christ could be everywhere. There is no doubt that Luther believed in the full deity and full humanity of Christ and 'accepted without reservation' 'the traditional terminology of the "two natures" and of their unification in the one person of the Lord to describe the mystery of Jesus Christ.'[30] But as Wells notes, 'The question, of course, was precisely how the two natures related to one another.'[31] Luther argued that Christ's humanity exists on three levels:

Thus the one body of Christ has a threefold existence, or all three modes of being at a given place. First, the circumscribed corporeal mode of presence, as when he walked bodily on earth, when he occupied and yielded space according to his size. He can still employ this mode of presence when he wills to do so, as he did after his resurrection and as he will do so on the Last Day, as Paul says in 1 Timothy [6:15], "Whom the blessed God will reveal," and Colossians 3 [:4], "When Christ your life reveals himself." He is not in God or with the Father or in heaven according to this mode, as this mad spirit dreams, for God is not a corporeal space or place. The passages which the spiritualists adduce concerning Christ's leaving the world and going to the Father speak of this mode of presence.

Secondly, the uncircumscribed, spiritual mode of presence according to which he neither occupies nor yields space but passes through everything as he wills. To use some crude illustrations, my vision passes through and exists in air, light, or water and does not occupy or yield any space.... He employed this mode of presence when he left the closed grave and came through closed doors, in the bread and wine in the Supper, and, as people believe, when he was born in his mother.

Thirdly, since he is one person with God, the divine heavenly mode, according by which all created things are indeed much more permeable and present to him than they are according to the second mode. For if according to the second mode he can be present in and with created things in such a way that they do not feel, touch, measure, or circumscribe him, how much more marvelously will he be present in all created things according to this exalted third mode, where they cannot measure or circumscribe him but where they are present to him so that he measures and circumscribes them. You must place this existence of Christ, which constitutes him one person with God, far, far beyond things created, as far as God transcends them; and on the other hand, place it as deep in and as near to all created things as God is in them. For he is one indivisible person with God, and wherever God is, he must be also, otherwise our faith is false.[32]

Luther here is making use of the *communicatio idiomatum*, a doctrine stating that what properly belongs to the humanity may be predicated of the deity and *vice versa*. But Luther not only applied divine attributes to the divine person who had a human nature, he applied them to the human nature itself. As Wells notes, Luther 'had argued that human nature, though itself finite and limited, was capable of receiving the infinite';[33] and the quotation above from Luther indicates that Wells' assertion is correct.

It is obvious that Luther had several profound insights into the function of the Lord's Supper. His condemnation of the Roman practice of denying the cup to the laity and of its assertion that the bread and wine are changed into the body and blood of Christ is valuable. So too is his emphasis on the Lord's Supper being Christ's testament to his people to assure them of the forgiveness of their sins. His advice on confession of sin and of partaking in a penitent spirit contains helpful advice for believers. Nevertheless, his comments on the humanity of Christ indicate that for Luther to advocate consubstantiation required him to believe that Christ's human nature possesses omnipresence, to not only be in heaven but also to be present in the Supper. Luther's suggestion, admits Letham, was an ingenious innovation, but with 'no clear precedent in Christian thought'.

> Its ingeniousness was also its Achilles' heel. The point of importance is that, if divine attributes such as omnipresence were communicated to Christ's human nature, how could that human nature still be human? Is not an indispensable aspect of humanity the property of being in only one place at one time? How could a body be omnipresent and still human. In the Lutheran position there are clear hints of the early Christian heresy of Docetism, the idea that Christ's humanity was only apparent and not real. In seeking to maintain a physical presence of Christ in the Lord's Supper while rejecting transubstantiation, Luther may have bitten off more than he could chew![34]

Ulrich Zwingli

Zwingli did not accept the Roman Catholic idea of transubstantiation or the Lutheran alternative of consubstantiation, which meant he faced hostility from both Roman Catholic and Lutheran theologians. In several places his teaching was condemned, including the Swiss canton of Uri and the German city of Nuremburg.[35]

His early writings on the Lord's Supper were in Latin, but his response to opposition was to publish his teachings in the common language so that 'the ordinary and simple Christian may learn the truth for himself'.[36] Zwingli preferred the name 'Eucharist', although he would use terms such as the 'Lord's Supper' and 'communion'.[37]

Zwingli affirmed that both baptism and the Lord's Supper had several virtues.

- They were instituted by Christ and he himself received them.
- They testify to historical events.
- They take the place, and name, of that which they signify.
- They represent high things: for example, the bread represents the body of Christ.
- There is an analogy between the signs and the things signified. In the Supper, there is a twofold analogy. First, just as bread and wine sustain human life and bring joy, so Christ sustains and rejoices the soul. Second, just as the bread is made up of many grains and the wine is made up of many grapes, so the many members of the church are constituted one body.
- They augment faith and are an aid to it.
- They act as an oath of allegiance to Christ and to fellow Christians.[38]

As with Luther and, later, Calvin, Zwingli realised that the central matter was the meaning of the presence of Christ in the Supper, particularly in relation to the physical body of Christ. 'The whole question has its source in the misunderstanding of the text: "This is my body."' [39] He was aware of three alternatives for those who took the bread: they were eating the body of Christ as it hung on the cross; they were eating the body of Christ under the bread; they were eating the body of Christ as it is resurrected.[40]

The first alternative is the Roman Catholic teaching, the second is the Lutheran, and the third is similar to the teaching of Calvin.

Those who say that Christians eat the body and blood interpret 'This is my body' literally. Zwingli notes that Christ often compared himself to objects; for example, he said, 'I am the vine', by which he did not mean he was a literal vine. Interpreting the body and blood literally means that Christ 'is torn apart by the teeth and perceptibly masticated'.[41] But since that does not happen, he cannot be present in such a manner.

Concerning the view that Christ's flesh is present under the bread, Zwingli argued that to take the word 'is' literally means that 'the substance of bread has to be changed completely into that of flesh. But that means that the bread is no longer there. Therefore it is impossible to maintain that the bread remains, but that in or under the bread flesh is eaten.'[42]

Responding to the third alternative, that of eating the body of the resurrected Christ, Zwingli argued against a literal interpretation of Christ's words by referring to the Ascension of Christ's human nature to heaven. His human nature has been in heaven since his Ascension, so references to the presence of Christ with his people must refer to his omnipresent divine nature.[43]

Zwingli also argued from 1 Corinthians 10 that eating the flesh and blood of Christ did not involve a literal eating. He notes that Paul says that 'amongst the other things which our fathers had no less than we was the same spiritual food and the same spiritual drink as we now enjoy'. But 'there cannot be the slightest doubt that they did not partake of the literal body and blood of Christ, for Christ did not come in the flesh until sixteen hundred years later. Therefore in their case this eating was simply believing in the one who was to give his flesh and blood on their behalf. Similarly in our case the eating and drinking of his body cannot be anything else but believing in the one who had already given his flesh and blood.'[44]

Furthermore, Zwingli regarded the 'is' in 'This is my body' as meaning 'signifies', which he regards as important for the emphasis on remembrance: 'Behold the end for which he [Jesus] bids them eat, namely, the commemoration of him.'[45]

Concerning John 6, in which Christ claimed that it was essential for his followers to eat his flesh and drink his blood, Zwingli argued that Christ was not speaking of the Eucharist;[46] rather he was teaching that he would be delivered up to death in order for his followers to have life.[47] Eating his flesh refers to faith in Christ, especially in his death.[48] Zwingli has in mind faith as trust.[49]

Zwingli stressed the corporate aspect of the commemoration: 'Since, therefore, this Lord's Feast, or in Paul's words, Lord's Supper, was instituted that we might call to remembrance the death of Christ, which he suffered for us, it is clear that it is the sign itself by which those who rely upon the death and blood of Christ mutually prove to their brethren that they have this faith.'[50] He regarded Paul's teaching concerning the body of Christ in First Corinthians 10 as referring to the body of Christians rather than the physical body of Christ:

> Paul seems to proclaim plainly there [1 Cor. 10-16-17] that those who eat this bread and drink this cup unite in one body with the rest of the brethren, which indeed is the body of Christ because that is the body of Christ which believes that the flesh of its author has been slain and its blood shed for it. He means, therefore, that they become partakers in the body and blood of Christ when they confess that they with the rest of the brethren trust in the death of Christ and the shedding of his blood. So they bear witness to the brethren that they believe this with faithful hearts and because they abhor all worship of idols and foreign gods, they should take the bread and cup of commemoration together with the brethren in the Lord's Supper, that brother may see that brother unites with him through his oath of allegiance as it were (whence it is called a sacrament) into one body, one bread, one profession.[51]

In emphasising the corporate nature of the Supper, his teaching at one level was a response to the Roman Catholic practice of the Mass in which the laity played a spectator role.

Zwingli described in *An Exposition of the Faith* what he understood by eating Christ sacramentally:

So then, when you come to the Lord's Supper to feed spiritually upon Christ, and when you thank the Lord for his great favour, for the redemption whereby you are delivered from despair, and for the pledge whereby you are assured of eternal salvation, when you join with your brethren in partaking of the bread and wine which are the tokens of the body of Christ, then in the true sense of the word you eat him sacramentally. You do inwardly that which you represent outwardly, your soul being strengthened by the faith which you attest in the tokens.[52]

Stephens helpfully summarises Zwingli's understanding of the Lord's Supper: 'thanksgiving for Christ's death for us, a confession of our faith, and a commitment to our brethren, to love them as Christ loved us.'[53]

Yet his teaching does not give sufficient weight to the biblical details. Bromiley identifies an important aspect of Zwingli's writings on the Supper when he says that while Zwingli gave effective criticism of the Roman Catholic and Lutheran views, he did not provide an alternative method, which gives the impression that he was only able to offer a bare sacramentalism. He so separated the sign from what it signified in the Supper that he 'did not show any clear sense of its unity'.[54] It is not fair to speak of Zwingli's interpretation of the presence of Christ in the Supper as 'the real absence',[55] because he did believe that Christ was present in his divine nature. But since Christ is present everywhere in his divine nature, it is possible that Zwingli did not regard Christ as present in a special sense at the Lord's Supper.

John Calvin

In his chapter on the Lord's Supper in his *Institutes*,[56] Calvin makes many pertinent points as he not only refutes the Lutherans and Roman Catholics but also explains his own understanding of what occurs at the Supper.

First, the Lord's Supper is a provision of our heavenly Father to 'assure us of his continued liberality'. Because Christ is the only food for our soul, 'our heavenly Father invites us to him, that, refreshed by communion with him, we may ever and anon gather new vigour until we reach the heavenly immortality.' Because no-one can see by nature the secret union between Christ and believers, the Father gives visible signs (the bread and the wine) in order to show 'that souls are fed by Christ just as the corporeal life is sustained by bread and wine'(4:17:1).[57]

Second, it is not sufficient to limit communion with Christ to being made partakers of the Spirit, and omitting all mention of flesh and blood (4:17:7).

Third, before the Incarnation, Christ as life was the source of life for all creatures. By the incarnation, Christ is the life both as God and man (4:17:8, 9) – 'in his humanity also fulness of life resides, so that every one who communicates in his flesh and blood, at the same time enjoys the participation of life.' The flesh of Christ 'is like a rich and inexhaustible fountain, which transfuses into us the life flowing forth from the Godhead into itself.'

Fourth, the Holy Spirit 'truly unites things separated by space' that is, Christ and believers. In the Supper, Christ exerts 'an efficacy of the Spirit by which he fulfils what he promises' – 'the sacred communion of flesh and blood by which Christ transfuses his life into us' (4:17:10). Although the physical body of Christ remains in heaven, the Holy Spirit, who unites us to Christ, is 'a kind of channel by which everything that Christ has and is, is derived to us' (4:17:12).

Calvin had two safeguards in attempting to understand Christ's presence in the Supper: 'First, Let there be nothing derogatory to the heavenly glory of Christ. This happens whenever he is brought under the corruptible elements of this world, or is affixed to any earthly creatures [such as "affixes him to the element of the bread, nor encloses him in bread, nor circumscribes him in any way"]. Secondly, Let no property be assigned to his body inconsistent with his human nature. This is done when it is either said to be infinite, or made to occupy a variety of places at the same time.'

Calvin disagreed both with the view that the Supper is only an act of remembrance and with the Lutheran view that Christ is physically present in, with and under the bread and wine.

Christ's own words of institution indicate that remembering

him in his death is an essential aspect of the Lord's Supper. Yet, to regard the Supper as only an act of remembrance does not explain other biblical passages such as Paul's teaching that 'the cup of blessing which we bless, is it not the communion of the blood of Christ? the bread which we break, is it not the communion of the body of Christ?' (1 Cor. 10:16). Paul's words point to a form of communion with Christ in his death. Those who teach that the Supper is only a memorial therefore deny that there is a real presence of Christ in the elements. Calvin responded to such that it is essential to distinguish between Christ and the elements so as to avoid confounding them, but it is not right to divide between Christ and the elements so as to make the one exist without the other in the Supper.[58]

Calvin asserted that the presence of Christ in the Supper was not a physical presence, for the human nature of the ascended Christ remains in heaven. He taught that the presence was spiritual, that by 'the incomprehensible agency of the Spirit, spiritual life is infused into us from the substance of the body and blood of Christ'.[59] This means that the presence is more than Christ's divine omnipresence. For Calvin, the presence of Christ is achieved by the Spirit, this secret agency being 'the bond of our union with Christ'.[60] So 'the body of Christ is given to us in the Supper spiritually, because the secret virtue of the Spirit makes things which are widely separated by space to be united with each other, and accordingly causes life from the flesh of Christ to reach us from heaven'.[61] The Spirit nourishes believers with life from the flesh of Christ as they partake of the elements.[62] The Spirit ensures that there is real communion between Christ and believers as they receive from Christ the benefits he purchased for them on the cross.[63] It is important to stress that Calvin affirmed the necessity of the believer's faith being active, in the sense of receiving from Christ, during the Supper.

There is a sense of mystery here, and much of what happens is unexplainable. Calvin's own words reveal the proper attitude:

Now, should any one ask me as to the mode, I will not be ashamed to confess that it is too high a mystery either for my mind to comprehend or my words to express. And, to speak more plainly, I rather feel than understand it. The truth of God, therefore, in which I can safely rest, I here embrace without controversy. He declares that his flesh is the meat, his blood the drink, of my soul; I give my soul to him to be fed with such food. In his sacred Supper he bids men take, eat, and drink his body and blood under the symbols of bread and wine. I have no doubt that he will truly give and I receive.[64]

It seems to me that Calvin was correct to object to both a mere remembering and to the consubstantiation interpretation of the Supper. In doing so he indicated that it is possible to deny that the elements are mere memory aids or that they are affected in some way. Some of what happens at the Supper is not comprehensible to the human mind. The Lord Jesus, through the Spirit, imparts to his participating people the benefits he died to give them, spiritual blessings such as assurance of forgiveness, the peace of God, and so on. But Jesus also gives himself, including his body and blood.[65]

Most Reformed theologians admit to a twofold sense of the presence of Christ: first, the second person of the Trinity must be present because of his inherent omnipresence; secondly, he is present through the working of the Holy Spirit employing the means of grace. But Calvin has been criticized for his third sense of Christ's presence. William Cunningham commented:

We have no fault to find with the substance of Calvin's statements in regard to the sacraments in general, or with respect to baptism; but we cannot deny that he made an effort to bring out something like a real influence exerted by Christ's human nature upon the souls of believers, in connection with the dispensation of the Lord's Supper – an effort which, of course, was altogether unsuccessful, and resulted only in what was about as unintelligible as Luther's consubstantiation. This is, perhaps, the greatest blot in the history of Calvin's labours as a public instructor.[66]

Robert L. Dabney also rejected Calvin's view and gave several reasons:

1. It is not only incomprehensible, but impossible, for it requires that matter, in this case the body of Christ in heaven, may exist without its essential attributes of locality and dimension.

2. The symbols of bread and wine symbolise the dead body of Christ, not the mystical union with Christ.

3. Old Testament saints, who possessed the same life as New Testament believers, had sacraments figured by eating and drinking, the same figure as in the bread and wine of the Supper. The Old Testament saints could not have shared in the life coming from the theanthropic Person of Christ because it did not exist in Old Testament times.

4. Feeding on Christ in John 6 is simply believing in Christ and does not refer to partaking of the Lord's Supper.

5. Calvin's view is inconsistent with the results of unworthy partaking. Dabney says that consistency requires Calvin's view to say that spiritual death is experienced in the soul of an unworthy partaker through the poisonous effects of Christ substantively present to the soul.[67] (Dabney was aware that Calvin denied there was any contact between an unbelieving communicant and Christ, which raises the validity of this objection by Dabney.)

In response to these criticisms, it is admitted that Calvin's view does contain aspects difficult to understand, particularly his idea that spiritual life comes to believers through partaking of the physical body and blood of Christ. Yet, as Sinclair Ferguson comments, there is the possibility that 'discomfort with Calvin's language masks a discomfort with the language of Scripture itself.'[68]

Robert Reymond notes that Calvin 'believed that the Scriptures declare the literal flesh and blood of Christ to be the Christian's life (John 6:27, 33, 51-59; 1 Cor. 6:15; Eph. 1:23; 4:15-16; 5:30;

see *Institutes* IV.17.9) and that therefore exegetical fidelity required him to accept that "his flesh [is] the food of my soul, his blood its drink" (*Institutes*, IV.17.32).[69] Reymond argues that the problem with Calvin's terminology is partly caused by his use of Jesus' comments in John 6 concerning eating his flesh and drinking his blood, given in a situation in which it is unlikely he was referring to the Lord's Supper.[70]

Calvin was aware that eating the flesh and drinking the blood of Christ mentioned in John 6 was not initially a reference to the Lord's Supper. In commenting on the chapter, he says that 'the ancients fell into a gross error by supposing that little children were deprived of eternal *life,* if they did not dispense to them the eucharist, that is, the Lord's Supper; for this discourse does not relate to the Lord's Supper, but to the uninterrupted communication *of the flesh of Christ,* which we obtain apart from the use of the Lord's Supper.'[71]

Yet he was also convinced that the teaching of Christ in John 6 was of crucial relevance to the Lord's Supper:

> And indeed it would have been foolish and unreasonable to discourse about the Lord's Supper, before he had instituted it. It is certain, then, that he now speaks of the perpetual and ordinary manner of eating the flesh of Christ, which is done by faith only. And yet, at the same time, I acknowledge that there is nothing said here that is not figuratively represented, and actually bestowed on believers, in the Lord's Supper; and Christ even intended that the holy Supper should be, as it were, a seal and confirmation of this sermon. This is also the reason why the Evangelist John makes no mention of the Lord's Supper; and therefore Augustine follows the natural order, when, in explaining this chapter, he does not touch on the Lord's Supper till he comes to the conclusion; and then he shows that this mystery is symbolically represented, whenever the Churches celebrate the Lord's Supper, in some places daily, and in other places only on the Lord's day.[72]

Yet Calvin's teaching does attempt to explain crucial aspects of the Supper, such as:

- the role of the theanthropic person of Christ as the God-man in relationship to communion with believers.
- the nature of communion with Christ now in heaven.
- the role of the Holy Spirit in taking of the things of Christ, not just the things of one of his natures, and applying them to us.

Ronald Wallace identified several features of Calvin's interpretation of the Supper. First, clarity is achieved. Wallace quotes Calvin's confidence of having this clarity:

> In this doctrine of the sacraments, their dignity is highly extolled, their use plainly shown, their utility sufficiently proclaimed, and moderation in all things duly maintained; so that nothing is attributed to them which ought not to be attributed, and nothing denied them which they ought to possess.[73]

Second, mystery is preserved. Calvin acknowledged that God was at work in the Lord's Supper in ways beyond human ability to understand.[74]

Third, absurdities, such as the assertion that the body of Christ was locally present in the elements, are avoided.[75]

Fourth, Calvin believed his views were in conformity to the rule of faith. Wallace notes in particular Calvin's concern to maintain the orthodox doctrine regarding the true humanity of Christ.[76]

Fifth, Calvin's view maintained a true eschatological tension, in that Christ has left the earth and will not return to it, even in the Supper, until his second advent.[77]

Sinclair Ferguson identifies the crucial question that Calvin is asking: 'With what Christ does the believer commune at the table?' Ferguson continues:

> His answer is: Christ clothed in the humanity in which he suffered, died, was buried, rose, and in which he has now ascended in glory. There is no other Christ than the enfleshed Word (**Logos ensarkos**). There is no other way of grace than through union and communion

with him as **ensarkos**. In the Supper, then, we commune with the person of Christ in the mystery of the hypostatic union; we do so S/spiritually, i.e. through the power of the Spirit.

Calvin need not be interpreted as saying more than this. We ourselves should not say less, otherwise we either deny the reality of the **koinōnia** of which the New Testament speaks (1 Cor. 10:16), or, just as seriously, we find ourselves denying the continuing reality of the humanity of the glorified Christ. The difficulty here lies not so much with what Calvin says in his teaching on the Supper, as in the way that much Christological thinking does not take adequate account of the fact that there is no other Christ. It does not take the truth of the bodily resurrection and ascension of Christ with full seriousness. Once this is grasped, Calvin's eucharistic theology becomes less puzzling, albeit the truth it represents (as the Reformer himself concedes) remains mysterious. But the mystery is no greater than other aspects of the Spirit's work.[78]

The teaching of Calvin is summarised by Alexander Barclay in the following propositions:

First, the body of Christ is in heaven. Christ cannot therefore be bodily present in the Supper, but he is effectually present in his power (*Virtus*), even as the sun is present with us through its power, although located in the distant heavens. In response to this proposition, it has to be noted that this can be read as distorting Calvin's view, for Calvin argued that the Holy Spirit mystically removes the 'space' separating the believer on earth from the body of the risen Christ in heaven, resulting in the believer partaking by the Spirit of Christ's risen body, not just its power.

Second, the flesh and blood are not eaten, nor is there to be supposed any transfusion or admixture of the substance of Christ. The bread and wine are signs, but exhibitive signs of the presence of Christ.

Third, to feed on Christ is more than a moral apprehension of the truth of Christ; more than a quickening influence of the Holy Spirit, convincing and enlightening the mind through the Word, and producing the new life of regeneration in the soul. Christ, though in heaven, yet in the fullness of his personality, embracing body and soul, vivifies and nourishes the believer, including body and soul.

Fourth, faith grafts us into the mystical body of Christ, which derives all its life from him, the Head, flowing out into the members. This union is mystical, but real.

Fifth, the Lord's Supper by its symbolical elements of bread and wine sets forth the truth of the Person of Christ, as the life and nourishment of the soul. By its symbolical actions of eating and drinking, it testifies our actual participation in Christ through the Spirit. These symbols are more than pictures or attestations. They not only signify and seal, but so exhibit and apply the reality, that there is a distinct spiritual effect.

Sixth, the Holy Spirit is the bond. He so acts that the substance of Christ's flesh and blood, though in heaven, affects the whole man. The influence is spiritual and real. The signs signify realities.[79]

Lessons from the Reformers

The obvious lesson that comes from a survey of the views of the leading Reformers is the *seriousness* with which they regarded the Lord's Supper; for them it was an important means of grace. 'As much as the Lutherans and the Reformed disagreed about the relations of Christ's humanity to His deity and thus the nature of His presence in the Supper, they agreed on one very important truth—in the Supper the living, Triune God meets His people and nourishes them. The question was not *whether*, but *how*.'[80] As Timothy George puts it, *we need to reclaim a theology of presence.* The Reformers differed as to what was involved in Christ's presence in the Supper, but they did stress that he was present. The Lord's Supper is not only a meal with symbols, it also involves communion with Christ. [81]

Connected to the above point is the lesson that a true understanding of the Lord's Supper cannot take place in isolation from other doctrines of the faith. In particular, such an understanding involves appreciating the person and work of Christ, the role of the Holy Spirit, and the functions of the church and its ministers. The Reformers remind us that it is possible for a religious rite to descend into an exhibition of clericalism, commercialism, scholasticism and spectatatorism (to use George's insights mentioned earlier). But they also remind us that it is possible to recover a comprehensive range of biblical doctrines which will lead to a restored biblical practice.

In response to the various views of the Reformers, several other comments can be made. First, the notion of consubstantiation is non-biblical, because it requires that Christ's human nature received divine properties, particularly the property of omnipresence, when he was exalted at his ascension. In effect, the idea of consubstantiation denies the ongoing humanness of Christ's human nature.

Second, the emphasis on memorialism is fine as far as it goes, but Paul's comments on communion indicate that what happens at the Supper is more than an act of remembrance.

Third, while we need not accept every aspect of Calvin's teaching, it is recognized that his emphasis on communion through the Spirit with the risen Christ who conveys spiritual life to his people through what is symbolised at the Supper is a biblical teaching. This emphasis of Calvin's also leads to another important aspect of the Supper, that it is primarily an activity of Christ in feeding his people, and then secondarily an act of his people in remembering him.

Fourth, we should not forget Zwingli's emphasis on the corporate nature of the Supper, that in addition to fellowship with Christ, believers have fellowship with one another.

Fifth, we need to return to the practice of more frequent communions.[82] The Reformers wanted weekly celebrations, and although they failed in the attempt, they were aiming to return the church to New Testament practice. Reformation should not be left to the past, rather it should be an ongoing phenomenon. The common objection to more frequent communions is the possibility of becoming so used to the practice that it becomes a mere ritual. But that objection can be made against any biblical feature of worship, whether it be the singing of praise, prayer or preaching.

Sixth, we need to restore the balance between Word and sacrament in Christian worship.[83] For the Reformers, the believers needed both the audible Word of God in sermonic form and the visible words of God in the sacraments. A service containing both a sermon and a supper conveys truth in both these ways. The audible explains what the visible depicts and the visible enables the worshipper to be involved in what is proclaimed.

Seventh, as far as Scotland was concerned, consubstantiation did not become an influential interpretation of the Lord's Supper within Scottish Presbyterianism. The other two views, associated with Zwingli and Calvin, were advocated, although it was the interpretation of Calvin that became the common understanding in post-Reformation Scottish Presbyterianism.[84]

5

Communion Seasons in the Scottish Lowlands

Prior to the composition of the Scots Confession, there had been an increasing opposition to the Roman Catholic practice of the Mass. Adamson mentions that the beginning of popular opposition can be 'attributed to the evangelical influence of Wycliffe's Bible, and to the Lollard propagandism which reached the Northern Kingdom [Scotland] in the fifteenth century. It is one of the Lollard tenets, recorded by Knox in his History, that to adore the Sacrament is idolatry.'[1] The desire for change was continued through the preaching and writings of Patrick Hamilton and others, and was enhanced by the influence of Genevan doctrine on many Scottish refugees on the continent at that period.[2] In 1560, John Knox, assisted by others, produced the Scots Confession and the First Book of Discipline.

Regarding the Lord's Supper, the Scots Confession denied transubstantiation, consubstantiation and mere memorialism, but affirmed the teaching of Calvin: the mystical union *'is wrocht by operatioun of the Holy Ghost, who by tre faith caryes us above all things that ar visible, carnall and earthlie, and maikis us to feid upoun the body and bloode of Christ Jesus, whiche was ones brokin and schedd for us, whiche now is in the heavin, and appeareth in the presence of the Father for us.'*[3]

The Book of Discipline affirms that the Supper should be held quarterly,[4] with the time of the Passover[5] not being of significance. The superstitions of the time are to be avoided and the ignorant are to be instructed and carefully examined before participation. Terms used are 'Supper' and 'the table of the Lord'. Concerning what took place, the compilers said:

> The Table of the Lord is then most rightly ministered when it approacheth most neare to Christs own action. But plaine it is, that at Supper Christ Jesus sate with his Disciples; and therefore doe we

judge that sitting at a table is most convenient to that holy action; that bread and wine ought to be there; that thankes ought to be given; distribution of the same made; and that all should likewise drinke of the cup of wine, with declaration what both one and the other is; we suppose no godly man will doubt…

That the Minister breake the bread and distribute the same to those that be next to him, commanding the rest, everie one with reverence and sobrietie to breake with other, we thinke it nearest to Christs action, and to the perfect practise, as we read in saint Paul; during which action we thinke it necessarie, that some comfortable places of the Scripture be read, which may bring in minde the death of Christ Jesus, and the benefit of the same. For seeing that in that action we ought chiefly to remember the Lords death, we judge the Scriptures making mention of the same, most apt to stirre up our dull mindes then, and al times. Let the discretion of the Ministers appoint the places to be read as they think good.[6]

The compilers were also concerned that ministers examine the intending communicants before the sacrament took place, with none to be admitted who could not 'formally say the Lords prayer, the Articles of the Beliefe, and declare the summe of the Law'.[7] The General Assembly of 1562 instructed that the Lord's Supper be held quarterly in towns and twice a year in rural parishes.[8]

The Book of Geneva was authorised by the same General Assembly for uniform use in the administration of the sacraments and solemnisation of marriages, and burial of the dead. It was revised and increased during the next two years, with further prayers and the completed Psalter included, so that in 1564 the General Assembly 'ordained that every Minister, Exhorter, and Reader shall have one of the Psalm-books, lately printed in Edinburgh, and use the Order contained therein in Prayers, Marriage, and ministration of the Sacraments'. This Book of Common Order, known as Knox's Liturgy, and modelled on the Book of Geneva, 'embodied the law of the Church from 1564 till 1645',[9] despite the attempt by King James I to bring about an Episcopalian liturgy, as seen in the five articles accepted by the General Assembly in 1618.[10] Public opposition was strong against

Communion Seasons in the Scottish Lowlands

this and subsequent additions, and the opposition resulted in a return to the liturgy of the Book of Common Order.[11] Although there was opposition to an Episcopalian uniformity, a more favourable response was given to the proposal that a uniform scheme involving doctrine, worship and church government be arranged for the Reformed churches in Scotland and England, which eventually resulted in the Westminster Directory replacing the Book of Common Order in 1645.

The communion service in a sixteenth-century Presbyterian church in Lowland Scotland was very different from services in subsequent centuries.[12] The sexes were segregated for worship in different parts of the church building. During the sermon and other preliminaries the congregation would sit or stand outside the fenced-off area that contained the tables. This area was not used until the minister left the pulpit and came down to begin the celebration of the Supper. When he had entered the area he then invited the communicants to come forward through gates on both sides of the fence. An elder stood at each gate and received tokens from the communicants as they entered the area.

The use of a table around which communicants sat is an old practice, having been traced back as early as the second century.[13] In Scotland, long after the Reformation, special communion tables were constructed. Up until the middle of the seventeenth century the table was surrounded by a fence called a 'travess' or 'flake', designed to keep out unwelcome participants. Presiding ministers were under General Assembly instructions to sit at the table rather than partake separately. Usually a table was not large enough to take all the communicants, and therefore the table was filled by successive groups of communicants. When pews were introduced into churches at the turn of the eighteenth and nineteenth centuries, the tables tended to disappear, although some can still be seen.

The use of a white cloth on the table also dates from early times; the first known mention of it is the year 384.[14] An ancient church leader, Isadore of Pelusium, said the white cloth represented the body of Jesus wrapped in the fine linen of Joseph

71

of Arimathea. The Reformers saw a different meaning: the white cloth suggested the purity and holiness of believers.[15] The custom of having a white cloth was not universal. Hunter suggests their expensive cost prevented churches replacing them when they came into a state of disrepair.[16]

Tokens were used to admit individuals to the table. To begin with, they were paper or cardboard tickets, but soon they were made of metal, with a congregational identity stamped on one side. In the middle of the nineteenth century, communion cards were introduced, but metal tokens are still used in the Highlands. The giving of a token by a kirk session indicated that the individual had passed the test for church membership. Visitors to a communion had to give evidence of church membership before they received a token.[17]

At the close of the sermon, the minister offered a prayer that included intercession, thanksgiving and the Lord's Prayer, after which the congregation joined in the reciting of the Apostles' Creed. The minister then left the pulpit while a psalm was sung and at the same time elders nominated for fetching the elements went to get them. 'Bringing the elements' was called the 'Great Procession' to distinguish it from the 'Little Procession' in which the beadle, carrying a Bible, preceded the minister into the pulpit. It was already an old custom at the time, being traced to the time of Justin Martyr.[18]

At the Table the minister read the words of institution and fenced[19] the tables before giving thanks for the bread and wine. This was followed by the 'fraction' (the breaking of the bread) by the minister, who first served himself if other ministers were not present. If another minister was present, he would serve the presiding minister at the next table. According to Burnet, the modern practice of elders serving the minister breaks with both Primitive and Reformed tradition; in the Reformed tradition the minister represents the Lord and so gives the elements to all, including himself. The elders are only there to pass on to the people what they have received from him. [20]

The minister passed the elements to those nearest him, and

they proceeded to pass them from one to another at the table. During this period of communicating, biblical passages were read. One reason for this was to prevent the worshippers from giving too much attention to the elements and not appreciating the spiritual realities they represented.

Preparations for the Sunday communion service included an examination either held publicly in the church by minister and elders or privately in homes by elders. The process in both urban and rural parishes could be time-consuming, sometimes taking over a month to complete.[21] The people were examined regarding biblical knowledge and daily behaviour, and with regard to the latter[22] it was deemed important to assess whether reconciliation with other believers was necessary. If there was not enough time to interview all the people, then the celebration of the sacrament would be delayed. Fasting was left to the individual conscience and was not required by the ecclesiastical authorities. The elders examined one another: 'In the Kirk-Session there was the meeting held for private dealing with one another. Each elder in succession left the room, and in his absence the others were asked if they knew anything against their brother, and, if there was no objection, he was called in and "encouraged to continue his work in the Lord".'[23]

On the Saturday a sermon designed to help prepare for the communion was commonly held, although it was not regarded as compulsory, with its role being regarded as beneficial. The morning communion service was followed by a thanksgiving service in the afternoon; the second service was regarded as very important and all who communicated in the morning were expected to attend.[24]

Communion seasons became a feature of Scottish Presbyterian church life from the early seventeenth century. The most noted occasion was at Kirk of Shotts in 1630 when several hundred people professed faith in Christ, at which event some of Scotland's best-known preachers, including John Livingston and Robert Bruce, were present. Communion seasons attracting large crowds took place in Ulster and south-west Scotland, two Presbyterian areas of influence, and continued to be held during the early years of the Covenanting period throughout Scotland. Many thousands were converted to Christ through these gatherings.

Yet, as time passed, all was not well in the Scottish Presbyterian experience of the Lord's Supper. The measures of the anti-Presbyterian government of Charles II prevented large communion gatherings from occurring, apart from occasional events held in defiance of these laws.[25]

A more serious threat came from the division within Presbyterianism caused by the Protestors/Resolutioners divide. The Protestors opposed those who accepted the future Charles II's acceptance of the Covenants because they suspected he was insincere. The Resolutioners regarded this outlook as bordering on treason. The Protestors were barred from the 1651 Assembly. Among the Protestors were leaders such as James Guthrie and Samuel Rutherford and among the Resolutioners were leaders such as Robert Baillie and James Ferguson. The division lasted throughout the reign of Charles II. The breach meant that Protestor and Resolutioner would not sit together at the Lord's Table. The celebration of the Lord's Supper was discontinued in many towns and rural parishes for several years, with even Edinburgh not having a communion between 1649 and 1655.[26]

After the 1688 Revolution, the Church of Scotland attempted to provide a Presbyterian minister in every parish. Some were inducted without difficulty, but in other areas there was opposition,[27] which meant that it took several decades for Presbyterianism to gain the ascendancy. Once it did, communion seasons regained their influence in Scottish Presbyterianism and retained it in the Lowlands until the nineteenth century.[28]

During the seventeenth century, common practices developed throughout the Lowlands concerning the Lord's Supper. From the end of the sixteenth century preparatory services had been held on the Saturday preceding the communion. The fast day, although not always on a Thursday, was introduced gradually from the beginning of the seventeenth century. Thanksgiving services were initially held on Sunday afternoons, with the change to Monday occurring after the revival at Kirk of Shotts in 1630, when many were converted at the special thanksgiving service on the Monday.[29] By the beginning of the eighteenth century, the communion season included a fast day on the Thursday, preparatory services on the Saturday, action sermons and the sacrament on the Sunday, and thanksgiving services on the Monday. A. R. MacEwan summarises a communion season in the Lowlands at that time:

> When a celebration was intimated in any one parish, hundreds and often thousands of people poured into it from the neighbouring parishes and remained for three, four or five days, listening from morning till night to a series of sermons which culminated in the religious rite…. It was the more serious and earnest of the people who frequented such assemblies. Young men when preparing for ordination would spend many weeks in attending Sacraments, riding or walking across country from one parish to another. When the faithful ministers of the day condemned those who 'ran from Sacrament to Sacrament', their condemnation rested upon the strain which their practice laid upon religious emotion. Their language, which was always respectful and kindly, might be applied with but slight modification to the modern practice of attending conferences, congresses and retreats.
>
> Those celebrations had a direct bearing upon the history of the Church. In every district they created a bond between the religiously disposed, who became acquainted with one another and exchanged views upon church affairs, gaining in this way an independence of parish limits and some width of outlook. They also gave great influence to the ministers who were most in request on such occasions, for the sermons were as a rule neither rhetorical displays nor appeals to sentiment, but careful expositions of Bible doctrine, with measured references to the questions which were before the Church of the day.[30]

The origin of large gatherings as a regular feature is usually connected to the Protestors in the 1650s.[31] Prior to this, large gatherings had not occurred in an organised way, although it was known for individual ministers occasionally to attract large crowds; for example, William Watson of Burntisland had about 1,000 communicants at communions between 1609 and 1613.[32] Two well-known large gatherings prior to the 1650s can be explained as being caused by other reasons. The great gathering at Shotts in 1630 was the result of local circumstances and no attempt was made to repeat it.[33] The other large gathering, at Mauchline in 1648, preceded the battle at Mauchline Moor on the next day, and the crowd at the gathering was swollen by hundreds of anti-royalist people.[34] But the Protestors made use of the practice, and were strengthened by the common discontent at infrequent communions. These large communion seasons were a means of drawing their supporters closer together and also encouraging others to join them.[35] Several ministers would be involved, and such great crowds would gather, often resulting in sermons being held in the open-air as well as in the church. The Lord's Supper was held in the church, and the communicants went in relays to participate.[36] 'At a communion in Burntisland in 1739 by Associate Presbytery ministers, we are assured, no less than 11,000 assembled from all parts of the realm. There were forty-three double tables, we are informed, at each of which sat one hundred and six communicants. The church, of course, could accommodate only a fraction of the number who had to take their turn at the table, the celebration occupying most of the day.'[37]

For those who could not get into the church, open-air sermons were arranged. The preacher spoke from a wooden pulpit, called a tent because it had a tent-like roof.[38] Sometimes several preachers spoke simultaneously from different tents placed in suitable places, at other times they preached sequentially from one tent.

Many who attended these services had no intention of sitting at the table; some came from curiosity, others to see friends, and others to see the excitement associated with the event.[39] In the eighteenth century, these occasions resulted in unwelcome extra features. Local inns began to supply drink for use on the Monday by those attending the celebration, and booths were set up to supply food for those who had travelled from a distance.[40]

But there were also reasons as to why many true believers did not participate in the Lord's Supper, and John Brown of Edinburgh detailed several of them in a volume of sacramental sermons, first in 1816 and then in 1853. One reason sometimes given was lack of preparation due to believers having failed to attend the preparatory services, with the result that they were not in a good frame of mind because 'their faith is weak, their hope is dead and their affections are languid', and so such 'deem it warrantable and reasonable to neglect communicating'. Brown comments this outlook is 'just as rational conduct as it would be in a fatigued traveller to refuse a cordial because he was faint, or in a person perishing for want to refuse bread because he was hungry.'

A second reason was fear of eating and drinking unworthily and thus sealing their own condemnation. Brown notes that the same principle should cause them to refrain from all religious exercises.

A third reason was 'the fear of that increased guilt which will be incurred by sins after communicating'. Brown affirms that such sins are serious, but not unpardonable, and if a person truly fears sinning, then he should carefully use the means God has appointed for dealing with personal sin, one of which is frequent communicating at the Supper. Brown likens the person with this outlook as being like a 'man who will not take nourishing food, lest, if attacked by a fever, he should suffer more than if his constitution were less robust.'

A fourth reason given for not participating was the argument that since no denomination conformed to the primitive standard it was unsafe to hold communion with them. Brown admits that Jesus has made no provision for this supposed case, but points out that 'if there is a danger of being unscripturally lax, there is also a danger of being unscripturally rigid.'

A fifth reason given was that of custom, of imitating the practice of others who did not participate in the Supper. It was not difficult for Brown to refute this idea since the sins of others will form no excuse for ours before the tribunal of God.

A sixth reason was the claim that failure to participate was not a refusal but a delay in obeying the command of the Saviour. To this objection, Brown responded by stating that 'to refuse immediate compliance with an injunction which requires it is disobedience'. Further, a present opportunity may be the last occasion for such to remember their Saviour.[41]

There were other occasional features associated with communion seasons. One was a special collection for the poor. Another was the practice on the Monday of one of the ministers summarising all the addresses that had been delivered at the communion.[42]

At the beginning of the nineteenth century, the evangelical revival in the Church of Scotland 'was at once a cause and an effect of a more positively doctrinal religion than that which had been recently in the ascendant. The "cold morality" of Moderatism gave place to a new proclamation of the doctrines of the Atonement and the Holy Spirit. The new fervour made itself felt at Communion seasons, when evangelical divines were often heard at their best.'[43] These divines included leaders such as Thomas Chalmers and popular preachers such as Edward Irving and Robert Murray McCheyne, with the latter writing a tract called 'This Do in Remembrance of Me'.[44] It still was the practice for large crowds in rural areas to travel large distances to attend these occasions.

As mentioned earlier, John Brown of Edinburgh published a volume of sacramental sermons, first in 1816 and then in 1853. He wrote of the practice in 1816: 'The observance was observed in a few cases, chiefly in large towns, four times a-year; in most country places among the Dissenters, and in some in the Establishment, twice; in many of the Established Churches only once.' Things had changed by 1853, especially among the United Presbyterians. 'The ordinance is more frequently administered – in very many congregations four times, in some six times, in at least one twelve times, in the course of the year; and in many instances, the practice of simultaneous communion has been introduced. The fast-day and other week-day services, if not altogether discontinued, are by no means uniformly connected with the communion; and "tent preaching," as it was called, has, except in some instances among the Reformed Presbyterians, disappeared from the Lowlands.'[45]

Within the next fifty years the communion season was to disappear from the Lowlands. Douglas Bannerman of the Free Church of Scotland, writing in 1887, noted that '[i]t must be plain to all of us that we are at a transition stage with respect to one characteristic of Scottish Church life, our communion seasons. The old "Sacramental Fast-Day," and other arrangements in the way of special preparation before the Communion and of thanksgiving after it, are rapidly disappearing from among us. In the Lowlands of Scotland, they will soon be things of the past.'[46]

Experiences of Duguld Buchanan

Before closing this chapter, it should be of interest to observe how an individual profited spiritually from attending communion seasons. Duguld Buchanan lived in Perthshire, on the borders of the Lowlands and Highlands. Today he is best known for his Gaelic religious verse and is regarded as one of the foremost Gaelic poets. He was a schoolmaster by profession, and in later years was a very effective evangelist, although he was never ordained. His diary has been translated into English, and extracts from it describe his experiences at some Lowland communion occasions shortly before he was converted in 1742 at the age of twenty-six and subsequently.[47]

'*July 1742*. On the second Sabbath of this month the sacrament was dispensed at Muthil. Thither he went to dedicate himself to the Lord at His table. The ministrations of Mr Halley were much blest to him.

'From Muthil he went, soon after, to Cambuslang. A remarkable work of grace was progressing there under the ministry of Mr M'Culloch, Mr Whitefield, and others. "I was greatly comforted by hearing people narrate their religious experiences to one another. On the Sabbath there was a great multitude gathered. Such a sight I never saw. Mr Whitefield lectured from Matthew 19, and there was an uncommon concern among the people."

'From Cambuslang he went to Comrie, to the sacrament. Here he heard Mr Halley of Muthil. He discoursed from Matthew 5. "The Lord helped me to make application of the third and sixth

verses. But not many days after, I raised all the foundations thinking it was a delusion." About this time, he found a treatise on
the doctrine of Justification by Faith, which helped him greatly.
It showed the different views people had of Christ when closing
with him for salvation. The author remarks, that the first actings
of faith are variously described in the Bible, such as looking unto
Jesus – coming to Christ – fleeing to the city of refuge – running
into His name, as into a strong tower – committing the soul into
his hands – and trusting in His name – so that the first actings of
faith in the soul may vary. Some have clearer views of Christ, and
are enabled to believe in Him more strongly. Others are weaker in
faith. As the manslayer, hasting for his life to one of the cities of
refuge, was ordered to flee to that which was nearest to him, so it
is the duty of sinners to flee immediately to Christ, and to that in
Him, of which they have the clearest discernment; and which in
that respect is nearest to them. Though the distinct actings of
faith may vary, yet in the main they agree; inasmuch as it is in the
one Christ they believe for justification of life. They all flee to the
one Christ, the one refuge, and so are safe. "This passage," he
says, "was the means of showing me several mistakes into which
I had fallen"...

'From Comrie he went to Kilsyth. "On Monday," he says – the
Monday after the communion – "I was suddenly enlarged in prayer,
and my soul was drawn out after a whole Christ. I came away
rejoicing in the Lord and in His goodness."

'But the clouds returned after the rain. "I soon became vain
and proud of my duties. The Lord did not suffer my pride to
swell. He discovered to me the iniquity that was in my heart, which
was the means of humbling me in the dust. He blasted my gifts. I
could scarcely ask a blessing on common mercies. He withdrew
from me in some measure His restraining grace; and left me to
wrestle with my heart idols. Then arose such a darkness and
deadness in my spirit, that I could not think, desire, or do anything."
This, he thinks, was a chastisement for spiritual pride.'

Buchanan had a profound spiritual experience on January 2nd,
1743, from 1 Corinthians 1:30. He does not indicate where he

was – at home or in a church service or elsewhere. He regarded this event as his conversion, and the verse from 1 Corinthians was 'my charter for the heavenly inheritance.'

"'*26th March* 1743, was set apart for fasting and humiliation in private, for my unsuitable carriage since my bands were loosed; and also because I intended to go to the sacrament of the Lord's Supper at Glasgow."

'This year he went to Kippen, the residence of earlier times; and where he heard the communion was to be dispensed. It was a happy season for him. He had sweet manifestations of God's love, and great delight in the preaching of the word, "by which," he says, "the secrets of his heart were made manifest." On the evening of the communion Sabbath he resorted to a glen, where, in former and less happy times, he was wont to pour out his heart to God. He perused the seventeenth chapter of the Gospel by John, and meditated on the contrast between his present and former devotions in the same place.

'Buchanan was at this period in the twenty-seventh year of his age, and living at Ardoch, but how employed we have no means of ascertaining. He found time, however, to make occasional excursions to neighbouring parishes, where the Sacrament of the Supper was being celebrated. These were times of refreshing to him, as the following entries show:

"'I went next Sabbath to the Port of Monteith to receive the seal of the covenant. So I received the seal of the everlasting covenant; and before I arose from the table, with what grief, joy, and wonder did I behold my dear Redeemer bruised under the Father's wrath, which justly belonged to me.

"'After that I went to Kilsyth. On Sabbath morning I heard Mr Robe preach the action sermon from Rev. i. 17, 18. I never felt more of the power of God than I did on that occasion. Afterwards I reviewed my whole exercises from the day in which I was first awakened, to that moment; and saw that the foundation of my peace was built upon the rock of ages; and then with the foolish virgins fell asleep for some time, until the Lord sent a messenger of Satan to buffet me.'"

'*August 1745.* "The Sacrament of the Lord's Supper being about to be dispensed in a neighbouring congregation, I went there, and got a soul-refreshing view of Christ at his own table, both in a way of correction and comfort, these Scriptures being presented to my view. Ezek. vi. 9 ; Amos ii. 13. At evening I went to secret prayer; and if ever I was sincere in anything, it was in dedicating myself to the service of God. Yea, I was made to believe that he accepted me in the beloved; therefore, I concluded that my mountain stood strong, and that I should never be moved. But little did I think, what storm was coming, and what a journey I had to go before I was to get another meal – no less than two whole years."

'"*July 22d, 1750.* I got intimation that the Sacrament was to be dispensed at Muthil. That was the place in which my soul was first made to lay hold on Jesus Christ; and where I was often instructed and comforted by the ministry of the word. Mr Gillespie of Carnock preached from 2 Cor. iv. 8, 'We are troubled on every side, yet not distressed.' The reading of the text was a sermon to me. He showed what distresses and perplexities arise from remaining corruption; and the subtlety of Satan, and why they are not in despair by all the devil, the flesh, and the world can do. I was melted down under the sermon, and thought all my bands were loosening, and the clouds dispelling. But immediately Satan raised an objection, that such a person as the minister described could not be a child of God. One other link added to Satan's chain, and he would have devoured me. But God who is all eye to see, as well as all ear to hear, and who knows my frame, remembered that I was dust. On my way home I sat down to rest, and in a minutes time, all my doubts were dispersed. The gates of brass, and iron bars of unbelief were broken in a thousand pieces, and my captive soul set at liberty.'"

Chapter 6

Theology of the Lord's Supper
in the Scottish Lowlands

In this chapter, I will consider the various ways in which the Lord's Supper was regarded in the Scottish Lowlands by prominent theologians and preachers. These will include famous teachers of divinity such as James Durham, George Hill, Thomas Dick, Daniel Dewar, John Brown and William Cunningham. I will also consider the opinions of well-known preachers: Robert Bruce, Thomas Boston and John Willison.

These authors come from different periods of history and from several Presbyterian denominations. From the early centuries of the Scottish Protestant church, I chose Bruce and Durham; Bruce was a Reformer from the sixteenth and seventeenth centuries, Durham was a Covenanter from the seventeenth century.

From the eighteenth century I chose Hill, Boston and Willinson, each being a minister of the Church of Scotland; Hill was a Professor at St Andrews in the first two decades of the century and was a leading Moderate; Boston was an evangelical minister of rural congregations in days of spiritual decline in the first three decades of the eighteenth century, but who died before the appearance of the Secession church; Willison, a minister in Dundee, was an evangelical minister of the Church of Scotland in the first half of the eighteenth century who refused to leave and join the Secession churches which were a protest movement against the spiritual apathy of the time.

From the late eighteenth century and the first half of the nineteenth century, I selected four ministers who were also professors of theology: John Brown belonged to the United Presbyterian Church, William Cunningham to the Free Church of Scotland, Daniel Dewer to the Church of Scotland, and

Thomas Dick to the United Secession Church.

Inevitably, these spokesmen are selective, since such views must be taken from published works, and the further back one goes the more scarce becomes the availability of writings on the topic. But they are diverse enough to be representative of conservative Presbyterians in Lowland Scotland, and given that each was theologically qualified their writings should contain their mature thought. I will also consider the teaching of the seventeenth century Westminster Confession of Faith, because it became the creed of Scottish Presbyterian denominations. But I will begin with the Scots Confession.

The Scots Confession (1560)

The compilers of the Scots Confession[1] set forth their understanding of the Eucharist in three chapters. In chapter 21, entitled 'The Sacraments', several features can be identified.

First, the Lord's Supper is one of two sacraments instituted by Christ:

> As the fathers under the Law, besides the reality of the sacrifices, had two chief sacraments, that is, circumcision and the passover, and those who rejected these were not reckoned among God's people; so do we acknowledge and confess that now in the time of the gospel we have two chief sacraments, which alone were instituted by the Lord Jesus and commanded to be used by all who will be counted members of his body, that is, Baptism and the Supper or Table of the Lord Jesus, also called the Communion of His Body and Blood.

Second, the Lord's Supper, as with the other sacraments, is not a mere sign, but in line with the emphasis of Calvin also involves interaction with Jesus Christ:

> These sacraments, both of the Old Testament and of the New, were instituted by God not only to make a visible distinction between his people and those who were without the Covenant, but also to exercise the faith of his children and, by participation of these

sacraments, to seal in their hearts the assurance of his promise, and of that most blessed conjuction, union, and society, which the chosen have with their Head, Christ Jesus. And so we utterly condemn the vanity of those who affirm the sacraments to be nothing else than naked and bare signs. No, we assuredly believe that by Baptism we are engrafted into Christ Jesus, to be made partakers of his righteousness, by which our sins are covered and remitted, and also that in the Supper rightly used, Christ Jesus is so joined with us that he becomes the very nourishment and food for our souls.

Third, unlike the teaching of transubstantiation, feeding on Christ in the Lord's Supper is enabled by the Holy Spirit:

Not that we imagine any transubstantiation of bread into Christ's body, and of wine into his natural blood, as the Romanists have perniciously taught and wrongly believed; but this union and conjunction which we have with the body and blood of Christ Jesus in the right use of the sacraments is wrought by means of the Holy Ghost, who by true faith carries us above all things that are visible, carnal, and earthly, and makes us feed upon the body and blood of Christ Jesus, once broken and shed for us but now in heaven, and appearing for us in the presence of his Father.

As with Calvin, this involves an overcoming of the distance between heaven, where Christ now is, and earth:

Notwithstanding the distance between his glorified body in heaven and mortal men on earth, yet we must assuredly believe that the bread which we break is the communion of Christ's body and the cup which we bless the communion of his blood.

Fourth, partaking of the body and blood of the Lord is a means of maintaining union with Christ and receiving life and immortality from God:

Thus we confess and believe without doubt that the faithful, in the right use of the Lord's Table, do so eat the body and drink the blood of the Lord Jesus that he remains in them and they in him;

they are so made flesh of his flesh and bone of his bone that as the eternal Godhood has given to the flesh of Christ Jesus, which by nature was corruptible and mortal, life and immortality, so the eating and drinking of the flesh and blood of Christ Jesus does the like for us.

Fifth, reception of the body and blood of Christ is not tied to the time of the sacrament, nor to the sacrament in itself, and remains beyond the understanding of natural man:

> We grant that this is neither given to us merely at the time nor by the power and virtue of the sacrament alone, but we affirm that the faithful, in the right use of the Lord's Table, have such union with Christ Jesus as the natural man cannot apprehend.

The activity of the Holy Spirit subsequent to the sacrament ensures that the fruit that could have been received at the sacrament but was not received because of human failings, will be given later by him:

> Further we affirm that although the faithful, hindered by negligence and human weakness, do not profit as much as they ought in the actual moment of the Supper, yet afterwards it shall bring forth fruit, being living seed sown in good ground; for the Holy Spirit, who can never be separated from the right institution of the Lord Jesus, will not deprive the faithful of the fruit of that mystical action.

As with Calvin, great stress is laid on the work of the Holy Spirit in connection with the Lord's Supper. Yet the work of the Spirit did not negate the need for the faith of the believer to be in exercise, nor did it mean that the Spirit was acting independently of the ascended Christ: 'Yet all this, we say again, comes of that true faith which apprehends Christ Jesus, who alone makes the sacrament effective in us.'

The compilers stress that they are neither followers of those who suggest the Lord's Supper is only a memorial ('Therefore, if anyone slanders us by saying that we affirm or believe the sacraments to be symbols and nothing more, they are libelous and speak against the plain facts') or of those who fail to distinguish between the person of Christ and the elements of bread and wine '(On the other hand we readily admit that we make a distinction between Christ Jesus in his eternal substance and the elements of the sacramental signs'). Unlike Roman Catholics who believe in transubstantiation, the Scottish Reformers 'neither worship the elements, in place of that which they signify', and unlike Zwinglians neither do they 'despise them or undervalue them, but we use them with great reverence, examining ourselves diligently before we participate, since we are assured by the mouth of the apostle that "whoever shall eat this bread, and drink this cup of the Lord, unworthily, shall be guilty of the body and blood of the Lord".'

Chapter 22 concerns the 'The Right Administration of the Sacraments'. The Scottish Reformers identified two features that are essential to a right administration:

> The first is that they should be ministered by lawful ministers, and we declare that these are men appointed to preach the Word, unto whom God has given the power to preach the gospel, and who are lawfully called by some Kirk. The second is that they should be ministered in the elements and manner which God has appointed. Otherwise they cease to be the sacraments of Christ Jesus.

These two requirements justified their separation from the Roman Catholic Church's practice: 'firstly, because their ministers are not true ministers of Christ Jesus (indeed they even allow women, whom the Holy Ghost will not permit to preach in the congregation, to baptize) and, secondly, because they have so adulterated both the sacraments with their own additions that no part of Christ's original act remains in its original simplicity.' The 'adulteration' is detailed:

- The addition of oil, salt, spittle, and such like in baptism, are merely human additions.
- To adore or venerate the sacrament, to carry it through streets and towns in procession, or to reserve it in a special case, is

not the proper use of Christ's sacrament but an abuse of it. Christ Jesus said, 'Take ye, eat ye,' and 'Do this in remembrance of me.' By these words and commands he sanctified bread and wine to be the sacrament of his holy body and blood, so that the one should be eaten and that all should drink of the other, and not that they should be reserved for worship or honoured as God, as the Romanists do.

• Further, in withdrawing one part of the sacrament—the blessed cup—from the people, they have committed sacrilege.

• Moreover, if the sacraments are to be rightly used it is essential that the end and purpose of their institution should be understood, not only by the minister but also by the recipients. For if the recipient does not understand what is being done, the sacrament is not being rightly used, as is seen in the case of the Old Testament sacrifices.

• Similarly, if the teacher teaches false doctrine which is hateful to God, even though the sacraments are his own ordinance, they are not rightly used, since wicked men have used them for another end than what God had commanded.

These features condemned Roman Catholic practice at the time:

We affirm that this has been done to the sacraments in the Roman Church, for there the whole action of the Lord Jesus is adulterated in form, purpose, and meaning. What Christ Jesus did, and commanded to be done, is evident from the Gospels and from St. Paul; what the priest does at the altar we do not need to tell. The end and purpose of Christ's institution, for which it should be used, is set forth in the words, 'Do this in remembrance of Me,' and 'For as often as ye eat this bread and drink this cup ye do show'—that is, extol, preach, magnify, and praise—'the Lord's death, till He come.' But let the words of the mass, and their own doctors and teachings witness, what is the purpose and meaning of the mass; it is that, as mediators between Christ and his Kirk, they should offer to God the Father, a sacrifice in propitiation for the sins of the living and of the dead. This doctrine is blasphemous to Christ Jesus and would deprive his unique sacrifice, once offered on the cross for the cleansing of all who are to be sanctified, of its sufficiency; so we detest and renounce it.

Chapter 22 concerns 'To Whom Sacraments Appertain'. The Lord's Supper is only for members of the household of faith who have the capacity to 'try and examine themselves both in their faith and their duty to their neighbours'. A description is given of what it is to partake unworthily: 'Those who eat and drink at that holy table without faith, or without peace and goodwill to their brethren, eat unworthily.' This stress on brotherly relationships was an important feature of preparation in the Reformation Church and is a rebuke to subsequent divisions within Scottish Protestantism which often displayed its separations at celebrations of the Lord's Supper. The Scots Confession stresses the responsibility of ministers to ensure, both by public teaching and personal contact, that participants were ready to go to the Lord's Table: 'This is the reason why ministers in our Kirk make public and individual examination of those who are to be admitted to the table of the Lord Jesus.'

Robert Bruce (c. 1554-1631)

Robert Bruce was an Edinburgh minister, whose two periods of banishment to Inverness in the seventeenth century were occasions of major growth of the Protestant church in the north-east Highlands,[2] with people travelling to hear his preaching from Ross-shire, Caithness and Sutherland, as well as the areas around Inverness. Bruce's sermons on the Lord's Supper, when published, became a crucial source of discovering the meaning of the Supper.[3] One of Bruce's prominent emphases was his teaching on the Lord's Supper, in which he followed the view of Calvin.

Bruce regarded the Lord's Supper as having four purposes. First, it was 'appointed chiefly for this end, to represent our spiritual nutriment, the full and perfect nutriment of our souls; that as he who has Bread and Wine lacks nothing for the full nourishment of his body: so he, or that soul, which has the participation of the body and blood of Christ, lacks nothing of the full and perfect nourishment of the soul'.[4]

Second, the sacrament is an act of witness both to hostile onlookers and to fellow Christians. It was instituted in order 'that we might testify to the world and to the princes of the world, who are enemies to our profession; that we might openly avow and testify to them our Religion and our manner of worshipping; and that we might also testify our love towards His members our brethren'.[5]

Third, the sacrament is designed to be spiritual medicine, to help those tempted to fall or who have already fallen. It was instituted 'to serve for our special comfort and consolation, to serve as a sovereign medicine for all our spiritual diseases, as we find ourselves either ready to fall, or provoked to fall, by the devil, the flesh, or the world; or, after we have fallen and are put to flight by the devil, and would fain flee away from God; God of his mercy, and of His infinite pity and bottomless compassion has set up this sacrament, as a sign on a high hill, whereby it may seem on every side, far and near, to call them again that have run shamefully away: and He clucks to them as a hen doth to her chickens, to gather them under the wings of his infinite mercy.'[6]

Fourth, the sacrament is an occasion for thanksgiving: 'render to Him hearty thanks for His benefits, and that He has come down so familiarly to us, bowed the heavens as it were, and given us the body and blood of His own Son; that we might render unto Him hearty thanks, and so sanctify His benefits to us.'[7]

Bruce claimed that there are both visible and invisible things in the Lord's Supper. The visible things are the bread and the wine. The invisible things are signified by the bread and wine; what is signified is Christ, 'in this respect, that His body and blood serve to nourish my soul to life everlasting'. It is not just the benefits of Christ's death that are signified, but also the person of Christ from whom these benefits come.[8] In the sacrament of baptism, the fruits are forgiveness of sins, mortification of sins, and the sealing of adoption, but the substance out of which these fruits grow is the blood of Christ. Similarly, in the sacrament of the Lord's Supper, the fruits are growth of faith and increase in holiness, but the substance out of which they grow is the body and blood of Christ. Christ is to the soul what bread and drink are to the body. Bread must be eaten before hunger is relieved and drink must be taken before thirst is removed; so Christ must be taken at the Supper before his benefits are experienced.

According to Bruce, the bread in the Supper has a power given to it by the institution of Christ, whereby 'it is appointed to signify His body, to represent His body, and to deliver His body'.[9] This power remains with the bread as long as the Supper lasts.

For Bruce, it was essential that the ceremonies of breaking the bread and pouring the wine take place, because they signified what had happened to Christ. Similarly, the distribution, giving and eating are essential, as they signify the 'applying of the body and blood of Christ to thy soul'. Bruce even says that to leave one of them out perverts the whole action.[10]

Because the conjunction between the elements and Christ is secret and spiritual, that which receives him is faith. Bruce recognizes that faith does not receive a greater Christ in the Supper than it does from the preaching of the Word, but he does say that it receives Christ better in that the receiver obtains a greater and surer hold of Christ through the sacrament. This happens each time a person takes part in the Supper.[11]

In addition to faith, Bruce argued that the Holy Spirit must be involved in giving Christ to the believer. He notes that the believer has a title to the body of Christ and the blood of Christ, a title that is not negated by their being distant, in heaven. Faith is the cord that covers the distance between the believer and Christ and couples them together. Bruce uses the illustration of the sun — we cannot touch the sun, yet are conjoined to it by its rays. The sun is Christ, and the rays are his virtue and power flowing from his body. These are conveyed to the believer by the Holy Spirit, whom Bruce likens to a ladder joining the believer and Christ.[12]

The Westminster Assembly

The Westminster Assembly met to draw up documents detailing a common set of doctrines and church practices for England, Scotland and Ireland. The members of the Assembly, which included several Scots, had produced their documents by 1645. In the Confession of Faith a chapter is devoted to the Lord's Supper under eight paragraphs. Paragraph 1 details five purposes of the Lord's Supper:

1. for the perpetual remembrance of the sacrifice of himself in his death,
2. the sealing all benefits thereof unto true believers,
3. their spiritual nourishment and growth in him,
4. their further engagement in and to all duties which they owe unto him;
5. and to be a bond and pledge of their communion with him, and with each other, as members of his mystical body.[13]

Paragraph 2[14] states that the Lord's Supper is not a sacrifice for sin as in the Mass, but is 'a commemoration of that one offering up of himself, by himself, upon the cross, once for all, and a spiritual oblation of all possible praise unto God for the same'.

Paragraph 3[15] is concerned with the actions of the minister in administering the sacrament and specifies several of these actions:

1. Jesus appointed his ministers to declare his word of institution to the people,
2. to pray, and bless the elements of bread and wine, and thereby to set them apart from a common to an holy use;
3. and to take and break the bread, to take the cup,
4. and (they communicating also themselves) to give both to the communicants;
5. but to none who are not then present in the congregation.

The last detail of paragraph 3 leads on to paragraph 4,[16] in which several Roman Catholic practices are condemned:

1. Private masses, or receiving this sacrament by a priest, or any other, alone;
2. the denial of the cup to the people;
3. worshipping the elements, the lifting them up, or carrying them about for adoration,
4. and the reserving them for any pretended religious use.

Paragraphs 5 and 6 concern the nature of the elements. In paragraph 5,[17] it is stated that the bread and wine as to their substance and nature remain unchanged, although they sacramentally represent Christ's body and blood. Therefore the notion of transubstantiation, specifically mentioned in section 6,[18] is unfounded.

Paragraph 7[19] repudiates consubstantiation and affirms a spiritual reception of and feeding on Christ and all his benefits by faith of worthy receivers. Unworthy receivers, according to paragraph 8,[20] only receive the elements and not what they signify; in addition they expose themselves to divine judgment.

The Confession does not support the view of Zwingli for it does not regard the elements as bare signs. But neither does it affirm the view of Calvin that the Spirit removes the barrier of space between the ascended Christ and his people on earth.

The Confession is also silent regarding the posture of participants and the frequency of the celebration. This is not because the Scottish delegates were undecided on these matters, for they had opposed weekly celebrations and had insisted that participants sit at a table(s) when taking the bread and wine.[21] There was a prolonged debate about the matter,[22] but it is evident that the Assembly as a whole was not prepared to accept that the practice of the Scottish Presbyterians was the only legitimate way. Nevertheless the General Assembly approved another Westminster document, The Directory of Public Worship, in which there was a chapter concerning the Lord's Supper, and in it the beliefs of the Scottish church were included. The frequency of the sacrament is a matter for local elders, with the morning of the day being best for holding it,[23] and when this was not possible, suitable other forms of preparation should be adopted.[24] The Lord's Supper should follow the sermon and should be preceded by a short exhortation in which the minister indicated who should and who should not partake.[25] The Directory stresses that the communicants should sit at or around a table.[26] The minister is to read the words of institution[27] and then offer a prayer by which the elements are sanctified.[28] His attitude throughout is to be earnest.[29] Instructions are given detailing the minister's actions and words concerning the elements, to ensure that his involvement follows the example of Christ, and once all have partaken he may give a short exhortation.[30] The Supper is to be concluded by a prayer of thanksgiving.[31] While the collection for the poor should not be forgotten, neither should it delay any part of the public worship.[32]

James Durham (1622-58)

James Durham was both professor of divinity in Glasgow University (he was appointed in 1647) and minister of St. Mungo's Church in the city. He contributed to a Scottish Reformed understanding of the Lord's Supper through a volume of sermons that were preached at communion seasons.[33]

Durham recognised both the similarity and the distinctiveness of the Lord's Supper as compared to other means of grace: 'It is true, there is no other thing on the matter communicated in it that there is communicated in the Word and baptism. Yet, if we look to the words "Take ye, eat ye, this is My body," they hold out Christ Jesus not so much giving any particular gift, but as actually conferring Himself in His death and suffering. And the main scope is to confer Christ and all that is in Him to the believer, which holds out in some way the excellency of this ordinance beyond others.'[34]

Durham noted the reasons why the Lord had instituted the Supper: 'And, for the consolation of them [his disciples at the inauguration] and of all His followers to the end of the world, He institutes this ordinance of the communion to be His love-token in His absence, so that all His people might be confident of His respect for them as well as to those then present, and so that all of them might thereby be put and kept in remembrance of Him until His coming again.'[35]

In another sermon Durham explains, by means of questions and answers, in what way Christ is present in the Lord's Supper. In the first question, Durham stresses the importance of covenant as a means of understanding the incarnation and sufferings of Christ and for partaking in the Lord's Supper:

QUESTION 1. In what respect is Christ present and discernible in the sacrament?

ANSWER 1. Not simply considered as He is the Son of God, nor in respect of any benefit from Him as Mediator, neither simply as Redeemer; but He is held out as incarnate; and so this sacrament differs from the Jews' Passover, which held Him out as to come, while this one holds Him out as having come.

ANSWER 2. It holds Him out not only as becoming man, but as suffering, as having His body broken.

ANSWER 3. He is made discernible in respect of the end for which He suffered, and had His body broken and His blood shed. "This is My body which is broken for you; this cup is the new testament in My blood, shed for the remission of the sins of many (to wit, all the elect)." It holds out Christ as Mediator, God-man, suffering for us.

ANSWER 4: It holds Him out as communicable, and in capacity to be participated of by us; therefore it is called the communion of His body, to tell us, that we may be united to Him, and made to share of Him—and we are bid to take and eat, and all to drink of it.

The last two look to the covenant, and hold out the sacrament in reference to it, and how our Lord Jesus, first by His sufferings was to purchase a people for Himself, and second, that He was to be communicable to His people. Therefore the cup is called the new covenant in His blood. The cup and the covenant go together, for though we may consider Christ without the sacrament, yet we cannot consider the sacrament without Christ and the covenant.[36]

In the second question, Durham considers 'to what is Christ made discernable and communicable?' He first states that Christ, although truly present, is not present in a corporeal manner to the bodily eye. But neither is he 'present and communicable by any local mutation, by taking us up to heaven to Him, or by bringing His body out of heaven to us'. Durham's last clause seems to be against the doctrine of consubstantiation, while the previous clause may refer to a rejection of an aspect of Calvin's theology or to correcting a misunderstanding of Calvin's teaching on believers being raised to heaven to meet with Christ, for Durham does state later that believers at the sacrament have a union with Christ in glory, which indicates he accepted a presence of Christ similar to that taught by Calvin.

Durham explains three ways in which Christ is present and communicable in the Supper:

(1) To our spiritual senses, to an enlightened understanding, which considers Christ's body broken and His blood shed.

(2) To the faith of his people He is present in His own ordinance. When His Spirit goes along and quickens their hearts, and their faith is in exercise, they are made to apprehend Christ's body, and to have a union with Him sitting in glory, as really as they partake of the elements with their hand and feed upon them with their mouths and stomachs. This union is as real as that between the head and the members, and between the root and the branches. These two (the Spirit on Christ's side and faith on ours) make up a real union; and therefore, though this presence is real, yet it is spiritual. Faith, looking and going through the elements, takes up Christ according to the end appointed, and this makes the union (even as faith will look and go through the Word, and, crediting the Word, takes up Christ in it and makes a union with Him). So, by virtue of this ordinance, there is a spiritual presence of and union with Christ Jesus.

(3) A presence to sense, not so much in respect of inward feeling as in respect of the powerful effects of His presence, though often inward feeling goes along with it. And therefore it is called the communion of His body, and the wine of heaven. In respect of the means and way He manifests Himself therein, it is to the eye, to the touch, to the taste, and to the ear; and there is a colour sensible, which is more than is in any other ordinance, where there is but the exercise of one sense; for the more of the outward senses He makes

use of, He brings with Him a proportionable blessing to the inward senses of the soul.[37]

Durham mentions four ways in which Christ's presence is discernible. First, he is present in the words of institution, for it indicates his authority and warrant that he will make himself over to his people. Second, he is discernible in the elements of broken bread (representing his body broken by suffering) and wine poured out (shows a most true and real death), which indicate the purpose of his death and make it over to the communicant. Third, he is discernible in that the sacrament is a seal which ratifies and confirms the promises contained in the covenant – receiving the bread and wine is a seal of our participation in Christ similar to how a sealed charter of a house indicates that the person has been given the house. Fourth, Christ is discernible in that he is communicated to his people.[38]

Durham then gives three reasons as to why Christ will have his broken body made thus discernible and apprehensible in the Lord's Supper. First, it is to evidence Christ's great love to his people; second, it is for the public professing and testifying of faith in a dying Saviour; third, it is for the edification and benefit of his people. With regard to edification, Durham mentions instruction in the sense that some may be helped through the sacrament who do not so well take up Christ in the Word, when they see him as a slain Saviour who is as needful as meat and drink. It is also edifying because participating strengthens faith, promotes the inward growth of grace, and gives consolation to those disturbed by whether or not they are elect since it reminds them of Christ's covenant offer of mercy.[39]

Another aspect of the communion service that Durham stressed was the appropriateness of covenanting with God. He urges his listeners: 'You are put to it by this very sacrament. Is it possible that you can take the communion for a seal and confirmation unless you covenant with God beforehand?'[40] He indicates how the sacrament is useful and helpful in this joining to the Lord in covenant:

'For the believer, all the promises are his, and it seals all the blessings to him because the condition of the covenant is found in him. Even as a pardon is given to a rebel on the condition that he lays down his arms, when he does lay them down and accepts the pardon the seal is appended to it, which makes it firm and sure.'[41]

'In the sacrament the Lord condescends in the most formal way to covenant; for in it He says, "Take My Son's blood to wash you who are guilty and filthy." And your taking is, as it were, shaking hands with Him and saying, "I am content, Lord to let this blood wash me." And thus, looking to the word of institution which gives footing to faith, and exercising faith thereon as your warrant, your faith is helped to take hold of Christ by and in the sacrament.'[42]

Durham urged Christians to make use of the Lord's Supper as a means the Lord will use to seal particular blessings to them, including the assurance of forgiveness of their sins, their right to the promises of God, and the prospect of heaven. The last aspect is a stimulus for holy living: 'Think to yourself, "O believer in Christ, shall I, sinful and unworthy I, ere long sit with Christ at His table in glory? And is this a sign and representation of it under a veil? What manner of person ought I to be in all holy conversation and godliness? Ought I not to love Him much, and to continue with Him in all His temptations.'[43] And he reminded his hearers: "Tis a cheerful thing to go from the table of the Lord with this sweet and heavenly meditation: "Christ and I will meet ere long at a table in heaven".'[44]

Thomas Boston (1676-1732)

Although not a theological professor Boston was a profound theologian who, through his writings, has influenced the thinking of ministers and Christian laypeople in Scotland for 300 years. The works of Boston contain complete volumes, some published in his lifetime, and sermons. He comments on the Lord's Supper in a collection of sermons he preached to his congregation on the Westminster Shorter Catechism.[45]

Boston saw importance in the elements of bread and wine

(signifying things) and in the actions of the administrator of the sacrament (the presiding pastor) and the communicants.[46] As far as the outward elements are concerned, Boston regarded as indifferent what type of bread was used and what strength there was in the wine. The bread and the wine signified the 'body and blood of Christ, ver. 24, 25 [of I Corinthians 11], even a whole Christ, with all his benefits, forasmuch as the divine nature after the incarnation was never separated from the human, though the soul was separated from the body, and the precious blood from the flesh'.

Boston also mentions several resemblances between the outward elements and Christ. Bread is nourishing for the natural life, Christ nourishes the soul; bread is prepared by being ground between millstones and baked in a fire, so Christ was ground between the upper millstone of the Father's wrath and the lower millstone of the malice of men and devils, and then cast into the fiery furnace of justice; bread is a common food for rich and poor, so Christ is common to all; bread is an essential means of provision, so Christ is essential for spiritual life; bread is enjoyable food to the healthy, so Christ is 'ever sweet to the soul that feeds on him'. Wine is forcibly squeezed out of grapes, so Christ's blood was squeezed out of his body by the Father's wrath; wine has medicinal virtue, so Christ's blood is 'the great medicine for the food of the soul'; wine is refreshing and strengthening to the body, so Christ's blood refreshes the soul pressed with guilt and under a sense of wrath; wine cheers, so Christ's blood enables his people to forget their sorrows. Although Boston made these devotional distinctions when explaining the use of bread and wine, he stressed that both elements had to be viewed together. Just as a person has to eat bread and wine before they can nourish him, so a believer must feed by faith on Christ's body and blood, because it 'is union with him by faith that makes us partakers of his benefits'.[47]

Boston regarded the actions of both pastor and communicants as being significant. The consecration of the elements is important, although there is no need to repeat the separate thanksgiving for both the bread and the wine, which was only a custom common at the time of Christ's inauguration of the sacrament. Consecration involves the reading of the words of institution and prayer with thanksgiving.[48] The consecration does not change physical elements into the body and blood of Christ, as is argued by those who interpret the sacrament transubstantially or consubstantially. Boston notes that such ideas are contrary (1) to the institution, in which Christ's body was distinct from the bread and wine, (2) to the doctrine of Christ being in heaven until his return, and (3) to sense and reason. Instead of a physical change, there is a relative change, with the elements to be seen as sacred symbols of Christ's body and blood.[49]

The pastor, in taking the bread and wine into his hand, represented 'the Father's chusing and designing the Son to be Mediator'. Believers should see Christ's acceptance of the call and his being completely furnished for all the purposes of his work. Breaking of the bread by the pastor is 'an essential rite' of the sacrament, signifying 'the breaking of Christ's body for us, and consequently the shedding of his blood'. There is no direction to pour out the wine, because 'the shedding of Christ's blood is sufficiently presented by breaking of his body'.

The giving of the bread and wine to the recipients 'signifies Christ's giving himself, with all his benefits, to the worthy receiver'. The receiving of the bread and wine by the believers 'signifies their receiving a whole Christ, as offered in the word, and exhibited in the sacrament, closing with him by faith'.[50]

Boston regarded the purpose of the Lord's Supper as fourfold. First, it is a memorial, both as a reminder to the world and as a means 'to revive, quicken and preserve the affectionate remembrance of his death in our hearts' – this purpose respects Christ's honour and our duty. Second, it is a badge of and a confirmation of the believer's union and communion with Christ himself – this purpose respects our privilege. Third, it is a spiritual feast for the believer's spiritual nourishment and growth in grace, with the eating being done by faith – this purpose respects our benefit. Fourth, it is a 'public testimony of our communion with all saints' – this purpose respects the whole church of Christ, and the duties they owe to one another as members of the same body.[51]

Boston also explained his understanding of self-examination. While it is important for Christians to engage in regular self-examination of their spiritual state, the Lord's Supper is an occasion for the examination of particular graces, which Boston described as 'sacramental graces', these graces being knowledge, faith, repentance, love and new obedience. Knowledge had to be competent (understanding of the fundamentals of the faith and of the purpose of the ordinance) and saving (knowledge of one's personal need of Christ as Saviour and the sanctifying effect of this knowledge on the person's life). Faith 'is the hand and mouth of the soul' that enables the believer to feed on Christ, and the marks of true faith are a superlative desire of Christ and his grace, both for justification and sanctification, and a receiving of Christ in all his offices. Repentance is necessary both for the activity of remembering a crucified Saviour and for receiving a sealed pardon from God; repentance involves departing from both outward and heart sins, not only because of the threat of wrath but because sin is against the nature of God. Love includes love to God and love to fellow humans. New obedience proceeds from love to God, is done for God's glory, is universal in the sense of including all of God's commands, and is constant in its practice.[52]

John Willison (1680-1750)

Willison was a Church of Scotland minister in Brechin from 1703 and in Dundee from 1718. In his collected works, there are several items connected to the Lord's Supper including *A Sacramental Directory*, *Sacramental Meditations*, *Sacramental Sermons*, *Sacramental Advices*, *A Sacramental Catechism*, and *The Young Communicant's Catechism*.[53]

In his *A Sacramental Directory*, Willison first comments on the infrequent nature of the ordinance at his time.[54] He contrasts this with the ordinary custom of the apostles to dispense the Lord's Supper every Lord's day, a practice that was followed by the church until the fifth century. He also notes that the Reformed churches in different countries had chosen quarterly, bi-monthly or monthly commemorations. In Scotland at the Reformation, the practice initially was monthly, but changed to quarterly in towns and twice annually in rural churches. He dismisses arguments for infrequent communions, such as that the Passover was an annual event, that reverence for the sacrament would be lost by frequency, that frequent communions would occasion much labour and toil for the administrators, and that additional costs would be required of congregations.[55]

Willison then reminds his readers of the need of preparation for partaking in the sacrament, especially through set times of self-examination of our state, our sins, our wants, our designs and our graces, as well as set times of humiliation for our sins. As with Durham, Willison stressed the usefulness of making a covenant with God through Christ before coming to the Supper. Other features of helpful preparation include meditation and prayer. Having spent a great number of pages describing preparation, Willison reminds his readers not to trust in their preparation.[56]

As far as the communion Sabbath itself is concerned, Willison advises believers to rise early for prayer and meditation, particularly on the free and undeserved love of Christ. Christ should be considered in all his offices and relations he bears to his people, such as surety, physician, ransomer, peacemaker, advocate, refuge, ark, reliever of burdens, helper, teacher, head and husband. Believers should come to the table with a holy awe and reverence of God, with holy fear and jealousy over themselves, with brokenness of heart for sin that caused Christ's sufferings, with burning love and affection to Christ, with much hunger and thirst for nourishment, with humility and self-denial, with charity and love to all including one's enemies, with honest designs to seal a marriage-covenant with Christ, with thankfulness and praise to God for providing such a Saviour, and with hope and expectation. At the table, believers should think of Christ's life and death; they should watch the minister's actions when consecrating the elements, breaking the bread, and giving the wine, realising that these actions are symbolic of what Christ did on the cross for them. Believers should rise from the table admiring their heavenly Father for giving his Son for them, with a thankful and praising spirit, yet aware of their shortcomings.[57]

Willison also gives directions for behaviour after the sacrament is over. Communicants should be more eager for prayer, since they still have a continued need of God, and also to reflect on how Christ visited them at the table. These visits can involve revelations of his attributes of greatness and purity, goodness and mercy. They can include sending the Spirit to melt their hearts in repentance or to sharpen their faith so that they lean more on Christ or to increase their love. Willison notes 'what a mistake many are in, who think there is no communion with Christ but by sensible consolations and manifestations of his love: for where there is a holy shame, grief, and sorrow, wrought in the soul for sin, it is as real an evidence of his gracious presence, as when the soul is affectionately melted into love, praises, and joy. Though Christ come not to you by the higher way yet be thankful if he come in the lower way.' His visits also occur when he strengthens them for his service and when he gives them special assurance of their salvation. Willison gives advice for future behaviour and attitudes in order to ensure lasting benefit comes from having partaken of the Lord's Supper. Believers are to keep close to Christ, earnestly pray for his presence, watch against sin and temptations, witness for him, serve him, pray for the growth of his kingdom, desire increasing longings for heaven, and delight in the company of God's people.[58]

Willison taught that the Lord's Supper consisted of two parts, with one being the outward sensible signs and the other the spiritual and heavenly things signified. The sensible signs were of three sorts: sacramental elements, sacramental actions and sacramental words. The elements are bread and wine. The actions are twofold, with some by the administrator and others by the receivers. The administrator (minister) takes the bread, prays for a blessing and consecrates the bread, breaks the bread and hands both bread and poured-out wine to the communicants. The actions of the communicants are their taking the bread and cup into their hands, their eating the bread and drinking the wine, their dividing the elements among themselves and giving to one another, and their doing all sitting in a feasting posture. The sacramental words are the words that Christ spoke at the first institution.[59]

As far as the presence of Christ in the sacrament is concerned, Willison uses a similar illustration as that used by Bruce (the sun and its rays) when he affirms:

> Though Christ is not bodily present, yet he is really and truly present in a spiritual and invisible manner. He is present by his God-head, and by his Spirit. He is present by his power and efficacy, communicating and applying the virtue of his death: and thus we are really made partakers of Christ in this ordinance. We partake of the sun when we have its beams of light and heart darted down upon us, although we have not the bulk and body of the sun put into our hands: so we partake of Christ in the sacrament, when we share of his grace, and the blessed fruits of his broken body, though we do not actually eat his flesh with our mouths.[60]

George Hill (1750-1819)

George Hill's *Lectures in Divinity* was used in the instruction of theological students.[61] In his lecture on the Lord's Supper, Hill notes that while remembrance is an important aspect of the Lord's Supper, there are also the elements of sacredness, seen in Paul's comments on partaking unworthily, and of communion, seen in the prospect of receiving blessings from Christ. Hill dismisses transubstantiation in line with other Reformed criticisms. In considering the meaning of consubstantiation, Hill comments on the understanding of the communication of properties in the person of Christ. He denies that the property of omnipresence was given to Christ's glorified human nature, instead advocating that 'in consequence of the intimate union between the two natures of him who is both God and man, every thing that is true concerning the human nature may be affirmed of the same person, of whom every thing true concerning the divine nature may also be affirmed'.[62] It is not appropriate, therefore, to argue that the properties of one of the natures can be given to the other.

Hill argues that the view of Calvin is contained in both the Thirty-nine Articles and in the Westminster Confession of Faith and its catechisms. He claims that Calvin's understanding allowed that the full benefit of the Lord's Supper is peculiar to those who partake worthily, which explains the necessity of self-examination. Yet Hill was aware of the possibility of dangerous deductions if Calvin's interpretation is abused: 'The notion of a communion with Christ in this particular ordinance, more intimate than at any other time, may foster a spirit of fanaticism, unless the nature and the fruits of the communion are carefully explained.'[63] He mentions some such consequences:

> The humble and contrite may be overwhelmed with religious melancholy, when the state of their minds does not correspond to the descriptions which are sometimes given of that communion. Presumptuous sinners may be confirmed in the practice of wickedness by feeling an occasional glow of affection; or, on the other hand, a general neglect of an ordinance, which all are commanded to observe, may be, and in some parts of Scotland is, the consequence of holding forth notions of the danger and guilt of communicating unworthily, more rigorous than are clearly warranted by Scripture.[64]

Hill argued that the frequency and occasion of holding the Lord's Supper was a matter for Christian prudence. But he did claim that Calvin's view stressed the Lord's Supper was when Christians should renew their personal covenant with God. In doing so, they 'behold in the actions which they perform a striking representation of that event, by which the covenant was confirmed; and they receive, in the grace and strength then conveyed to their souls, a seal of that forgiveness of sins, which, through the blood of the covenant, is granted to all that repent, and a pledge of the future blessings promised to those who are "faithful unto death".'[65]

John Brown (1784-1858)

John Brown was Professor of Exegetical Theology in the United Presbyterian Church and Senior Pastor of a United Presbyterian congregation in Edinburgh. Among his many works he wrote a volume on the Lord's Supper, the chapters of which were structured in the order of a communion season, beginning with chapters on preparation, then on the administration of the sacrament, and then on what should be done after the sacrament. The volume was published first in 1816 and then reprinted in 1853.

Concerning any guilty of unworthy communicating, Brown described such a person as one 'who engages in this religious service, from improper motives,—ignorant of its nature and design,—destitute of faith in the doctrines which it symbolically teaches,—unactuated by those holy tempers which it is intended to exercise and improve,—or with a view to gain unworthy ends.'[66] He further develops these features.

Improper motives included partaking out of custom, partaking because Christianity is the religion of the state, partaking because one did not wish to be regarded as an infidel, partaking because one expected pardon of sin for doing so. A true motive must include a regard to the Divine authority instituting the ordinance and requiring us to observe it.

Ignorance concerns lack of knowledge of the first principles of Christianity and a person in this condition cannot understand the significance of the emblems. There is no benefit to the person who partakes ignorantly. But faith in the doctrines of Christianity is more than head knowledge, although accuracy of understanding concerning these doctrines is important. Nevertheless, it is the case that a 'man whose professed creed is rigidly orthodox, and who is zealous, even to rancour, in defence of it, may yet notwithstanding be an unworthy communicant'. Therefore a 'faith of these truths producing a reliance on the Saviour for pardon, and acceptance, and purity, and consolation, and eternal life, and a submission of the understanding and affections to his authority, is absolutely necessary for advantageously and acceptably observing the Lord's Supper'. Appropriate affections include deep veneration, love to Christ, penitence and love for other Christians.[67]

Brown did not regard the meaning of 'guilty of the body and blood of the Lord' as being a mere profanation of the symbols; rather the clause referred to murder. He is aware that it cannot be understood literally in this way, but explains 'that the unworthy communicant is under the influence of the same malignant dispositions which animated the murderers of our Lord; and that, placed in their circumstances, he would have imitated their conduct'.[68]

Yet Brown did not regard unworthy participation as resulting in 'eating and drinking damnation'; rather to eat unworthily resulted in temporal judgments such as bodily illness and death. Those who received these judgments are nevertheless described by Paul as being asleep, a term used for dead believers. But even for true Christians, such judgements will while they last be intolerable.[69]

With regard to self-examination before the Lord's Supper, Brown taught that its design 'is to discover both whether we are *habitually*, and whether we are *actually*, prepared for it'. Therefore a Christian should examine himself concerning his opinions of basic Christian doctrines, his affections in relation to Christ, the law, sin and fellowmen, and his conduct towards God and others. The Scriptures are the criterion for assessing ourselves; seriousness and impartiality are essential for self-enquiry; and the assistance of the Holy Spirit is necessary, and for his help we need to pray frequently and fervently. Brown also listed several motives for engaging in self-examination: the authority of God requires it, it is beneficial for each person to know what state he is in, it is a means of gaining assurance of salvation. Failure to examine oneself is one reason why many Christians receive little benefit from partaking in the Lord's Supper.[70]

Brown also gave two examples of fencing the table. One benefit of this practice was the help it could give to any who were still confused about their spiritual state even although they had engaged in self-examination. Brown acknowledged that 'this service not being of direct Divine appointment is, of course, not absolutely necessary to the right dispensation of the Lord's Supper; yet its use is sufficiently apparent. It is not intended to be a substitute either for church discipline or self-examination—though it is feared it sometimes has been thus abused. It is intended to do what church discipline cannot do, and what self-examination may not have done. If judiciously performed, it can scarcely do harm—it may do much good—and it is certainly quite in the spirit of the apostolic injunction, "Let a man examine himself, and so let him eat of that bread and drink of that cup".' Brown in his fencing gave four qualifications for participating: the person must deeply and habitually feel his need of the Saviour; he must cordially acquiesce in the scriptural mode of salvation; he must have experienced the regenerating and sanctifying influences of the Divine Spirit who effects a complete transformation of the sentiments, tempers, dispositions and habits; he must pay a religious regard to all the commandments of God. Further, Brown drew attention to passages such as Psalm 15, the Beatitudes (Matt. 5:3-9) and Paul's contrast between the works of the flesh and the fruit of the Spirit (Gal. 5:19-24).

In his second example, Brown based his comments on believers being the family of God. The Lord's Supper is a family feast. This means that all believers have an intimate relation to Jesus Christ. As his family they love him and his commandments, they have a family likeness, they obey their Lord, they have fellowship with other members of the family, they show kindness to the family members.

In the two examples he gives of fencing the table, Brown in the first describes believers from an individual point of view (unless one knew otherwise, there is no hint in the address that believers live in a community of Christians) and in the second he stresses the corporate aspect of believers as church members.

John Dick (1764-1833)

John Dick was a minister of a Glasgow congregation of the United

Associate Church and Professor of Theology for the United Associate Church. His *Lectures in Theology* were published in the 1830s,[71] and in Volume 4 there are three lectures on the Lord's Supper. In the first lecture he comments on the development of the idea of transubstantiation, which began with Radbert, an abbot in France in the ninth century. Dick notes that the 'doctrine of transubstantiation, which was at first rudely exhibited, required time, and labour, and ingenuity, to mould it into its present form'.[72] Nevertheless, Dick objects to the doctrine for several reasons.

First, the doctrine destroys the nature of a sacrament because it requires that the sign has become the thing signified when the bread becomes the body of Christ. Second, the doctrine is against the dictates of reason, for it requires that Christ's body be in more than one place simultaneously and be in more than one state simultaneously (perceived in heaven as glorified on the throne of God but hidden and humiliated on the altar on earth). Third, the doctrine contradicts the testimony of our senses, for they 'assure us that there is no change in the elements'. 'We see bread and wine in the Eucharist; we smell them, and we taste them.'[73]

In Lecture 2, Dick notes three consequences of the doctrine of transubstantiation. First, it gives rise to idolatry, when the bread is adored and worshipped. Second, there is the notion that the Eucharist becomes a sacrifice for the sins of both the living and for the dead in purgatory. Dick dismisses with contempt supporting arguments for this concept: first, apostolic tradition is 'any thing which was said or done by some dreaming dotard or superstitious fool in remote ages, and which other dotards and fools were pleased to admire, and to retain as wise and good'; second, the biblical examples given for the doctrine, such as when Melchizedek gave an unbloody sacrifice of bread and wine to Abraham, are interpreted against the law of sound criticism; third, the perpetuity of Christ's priesthood does not require a perpetual sacrifice, as claimed by advocates of transubstantiation, for his priesthood also involves intercession. The third consequence of the doctrine is withholding the cup from the laity; support for this comes from the idea of *concomitance*, in which 'although the bread is said to be changed into his body, and the wine into his blood, yet his body and blood are not to be considered as in a state of separation.' If this were true, there would be no need for Roman Catholic priests to drink the cup. The idea also ignores that the command to drink the cup is as express as the command to eat the bread.[74]

Dick devotes less attention to the views of Luther, Zwingli and Calvin. Consubstantiation, while not being the same as transubstantiation, is 'equally unintelligible and unscriptural'. It is liable to many of the objections made against transubstantiation: 'It supposes the body of Christ to be at the same time in heaven and on earth, in Europe and in America; it supposes it to be in a state of glory, and in a state of humiliation; it supposes it to be present, and yet to be imperceptible to any of our senses, and therefore present after the manner of a spirit…'[75]

Dick noted that Zwingli had adopted the view 'that the bread and wine were no more than a representation of the body and blood of Christ; or, in other words, the signs appointed to denote the benefits that were conferred upon mankind in consequence of the death of Christ; that, therefore, Christians derived no other fruit from the participation of the Lord's Supper, than a mere commemoration and remembrance of the merits of Christ, and that there was nothing in the ordinance but a memorial of Christ'. This opinion alarmed other opponents of transubstantiation and consubstantiation, and Dick comments on some attempts to show that Zwingli did not deny an efficacy in the sacrament. There was 'a disposition in that age, to believe, that there was a presence of Christ in the Eucharist different from his presence in other ordinances of the gospel; an undefined something, which corresponded to the strong language used at the institution of the Supper, "This is my body, —this is my blood." Acknowledging it to be figurative, many still thought a mystery was couched under it. It was not, indeed, easy for those who had long been accustomed to the notion of the bodily presence of Christ, at once to simplify their ideas; and perhaps, too, they were induced to express themselves as they did, with a view to give less offence to the

Lutherans. Whatever was their motive, their language is not always sufficiently guarded.'[76]

Dick also stated his dilemma over the views of Calvin. For Dick, Calvin's teaching 'supposes a communion of believers and the human nature of our Saviour in the Eucharist; and endeavours to remove the objection arising from the distance of place [between Christ in heaven and believers on earth], by a reference to the almighty power of the Spirit, much in the same way as Papists and Lutherans solve the difficulty attending their respective systems'. Calvin both obscured the meaning of the Lord's Supper and destroyed its simplicity by using 'ambiguous language'. To say that believers had mysterious communion with Christ's human nature was a 'notion as incomprehensible to himself [that is, Calvin] as it is to his readers'. Calvin's error was the failure to maintain the figurative sense of Christ's words concerning his body and blood, with the consequence 'that to mix together the figure and the literal sense, sometimes bringing forward the one and sometimes the other, creates confusion in the minds of others, and, instead of illustrating the subject, involves it in obscurity.'[77] It is evident from Dick's comments that he preferred the view of Zwingli rather than Calvin's view, and this becomes clear in his third lecture.

In his third lecture, Dick further considers what takes place at the Lord's Supper. He refers to the Westminster Confession's teaching ('the body and blood are as really, but spiritually, present to the faith of believers in that ordinance, as the elements themselves are to their outward senses') and the Larger Catechism's teaching (believers 'feed upon his body and blood, to their spiritual nourishment and growth in grace') and interprets them as saying that the 'incarnate Saviour is apprehended by their minds, through the instituted signs: and that, by faith, they enjoy peace and hope; or it means something unintelligible and unscriptural'. Dick is aware of the meaning of the various Reformed Confessions and objects to their teaching on the presence of Christ.[78] Dick refuses to affirm the presence of Christ from the words of institution because they merely import that the elements are signs, and the function of a sign is to represent an absent object. He does not deny that Christ is present, but states that he is present in the same way that he is present in the other means of grace, that is, by the Spirit.

Concerning the possibility of sacramental actions, Dick sees no significance in Jesus taking hold of the bread, which means that 'the taking of the elements by the minister before prayer, appears to me to be a matter of indifference', which is a change of understanding from the emphasis of the Scottish Reformers and Covenanters. Another difference from his predecessors was Dick's objection to interpreting the Saviour's words of blessing as referring to the consecration of the bread; rather he sees the action as Jesus blessing God and giving thanks for the bread. Therefore it is questionable whether a minister should engage in the practice of blessing the elements, but it is essential that he should give thanks. Jesus' words concerning the bread and the cup indicate that they are only symbols. It is essential to retain the practice of breaking of the bread, and the bread and the cup must be placed in the hands of the communicants, who should be sitting at a table and not kneeling.

Dick regarded the Lord's Supper as a memorial of Christ's death, as a public declaration of faith in Christ, as a solemn engagement to serve him, and as an expressive sign of the communion of Christians with one another in love. Qualifications for participating, in the judgment of the church, included baptism, knowledge, profession of faith in Christ, and appropriate behaviour. In the personal judgment by individuals, there needs also to be penitence if a person is not prepared for participating because of spiritual problems. But this does not mean that self-examination is required of every person before a communion. This means that the function of the practice of Fencing of the Tables needs to be considered. Dick did not deny that the practice had its good consequences, but noted that there was no biblical authority for the practice, that it was not necessary for the ordinance or to imagine that it added anything to its perfection or solemnity, and that a better means of ascertaining one's state or character was through regular teaching by the minister as he expounded the Bible. Dick both affirms the new practice in his church and criticises the former practice when he says, 'The plan at present pursued in our Church is preferable to that of our predecessors, who, taking the decalogue as their standard, excommunicated sinners of every description and degree, many of whom were known not to be present, and would have disclaimed the privilege which was publicly denied to them. What had they to do to judge those who were without; ought they not to have judged those alone who were within?'

Concerning the frequency of the communion occasions, Dick disagreed with the argument that the Bible taught it should be celebrated weekly. Instead churches 'are left at liberty to order their procedure according to their own views of expedience and utility'. But the 'sacred feast should not be treated as if it were of no value, and so rarely celebrated as to be almost forgotten; nor should it be magnified above other ordinances, and represented as of indispensable necessity on every occasion'.[79]

Dick in rejecting transubstantiation and consubstantiation noted that both ideas are contrary to what ordinary people sense and reason about physical objects. His rejection of Calvin's understanding of the Lord's Supper is because it does not accord with the teaching of Scripture and common sense. In the main he aligned himself with the views of Zwingli. Concerning liturgical practices, Dick was prepared to replace actions if no longer of value. Since the denomination of which Dick was a member eventually helped to form the United Presbyterian Church in the second half of the nineteenth century, it is not surprising that the new denomination became the first of the mainline denominations in Scotland to change its practice at the Lord's Supper.

Daniel Dewar (1788-1867)

Daniel Dewar[80] was Principal of Marischal College and University in Aberdeen. In 1866 he published his *Elements of Systematic Divinity*, and in Volume 3 he discussed the Lord's Supper in four chapters. Dewar regarded the occasion of the initial Lord's Supper as taking place during the Passover. He did not regard the Saviour's action of blessing the bread as an act of consecration of the element;

rather it was his giving thanks to God. The action of breaking the bread is to be practised because it was a deliberate act of Jesus when instituting the Supper. The Supper is an emblematic commemoration of Christ's death and an emblematic representation of our partaking of its blessings through faith. The participants should be sitting.[81]

Dewar devotes a chapter to the history of interpretation of the Supper. He mentions the contribution of Radbert to the development of transubstantiation and also says that a form of consubstantiation existed in the eleventh century as well as a symbolic interpretation, similar to memorialism, associated with Ratrum.[82] The leading opponent of transubstantiation at that time was Beringer, whose views were similar to the subsequent teaching of Calvin, and Dewar details Beringer's attempts to oppose transubstantiation. Dewar has another chapter on the doctrine of transubstantiation itself, in which he gives the usual Protestant objections to it. Many of the objections to transubstantiation also can be used against consubstantiation.

As far as these chapters are concerned, Dewar does not indicate whether he prefers the views of Zwingli or those of Calvin, although his comments indicate he was aware of the distinctions between them. In commenting on the teaching of Beringer, Dewar notes his similarity to the teaching of Calvin in that Beringer did not only 'lay great stress on the symbolical character of the institution, and to teach that not the true body and the true blood of Christ were in the Holy Supper, but a symbol of them', but also 'proceeded further than this, and held that Christ is spiritually present with His people in the Lord's Supper, to hold fellowship with them'.[83]

William Cunningham (1805-1861)

William Cunningham was Professor of Church History, as well as Principal, in the Free Church of Scotland College in Edinburgh and is regarded as an authority on the Reformers. He gives his views on the Lord's Supper in an article in which he considers the various teachings of the Reformers on the sacraments.

Cunningham deals with baptism and the Lord's Supper simultaneously and indicates where this is otherwise. Cunningham expresses his disapproval of both transubstantiation and consubstantiation. He acknowledges that there are statements in Zwingli's writings that indicate he regarded the elements as bare signs and the reception of them as a mere commemoration of what Christ had done for sinners. This view was regarded as defective by subsequent Calvinistic leaders. Cunningham also suggests that Zwingli, towards the end of his life, moved towards a position close to the other Protestant Reformers. Cunningham's assessment was that Zwingli came short in his doctrine because he did not bring out 'fully what God does, or is ready and willing to do, through their [the sacraments'] instrumentality, in offering to men, and conferring upon them, through the exercise of faith, spiritual blessings.'[84] But while indicating the inadequacy of Zwingli's teaching regarding the Supper, Cunningham does not endorse Calvin's suggestion that 'something like a real influence exerted by Christ's human nature upon the souls of believers, in connection with the dispensation of the Lord's Supper', a teaching that Cunningham regarded 'as unintelligible as Luther's consubstantiation'.[85]

Responding to the Roman Catholic criticism that the Protestant interpretation suggested the sacraments are superfluous and unnecessary, Cunningham said they were necessary because observation of them was commanded by Christ and therefore neglect of them was sinful.[86]

Cunningham noted that the sacrament can be regarded in two different aspects. First, it can be observed and second it involves participation. As far as observation of the rite is concerned, God 'is just telling us that Christ's body was broken, and that His blood was shed, for men; and that, in this way, full provision has been made, not only for restoring men to the enjoyment of God's favour, and creating them again after His image, but for affording them abundance of spiritual nourishment, and enabling them to grow up in all things unto Him who is the Head.'[87] When it is celebrated, the Lord's Supper is not only a sign indicating what

Christ has done or can do but is also a seal; as a sign the Lord's Supper is a proposal or document containing God's terms made in the covenant of grace, and as a seal it is similar to an ancient seal that was appended to a signature made to a document, being evidence to us of 'the reality and certainty, or reliability of the whole transaction'.[88]

Cunningham says that the sacraments are signs and seals both on the part of the believers and on the part of God. He notes that both baptism and the Lord's Supper highlight an individual tendency that equips them for being instruments in the hand of the Spirit for 'guiding us to a personal application of divine truth to our own condition, and circumstances, and thus sealing or confirming our faith, love, and hope'. When a believer partakes in the Lord's Supper, he is 'making a personal profession of his faith in Christ, and giving a personal promise and pledge to persevere in faith and obedience. The natural tendency of this is to lead him to realise more fully his actual position, obligations, and prospects as a believer, and this warrants the confident expectation that the Spirit will actually employ it for accomplishing this result.' As far as God's involvement is concerned, his allowing in his providence a person to participate in the Lord's Supper is not evidence of true conversion; rather God is singling him out and addressing him personally and intimating his willingness to give him all needful spiritual blessings, as detailed in the Scriptures.

As far as participation is concerned, believers do this for two reasons: (a) because they are commanded to do so and (b) because it is a means of grace or privileges that God appoints and bestows. As obedience, it is both an act of worship and a public profession of Christianity.[89] There is difficulty understanding how the sacrament is a means of grace. Cunningham objects to the Romish doctrine that the sacrament conveys grace *ex opere operato*, that it automatically provides spiritual nourishment. In explaining how the Lord's Supper is a means of grace, Cunningham stresses that the sacrament is only for believers, approving of the Westminster Confession's statement that 'the word of institution contains a promise of benefit to worthy receivers'.[90] Therefore, 'participation in [the sacraments] assumes the previous and present existence of faith in all who rightly receive them; and that they produce their appropriate, beneficial effects only through the operation and exercise of faith in those who partake in them'.[91] These beneficial effects do not include such spiritual blessings as regeneration or justification, because as believers in Christ they already have them. The blessings conveyed are those they still stand in need of. Cunningham divides these blessings into two kinds; there are blessings connected to the fact that each believer is still a sinner ('forgiveness of the sins which they continue to commit,' 'a growing sense of God's pardoning mercy') and blessings connected to Christian progress in life ('grace and strength to resist temptation, to discharge duty, to improve privilege, and to be ever advancing in holiness'). The conveyance of these blessings is not limited to the Lord's Supper, for they are conveyed through each means of grace. Nevertheless, the main purpose of the Lord's Supper, in being instrumental in conveying these blessings, is to strengthen and confirm the faith of believers.[92]

Cunningham was concerned about attempts to elevate the Lord's Supper above other means of grace (seen in the Tractarians of his time, whom he critiques throughout his lecture). He was also concerned about attempts to give to the Lord's Supper a deeper shade of mystery than the Scriptures gave to it. But it is open to question if, in his emphasis on the necessity of the believer's faith being active, he has not relegated the action of God at the Supper to one primarily of response to faith and not of initiating the interaction with each of his people. It is also difficult to understand what he means by avoiding a deeper shade of mystery. If there is a shade of mystery, then it is a mystery. And what takes place at the Lord's Supper is mysterious, otherwise there would not be the diversity of understandings regarding what occurs at it.

Conclusion

From this summary, several comments can be made regarding the Lord's Supper in the Presbyterian churches in the Lowlands.

First, it is evident that subsequent to the Reformation down to the nineteenth century, the period in which the communion season was a feature of Scottish Presbyterian life in the Lowlands, there was a consistent opposition to the doctrines of transubstantiation and consubstantiation.

Second, initially the views of Calvin were taught and the view associated with Zwingli was not advocated, although later there does seem to have been a difficulty understanding what Calvin meant. It was accepted that the Supper was more than a remembrance, for it was communion with Christ, but what that involved is not explicitly stated by Durham, Boston, and Brown. Willison, in describing the presence of Christ in the Supper as referring to presence by his Godhead and his Spirit, indicates he is not entirely in agreement with Calvin's view of the presence of Christ's humanity, although he does use the same illustration as Bruce, that of the sun and its rays, to indicate how Christ's power is effected.

With Dick of the Secession Church and Cunningham of the Free Church, there is a clear rejection of Calvin's teaching, with both claiming that the contents of the Westminster Confession support them. I suspect that this is doubtful, for while the Confession's statements do not include Calvin's notion of believers ascending to heaven to have fellowship with Christ's human nature, they do emphasise communion with Christ by the Spirit. Nevertheless, the Westminster Confession differs in this regard from the Scots Confession and this in itself indicates a development in how the Scottish Presbyterian Church understood the Supper.[93]

Third, the passing of time saw a willingness to adapt or remove many of the practices introduced by previous generations of Christians, whether by the Reformers or church leaders in subsequent periods. Some of these practices were not mentioned in the Bible, such as the number of days associated with the communion and practices linked to the communion such as fencing the table. It was realised that these practices were not authorised by Scripture but had been introduced because they had been useful at the time. These changes were made because the practices were no longer of value due to different circumstances. But consideration was also given to items mentioned in the Bible, which had initially been perceived as part of the Supper, such as whether or not the Lord Jesus consecrated the bread when he blessed it. Some concluded, such as Dick and Dewar with the example mentioned, that previous understandings had been wrong.

7

The Lord's Supper in the Scottish Highlands[1]

It is difficult to describe the activities of the Scottish church in the Highlands for almost any period of Scottish history, except for comparatively modern times. This is due to the dearth of recorded material, with this dearth being 'particularly acute for the period of the Reformation'.[2] There are no surviving records from the late sixteenth century of the meetings of kirk sessions, presbyteries and synods of the Highland area.[3] Yet it is possible to discover from other sources the way the Reformed Church attempted to meet the needs of the Scottish Highlands. In 1562, the General Assembly was informed that the north was destitute of ministers for the most part.[4] Yet by 1574, 'with the exception of Argyll and the Isles, 988 parishes were equipped with the services of 289 ministers and 715 readers, with 20 ministerial charges unfilled and 97 vacancies for readers'.[5] The parishes in the Highlands were very much larger than in the Lowlands, nevertheless the situation in the Highlands shortly after the Reformation compared favourably with other parts of Scotland.[6] Communion services, held infrequently, were occasions when all parishioners were expected to give their attendance.[7]

In the Highlands, three forms of church polity were found at the close of the seventeenth century: Presbyterianism, Episcopacy and Roman Catholicism. Each had its areas of strength and weakness. The areas where Presbyterianism was stronger included Easter Ross, Sutherland, and parts of Argyll. Support for Episcopacy could be found in Perthshire, Ross-shire, Inverness-shire, Caithness, and northern Argyll. Roman Catholic support was spread over a wide area from the Outer Hebrides to Aberdeenshire.[8]

Major events in Scottish political and ecclesiastical history had their effects on religious life in the Highlands. After the ejection of Presbyterian ministers upon the restoration of the monarchy in 1660 and the recovery of Episcopalianism, the Lord's Supper was seldom observed in the Highlands.[9] Although most of the believers in strongly Presbyterian areas sided with the ejected ministers,[10] the replacement ministers in virtually every parish conformed to Government requirements.[11] Evidently, celebrations of the Lord's Supper were not a priority, for the Bishop of Ross, for example, had to exhort the ministers 'to use all diligence in celebrating the holy Sacrament of the Supper'.[12] Kennedy comments regarding this requirement that the ministers, who prior to the Restoration judged their congregations quite unfitted for such service, 'now, while their congregations are in no better state than before, resolve to yield obedience to the Bishop'.[13] Nevertheless, support for the ejected ministers was not only strong among the poor; many landowners supported the ministers and were fined for doing so.[14] From the period between 1661 and 1688, when the Covenanters were being persecuted elsewhere in Scotland, there are a few traditional accounts of communion occasions in the Scottish Highlands.

These gatherings, or conventicles, are associated with ministers who were ousted from their congregations by the civil government's imposition of Episcopalian polity on the Presbyterian church. One of these ministers was Thomas Hog (1628-92), a church leader of significance in the growth of evangelical Presbyterianism in the Highlands. He was ousted from the parish of Kiltearn in Ross-shire and moved to Auldearn in Moray where he continued to preach to large congregations in the open-air, despite such action being illegal. Hog also decided to have an open-air celebration of the Lord's Supper, to which 'a considerable number of people from a wide circuit of country—including some all the way from Easter Ross—joined in the sacred ordinance. The occasion was marked by signal tokens of the Lord's presence, and "the communicants…returned to their habitations with joy unspeakable; and the spirit of their adversaries was so bound that they gave them no disturbance"'.[15]

Another of these conventicles occurred in Rosskeen, Ross-shire, in September, 1675. The events of the Sunday are summarised by Dr. John Kennedy of Dingwall:

Mr. Anderson preached the preparation sermon on Saturday, Mr. MacKilligan officiated on Sabbath in the forenoon, and Mr. Fraser in the afternoon, and Mr. MacKilligan preached the thanksgiving discourse on Monday. During this last service, there was such a plentiful effusion of the Spirit, that the oldest Christians then present declared they had never enjoyed such a time of refreshing before.[16]

This occasion seems to have been an occasion of great spiritual refreshment. Wodrow, the historian, records that at the 'last sermon there was a plentiful effusion of the Spirit upon a great many present; and the oldest Christians there declared they had never been witnesses to the like. In short, there was so sensible and glorious discoveries made of the Son of man, and such evident presence of the Master of Assemblies, this day and the preceding, that the people seemed to be in a transport, and their souls filled with heaven, and breathing thither, while their bodies were upon the earth.'[17] This event is remembered by a commemoration pillar on the site, and part of the inscription states:

This stone marks the only place in Ross-shire, in which the Sacrament of the Lord's Supper is known to have been dispensed to the Covenanters, during the days of the persecution. Respecting the command of their Divine Redeemer more than they feared the fury of the oppressor, they met here on a Sabbath in September, 1675. Soldiers were sent to apprehend them but they did not arrive till the Communion Service was over, and the congregation dispersed.

Douglas MacMillan describes a third occasion when the Lord's Supper was celebrated, this time in Sutherlandshire:

Although all the parish ministers in Sutherland had actually conformed and so, to a large extent, had lost the confidence of the people, a minister from Warwickshire found his way to the Cape Wrath district of Sutherlandshire.... The English minister, George

Squair, himself a fugitive from Charles II's religious policies, became so concerned with the spiritual needs of the people that he set himself to learn Gaelic and became an accomplished preacher in the language. His preaching through the northern districts was greatly blessed and the time arrived when he proposed to hold a Communion.... The place selected for the purpose was, according to Dr. Donald Munro, 'an isolated spot among the wild hills of the parish of Eddrachillis'. Another historian speaks of this Communion and tells us: 'The whole service was a memorable one.... Not only was there no interruption of the service, but all there felt so much of the Lord's presence, and their bonds were so loosened, and their fears so dispelled, that all, without a single exception, felt constrained to say with Thomas, "My Lord and my God," and without exception, commemorated the dying love of their Redeemer.'[18]

In the Highlands, two other services were included in addition to the services common in Lowland communion seasons: (a) in some areas, a fellowship meeting on the Friday was held; (b) in line with the government's policy, as well as that of the General Assembly of the Church of Scotland, English services were introduced, duplicating each Gaelic service.[19] The communion season in each locality took place when the demands on the people were not strong, the period between the end of Spring work and the beginning of harvest. Each locality held its communion at a different time, so it was possible for the people and the ministers to attend communions in neighbouring parishes.[20]

There are accounts of communion seasons in subsequent decades in the Scottish Highlands. Donald Sage recollected that during his boyhood, in the period between 1789 and 1800, there was a communion service in Kildonan in the north Highlands at which between three and four thousand people were in attendance. The sacrament was held annually. He also records that it was common for people to come from a wide geographical area, with some of those attending coming from communities that were fifty miles away from Kildonan. Some of these communities were to the south, others were to the north, of Kildonan, which means that some of these communities were between eighty and one hundred miles apart. Sage also mentions a distinction in the practice of the Lord's Supper that prevailed in the north of Scotland:

> In the north of Scotland a distinction prevailed in the annual administration of that ordinance which in the south was utterly unknown. That distinction was made between the public and the private or parochial administration of the Lord's Supper in any parish. The ordinance was considered as administered publicly when communicants from other parishes joined with those of the parish in its observance, and when, on that account, there were two distinct services, one in Gaelic and the other in English, and two different congregations, the one without, the other within doors. My father administered the sacrament for the most part publicly, and it was customary on those occasions for the minister on Sabbath to keep open table, as the services were much prolonged on that day, and a number of the parishioners lived at a distance from the church.[21]

Later in his description he mentions a tension between his father, who was the minister, and his elders concerning the former's intention to hold a private communion in the spring instead of the usual public one in the summer. The disagreement was so strong that when the communion was held in the spring only one of his elders assisted him. An ironic aspect of the event is that the numbers attending were so large they could not all get into the church building. Yet the minister refused to allow any open-air preaching.[22] John Macleod notes that the minister's outlook was not shared by the congregation. Sage is presenting the situation from the point-of-view of the Synod of Sutherland and Caithness, which was attempting to counteract the activities of lay-leaders. The minister announced the communion only a week beforehand, an attempt to prevent these lay-leaders from being involved.[23]

Tension over the introduction of private communions was not limited to the far north. John Kennedy, in his account of his father called *The Minister of Killearnan*, summarises the response to these shorter communions:

Feeling the desirableness of having it oftener than once, and it being impossible to find two days, with a sufficient interval, on which the people could comfortably assemble in the open air; and anxious, besides, to be rid of the distractions that necessarily attend the public communion, he resolved to dispense the sacrament of the Lord's Supper in winter. At that season a large number of strangers could not attend, and could not be accommodated even if they did; and it was called, on that account, 'the private communion'. A strong prejudice against it generally prevailed at first. It looked to some like an attempt to shut out strangers from the privileges of the sacred feast, and to those who viewed it thus it wore a most unchristian aspect. Forgetting that it was only added to the other mode of celebrating the ordinance, they opposed it as if it were its substitute. Some ministers, yielding to the unreasonable prejudice of their people, refused to adopt it; but, in course of time, the feeling against the private communion wore away, and what was at first a solitary and disliked exception, became afterwards the rule.[24]

By the time the nineteenth century began, the communion season was an established event in the Christian outlook of Highland Presbyterianism. Eyewitness accounts of Highland communions in the early nineteenth century have been recorded. One such account is by John Kennedy of Dingwall describing the communions in his father's congregation in Killearnan during the second decade of the century:

During the first half of his ministry at Killearnan, the sacrament of the Lord's Supper was dispensed only once a year, and generally on the first Sabbath of August. Great crowds were accustomed to assemble on such occasions. As many as 10,000 people have met on a communion Sabbath, and nearly 2,000 communicants have sat at the table of the Lord. These large assemblies were, of course, in the open air.[25]

Another account is from a friend of Sir Walter Scott named William Laidlaw who described a service in Ferintosh, Ross-shire:

The people gather here in their thousands to the Sacraments, as they did in their thousands in Ettrick in Boston's time. We set out on the Sabbath to the communion at Ferintosh, near Dingwall, to which the people resort from fifty miles distant. Dr. MacDonald[26] ... preached the sermon in the church in English, with a command of language, and a justness of tone, action, and reasoning – keeping close to the pure metaphysics of Calvin – that I have seldom, if ever heard surpassed. He had great energy on all points, but it never touched on extravagance.

The Gaelic congregation sat in a dell or cleuch of a long, hollow, oval shape bordered with hazel, birch and wild roses. It seemed to be formed for the purpose. We walked round the outside of the congregated thousands, and looked down on the glen from the upper end, and the scene was really indescribable.

Two-thirds of those present were women, dressed mostly in large, high, wide, muslin caps, the back part standing up like the head of a paper kite, and ornamented with ribbons. They had wrapped round them bright coloured plaid shawls, the predominant hue being scarlet.... I never saw such a scene. We sat down on the brae among the people, the long white communion tables being conspicuous at the bottom. The congregation began singing the psalm to one of the old plaintive wild tunes that I am told are only sung in the Gaelic service. The people all sing, but in such an extended multitude they could not sing together. They chanted as if it were in masses or large groups. I can compare the singing to nothing earthly, except it be imagining what would be the effect of a gigantic and tremendous Aeolian harp, with hundreds of strings! There was no resisting the impression.

After coming a little to myself I went and paced the length and breadth of the amphitheatre, taking averages and carefully noting, as well as I could, how the people were sitting together, and I could not in this way make less than nine thousand five hundred, besides those in the church, amounting, perhaps, to one thousand five hundred. Most of the gentlemen of the neighbourhood, with their families, were there. I enjoyed the scene as something perfect in its way, and of rare beauty and excellence.[27]

Another eyewitness account is from William Howitt:

We thought ourselves fortunate in August, 1838, when we happened to fall in with the celebration of this annual ordinance in the Highlands. We were at Beauly, about a dozen miles west of Inverness, on Sunday morning, and were enquiring of the landlady of our excellent inn how far it was to the celebrated Falls of Kilmorack.

"Oh," said she, "it is a bare two miles, and you will be just in time to see the Sacrament administered there in the open air to the Gaelic congregation."

Most of the people were on foot, none was barefooted. On week days, we scarcely saw a woman with shoes and stockings, but to-day, none was without. And, with the exception that hardly one had a bonnet on, the young women were not much to be distinguished from those of our smartest towns. They all had their hair neatly braided with a comb of tortoiseshell. Many of them had silk gowns and handsome worked muslin collars, others were dressed in white....as we approached [the burial ground of Kilmorack], we beheld upwards of a thousand people collected and conspicuous in the bright and varied hues of Highland costume.

We stood, and for a moment, almost imagined we were come upon a band of the ancient Covenanters. A more striking picture we never saw.

We entered the burial ground....Beneath a spreading tree near the garden wall stood a movable booth of wood. From this booth the minister was now addressing the assembly while two other ministers occupied a seat behind him....A more serious and decorous congregation never was seen.

When those who had gone forward communicated, the minister addressed them, and they retired from the table, and a fresh company took their place. Another minister then came forward and there followed a new succession of psalms, prayers and addresses.

We left about three o'clock, but were told that not till six o'clock would the service close.

Shortly after we left, the distant voice of the minister and the wild cadence of the Gaelic psalms, like the breezy music of an Aeolian harp, reminded us that it was the sacred anniversary of a grave and religious people.[28]

Each of these descriptions are of communion seasons on the east coast of the northern Highlands. The reason for this is that

Presbyterianism on the east coast was influenced by evangelicalism for two centuries before similar occasions were experienced on the west coast. The state of things on the west coast during the early 1800s was very different:

> In many parts of the Western Highlands and Islands at that time, the people lived in practical heathenism. With very few exceptions, the pulpits were occupied by ministers having no religion—genuine Moderates, who took advantage of their retired situations in the country to take to themselves all sorts of license, shewing an utter disregard for the duties of their office, and often for the laws of morality. It was not rare to find among them men who were habitual swearers and drunkards. Instances were known where the parish minister added considerably to his income by distilling and smuggling whisky. The people as a rule neglected the ordinances of religion, and spent the Sabbath either visiting in each other's houses, or when the weather permitted, lounging lazily on the hill-side, never considering it their duty to go to church, excepting on sacramental occasions, when all and sundry were admitted, sometimes in a state of drunkenness, to the communion table.[29]

Changes were taking place due in part to local revivals and to evangelistic efforts such as those connected to the Haldane evangelists. And the Disruption movement of 1843, when the Free Church of Scotland came into existence, 'awakened in many quarters a great desire to hear the preaching of the gospel, which was new to multitudes in the West Highlands'.[30]

The above accounts of communion services by Laidlaw and Howitt were observations of passing travellers. But what was the point-of view of Christians? Two descriptions of communion seasons, one describing seasons in the eighteenth century, the other seasons in the nineteenth century, will give their assessments. The first is by John Kennedy as he describes a Ross-shire communion season in the eighteenth century:

> A Communion season is approaching. It has been timeously announced, that it may be known 'far and wide,' and that the praying people may be bearing it on their spirits before the throne of grace.

The minister preaches a suitable course of sermons on several preceding Sabbaths. The Lord's people are stirred up to seek a special manifestation of His power and glory. A few who propose to seek admission to the Lord's Table are deeply exercised at the solemn step they contemplate, and faithfully and tenderly are they dealt with both by ministers and elders. As the appointed time draws nigh, special meetings for prayer are held, and, with holy solicitude, all the preparatory arrangements are made. The *Fast-Day* [Thursday] is come. Eminent ministers have arrived to take part in the solemn services. Many of the Lord's people are gathering. From as many as forty parishes they come; but lodgings they will easily procure, as the parish people are striving for the pleasure of entertaining them. Suitable discourses are preached in Gaelic in the open field, and to a small English congregation in the church, and in the evening prayer-meetings are held in the various districts of the parish. On *Friday*, the day of self-examination, the only public service is in the open air. A large crowd is gathered. 'In the tent' there are several godly ministers. The service is that of the fellowship meeting, such as has already been described [local meetings for fellowship which will be discussed later], but now with special reference to the solemn duties of a Communion Sabbath. There are two questions proposed successively to secure variety. Strangers [well-known visiting Christian men] only are called to speak, and even of those only the 'flower', for there are so many. Not fewer than thirty will have spoken before the service is over. Blessed indeed to many souls have these 'Friday meetings' been. The services on *Saturday*, the day of preparation, are conducted as on Thursday, but, owing to the gathering influx of strangers [visiting Christians and others], the congregation outside is greatly larger than on the Fast-Day. At the close of the service tokens are distributed. Prayer meetings are held throughout the parish in the evening; and while the ministers are preparing for the solemn work of the Sabbath, many are the petitions that ascend in their behalf to Him who hath 'the treasure' to dispense, and of whom is 'the excellency of the power'. In many instances, these prayer-meetings have been protracted all night. So sensible were the people of the presence of the Lord that they could not forsake the place where they enjoyed it; and they found 'the joy of the Lord' a sweet substitute for sleep. On *Sabbath*, the day of Communion, an immense crowd is gathered before the tent. As many as eight thousand are there. The 'Beauty of the Lord' is on the assembly of His people; and before the service is over, many a soul has had reason to say, 'It is good to be here.' On *Monday*, the day of thanksgiving, a crowd almost as large as that on Sabbath is assembled; and often has 'the last' been found to be 'the great day of the feast'. The closing service of the Communion season is now over, and then comes the solemn parting! How affecting do the Lord's servants and people feel the scene before them to be, as the multitude disperses, never to meet all together again till the vast congregation of the 'last day' has assembled. What touching farewells are now exchanged between the Christians who enjoyed with each other, and together with the Lord, such sweet communion since they met a few days before! There are few tearless eyes, but the weeping is expressive of gratitude as surely as of sorrow.[31]

As an example of what a minister did on these occasions, the following description of Angus Macintosh, a minister from Tain, gives an impression:

Dr. M'Intosh enters the tent, and after praise he offers up a solemn, moving prayer. He reads his text, and for a time he is calm, with little action; and his deep-toned, melodious voice is heard by the most distant of eight or ten thousand people. He begins by showing the great doctrines revealed in his text, and the great lessons taught in it. Then his application commences; his eye kindles, and his voice is louder; his very countenance shows how thoroughly he believes what he says. At one time you see deep awful compassion,— a cloud on the countenance; at another, the sun breaks through the clouds, and there is a beautiful smile. He comes to the fencing of the tables, and after a few solemn words addressed to the worldly professor, deals with God's children. He follows the perplexed enquirer through all his wanderings; he comes down to the first breathing of the divine life in the soul; and he encourages the weakest to come with all his darkness and perplexity to meet Christ at his table. After the communion, he generally concluded with an address; and here he specially shone. After a few pithy words to the communicants, he turned to the thousands of the young and thoughtless before him, and he spoke to them God's message with a power, an unction, and an authority which made the most careless listen. In telling sinners of their danger, he spoke as one who saw it vividly; his fine eye was frequently filled with tears, and his voice and manner made them feel as if thunder were rolling over their head. This was followed up by holding forth Christ as the living, present, all-gracious Saviour; and by the most melting appeals to the worst and vilest to come to Him even now, with all their sins, that they might even now be saved. He seemed unwilling to part with them till they fled for refuge to Christ, and with a thorough knowledge of their own language and phrases, he plied them with illustrations and arguments.[32]

In the early twentieth century, the influence of Highland communion seasons began to decline. Donald Munro, who knew a great deal about these communion seasons both from personal experience and anecdotal account, recorded his understanding of these occasions as he looked back on more spiritually prosperous times:

> Seldom could one witness a more inspiring sight than the immense concourse that assembled on a sacramental Sabbath in the days of the fathers. Under the canopy of heaven they met, in some wooded dell, at the famous 'Burn' of Ferintosh, on the grassy seashore, or on the hillside in some natural amphitheatre which seemed to have been created for the purpose. The very surroundings often seemed to lend impressiveness to the solemn service, for sometimes there was no sound to break the stillness which brooded over the secluded spot save the sighing of the gentle breeze, or the boom of the waves as they rolled on to the pebbly strand. In front of the preaching-tent stretched two long rows of Communion tables, with their snow-white linen, around which a dense mass of people, sometimes amounting to several thousands, sat. The picturesque appearance of the vast gathering might appeal to the superficial observer, for some of the venerable-looking men were attired in blue cloaks, and others had wraps and plaids of various shades, while over the caps of elderly matrons were large muslin kerchiefs.
>
> At the appointed hour, generally 11 o'clock, the presiding minister entered the tent. He was generally one of the most outstanding preachers in the north, for as a rule only men of weight and experience, such as Dr. Angus Macintosh, Mr. Kennedy, Killearnan, and Dr. MacDonald, were asked to preach the Gaelic Action. This

was what the sermon prior to the participation in Communion, was called and, generally, it dwelt on some aspect of the atonement. The preacher came direct from the ivory palaces of secret communion, and the fragrance which accompanied him was diffused around. The very reading of the opening Psalm had a subduing effect on the assembled thousands, while the singing of it to one of their plaintive melodies, led by a choice precentor as the leader of the praise was called, was most thrilling. The prayer which followed, so fervent and unctuous, found a response in many a contrite heart. It must have been a most cheering sight which met the eye of the preacher as he stood up to announce his text. An earnest, expectant look was depicted on many a countenance, for not a few came there to hear a message from God. The prayerful atmosphere which pervaded the congregation was intense, and the preacher was conscious of it. From the very beginning of the sermon, in which the glory of Christ's person and the merits of his atoning sacrifice were treated with rare clearness, fullness, and tenderness, the interest of the hearers was aroused; and as the subject was unfolded their riveted attention showed how nice [that is, precise] doctrinal distinctions and apt illustrations were appreciated. But as the service proceeded, the breathless silence, the awed look, the deep sigh, or the trickling tear indicated how profoundly the hearers were being impressed. Sometimes a wave of emotion would pass over the congregation, under which they would be bowed down as the ripe corn before the autumn breeze. At other times, as the preacher became more absorbed in his theme, and rose, as it were from peak to peak, in his upward flight, some in the congregation were carried away in ecstasy of soul—the things of time were receding, eternal things were so real that they felt as if transported to the very gates of heaven, and seemed to gaze through shining vistas into the celestial city.[33]

MacMillan says that there 'were times when the Communion services were very long as relays of believers came forward, sat at the long Communion table, and then rose to give way to another waiting group. Each "table", or "sitting", was spoken to in a "pre-communion address" and then, having partaken, they were encouraged to faith and godliness in a "post-communion" word of encouragement.'[34]

MacMillan also records the assessment Dr. Munro gave of another feature of the occasion: 'an outstanding feature of the day's service was the concluding address, which followed the administration of the ordinance. That was a part of the day's duties in which many of the noted ministers of the north excelled. Most moving were the appeals to the unconverted, for they flowed from a glowing heart in a molten stream.'

Having given in this chapter a brief description of the development of communion seasons in the Highlands, in the next chapter I will detail some of their features.

8

Features of Highland Communion Seasons

In the Highlands services of communion seasons were not only attended by members and adherents of the local congregation, but also by members and adherents from other congregations from the same geographical area, and even some from further away. It is not clear when this practice began. Donald Macleod suggests it began during the banishment of Robert Bruce, a leading Scottish Reformer, to Inverness first in 1605 and again in 1622.[1] Bruce preached during these periods of exile and it was common for thousands, from all over the Highlands, to gather each Sunday to listen to his sermons. Macleod notes that 'these migrations became a staple feature of religious life not least because Bruce was followed by a long succession of outstandingly gifted preachers, particularly in Ross-shire. From Hog of Kiltearn to Kennedy of Dingwall these Highland preachers matched in stature the very best of the south and could command huge audiences wherever they went. Such men were frequently asked to "assist" at Communions.'[2]

The large gatherings were not welcomed by every presbytery and synod. In the previous chapter I mentioned the tension between the father of Donald Sage and his elders over changes he made to the communion practice. The Synod of Sutherland and Caithness, in an Act of 1737, tried to deal with the problem of large crowds by holding two communions on the same date but in different parishes.[3] Their suggestion was not successful, and the Act was set aside in 1758.

The significance of larger communion gatherings in the Highlands lasted for many decades. For example, the Communion season at Creich in Sutherland was 'one of the great events of Church life of the Northern Highlands', and was so for over a century, covering part of the eighteenth and most of the nineteenth centuries. One reason for its prominence was its timing, the third week of August, which meant it was the last of the summer communions, with the harvest following immediately. A surprising aspect of Creich is that for over thirty years prior to the Disruption in 1843 the minister of the parish was not an evangelical. In order to please his parishioners he gratified the people by asking to his communion the popular evangelical preachers of the day.[4]

It was not only at communion seasons on the east coast of the Scottish Highlands that large gatherings were found. Once the gospel had become powerful on the west coast, the same phenomenon of large gatherings occurred. Communion seasons at Plockton on the west coast of the Highlands, during the ministry of Alexander Macdonald (1827-44), are described as 'peculiarly interesting and most precious. The numbers present varied from twelve to fourteen thousand, gathered from fourteen parishes.'[5]

These great assemblies were popular because 'they provided for so many not only high occasions in their religion, but high occasions in their ordinary lives which had so little variety or diversion. The longer the intervals between these irregular "works," the more keenly the people looked forward to them. Many met friends as at no other time in the year, and picked up the latest news. People got a welcome change of scene, if not of air, from the humdrum of their daily labour. In the Highlands these gatherings "helped to destroy the lingering elements of distrust and clan antipathies by bringing people together under conditions eminently conducive to friendliness."'[6]

An accompanying aspect of these large gatherings was the hospitality shown by local Christians to visiting believers. Given that the historical period in which these occasions took place was one of poverty for the lower classes, the resourcefulness and kindness of local believers in providing food and accommodation is admirable.

Positive aspects of Highland Communion seasons

Prayer

Meetings for prayer accompanied the regular services. These meetings were led by laymen and were usually held early in the morning before the services of the day, or in the evening after they were over. These prayer meetings were marked by earnest petitioning to God that he would come to the communion season in great blessing. The preachers too were prayed for earnestly.

One crucial emphasis of the communion season was the stress on personal prayer. For example, during communion seasons in Lewis in the 1830s, it was common that 'every retired spot for miles around would be occupied by a secret worshipper, wrestling with God for the blessing on his own soul and that of others'.[7]

The Fellowship Meeting

In the Highlands the Friday of each Communion season was given over to 'The Men's Meeting'. It had this name because visiting elders and other Christian men, as well as local elders and men, spoke to the congregation rather than the people listening to preaching from the ministers.

A second name for this gathering, the 'Fellowship Meeting', indicates its purpose while a third name, the 'Question Meeting', indicates its format. One of the men selected a passage of Scripture, which became the question to which the other men spoke as they discussed various aspects of a believer's relationship with God. The point of this meeting was to suggest marks or evidences of a genuine work of saving grace. Concerning the abilities of these men to speak about personal religious experience, Macrae says:

> Among the men who spoke on such occasions were many who were distinguished for their gifts and piety, and who used the opportunity to bear testimony to the reality and power of the Gospel in the hearts and lives of men. They could probe into the secrets of the heart, and lay bare alike the marks of grace and of counterfeit grace,

because the secrets of their own hearts had been laid bare to themselves by the searching Word and Spirit of God. Some of them spoke of the deep things of the soul with such brokenness and tenderness, and under such a subdued sense of the Lord's presence, that Friday was often the most helpful day of the season.[8]

The origins of this type of meeting are obscure. One possibility is linked to pious soldiers from Sutherland who fought in the army of Gustavus Aldophus in the Thirty Years War (1618-48). During their period of service they began the practice of meeting together for mutual edification, and when they returned to Sutherland they continued the practice as a means of preparation for the Communion.[9]

Another possible origin concerns meetings for mutual edification at communion seasons that were advocated by John Livingstone, when he was ministering in Ireland in the 1630s: 'Crowds would gather on the Saturday before communion to hear a sermon, and spent the Saturday and Sunday nights "in severall companies, sometimes a minister being with them, sometimes themselves alone in conference and prayer"; "it is hard to judge whether there was more of the Lord's presence in the publick or private meting.'"[10] The practice spread to Scotland, and according to Macaulay,

> Shortly after 1638 there arose a hot discussion regarding certain religious meetings, which seem to have originated with Presbyterians from Ireland, who, when their ministers were driven from them, had acquired the habit of meeting among themselves for religious exercises. The question of their legality came before the Assembly at Aberdeen in 1640, and caused a great stir among the brethren. Henderson did not like it, and would have put an end to it, but such men as Rutherford, Dickson, Livingston and even Blair had other views.
>
> Notwithstanding an adverse judgment by the Assembly of 1647, the issue was the firm establishment of the Fellowship meeting in which the laity had religious communion and discussion among themselves, and which became a vitalizing element in Scottish religious life.[11]

There was contact between evangelicals in the Highlands and Lowlands. John Macleod refers to the religious letters of John Munro, a resident of Edinburgh, sent to his brother Thomas, a leader of the Men in Dunrobin, near Golspie, who opposed the attempt of the Synod of Sutherland and Caithness to ban the Friday Fellowship meeting at communion seasons.[12] The complaint of the Synod indicates that one feature of the Fellowship meetings was to deal with cases of conscience, although others in addition to attendant ministers also attempted to give answers to the problems. Macleod suggests that the Highland Fellowship meeting was a modification of the Lowland meeting.[13]

There is also a connection to monthly Monday meetings for men organised by Thomas Hog of Kiltearn in Ross-shire.[14] Gustavus Aird comments concerning who was admitted to the monthly meeting: 'Originally, none were admitted to the Monday monthly question meeting until they spoke to some of the elders, and then to the minister, and gave some account of their experiences. This was succeeded by their becoming communicants.'[15]

Even after Friday question meetings occurred, the occasion was preserved for the local people:

About a century ago [1790s], the Friday meeting was held in the Church, and none were there but the persons belonging to the parish and who were admitted by the minister and the elders to attend the Monday question meeting. In the parishes adjoining the parish in which the Communion was held, the question meeting on Friday was held. They did not go on that day to the parish where the Communion was, but kept the question meeting in their own parishes, and went on other days where the Communion was held….I suppose, early this [nineteenth] century, Friday began to be kept as a public meeting, but it was not so originally.[16]

Aird's description suggests that the attempt by the Synod of Sutherland and Caithness in 1737 was successful in reducing the numbers that attended the Friday services in subsequent decades, until it became a public meeting in the early nineteenth century.

Aird says concerning the geographical spread of the observance of the question meeting:

> But, as far as is known to me, the question meeting day was only observed in some parts of the Highlands, especially a large portion of Ross-shire, Inverness-shire and Nairnshire.[17] These week-day services were never kept in Lewis until the late Mr. McLeod, Rogart, was settled in Uig. Neither were they kept, I believe, in Skye until Mr. Shaw's time in Bracadale [1812-25], and then in Mr. Roderick McLeod's time there [1823-39] and in Snizort [1839ff.]. So that I think they originated in consequence of the Revival of Religion, but now it is very difficult, if not impossible, to fix on the exact dates of the origin of all the days connected with the Communion.[18]

Possibly local influences contributed to an area-wide desire for such meetings. For example, Alexander Macdonald, the minister in Plockton from 1827-44, held a monthly fellowship meeting on a Monday. On the Sunday previous to each fellowship Monday, people flocked to his services from the surrounding parishes (they did not have evangelical ministers) in order to hear him on the Sunday and attend the fellowship meeting on the Monday. The fellowship meeting 'was a great help to them'.[19]

Such meetings were frequently the means of removing the perplexities of anxious enquirers and seekers after the Saviour. As they heard the inward workings and experiences of God's people being discussed, so their own spiritual questions and strivings were often dealt with and explained for them. The topics handled varied enormously from speaker to speaker and, as most of them were mature, exercised believers of long standing, the richly experiential quality of the individual contributions provided a means of comforting and assuring sorely tried or downcast Christians.

J. P. MacQueen mentions several features of fellowship meetings in Sutherland:

> 1. The Sutherland 'men' insisted on the simplest, lowest and most obvious marks of grace, consistent with one's being in a state of

grace, and not the highest marks. They frowned emphatically on any abuse of the fellowship-meeting, as supposedly and wrongly affording an opportunity to give blows, metaphorically speaking, to a brother layman or minister present. They regarded such conduct as manifesting a lack of becoming courage and candour in not having the gracious manliness to speak to such a brother privately, and not publicly.

2. When a God-fearing minister was obtainable, he was expected to give a doctrinal exposition of a suitable, simple, not complex or disputable, passage of Scripture, 'given out' by one of the 'men' (a layman), generally regarded as among the oldest, more experienced, and judicious, among the godly. The suitability, or otherwise, of the passage was left entirely to the judgment of the minister 'opening the question'.

3. As distinct from the present day, not one of the 'men' read the passage, as owing to the widespread illiteracy, it would be regarded as literary snobbery to read the verse, thus esteeming oneself more advanced than his brethren, which is diametrically opposed to Christian humility and precept.

4. All 'the men' were expected to be short and edifying in their remarks, and it was regarded as violation of good manners, brotherly love, and courtesy, when any brother took up too much time, while there were present so many 'men' to speak, whom all present wanted to hear. The one who thus overleaped the bounds of sobriety and propriety was regarded as esteeming his own natural gifts and eloquence as far above those of his brethren, and this was regarded as the opposite of spiritual-mindedness, gracious unction, and solemn heavenly liberty, in speaking, with pithy brevity. The other extreme of being too long in speaking was unbecoming abrupt shortness and brevity, as, according to the Sutherland 'men', showing a lack of becoming reverence. 'Let brotherly love continue,' was their outstanding and constant resolution.

5. The minister who 'closed the question', summed up, and he was expected lovingly, but firmly, faithfully, candidly, and conscientiously, to point out any flaws, errors, or irregularities, in the preceding statements of the brethren.[20]

The fellowship meeting gave to laymen the opportunity of using their gifts for the benefit of the church. Dr. Kennedy comments regarding this:

> Of the question, "How far lay agency may be employed for the edification of the church," the wisest practical solution has been furnished in the service of the fellowship meeting. It is surely desirable that, if there are talented and godly men in a congregation, an opportunity should be afforded for securing to others the benefit of these gifts with which the Lord has endowed them. If He has made them 'apt to teach', then an opportunity to teach should be given them by the church. This should be provided, so as not to invade the province of the ordained teacher, and so as to conserve and support the authority of his office. By no summary process ought a man to be converted into a preacher, however shining his gifts, and however eminent his godliness. But is he therefore to be kept silent? May no opportunity be given to him to exhort his brethren, publicly as well as privately, so as to secure to the Church at large the benefit of his stores of Christian knowledge and experience? All these conditions have been met in the service of the fellowship meeting. There an opportunity to exercise their gifts for the good of the Church, and without the least prejudice to the position and influence of the minister, was given to such as the Lord had qualified.[21]

Expectations of preparation

A pastoral letter sent to his congregation by John Kennedy of Dingwall, when abroad for his health, gives insight into how the communion was approached.

He reminds believers that they should anticipate communion with the risen Christ at the Supper: '[Christ] is alive to present to His Church the new covenant, which he sealed by His blood, with all the fullness of its precious blessings, as a free gift to each one of you who "have believed through grace."' They should know that special privileges await them at the Table, they have 'the fullest and the closest manifestation of the glory and love of Jehovah the Father given on the earth'. Because this is the case, 'What a solemn movement it is to advance into such a light so shining, and what an inestimable privilege it is to be allowed, and called, to enter the brightness in faith, but with godly fear!'

The seriousness of their profession is pointed out:

> Before you is the prospect of making a solemn profession of dedicating yourself unreservedly to the Lord. To be honest in this profession, you require to be free of all conscious cherishing of sin, and especially of all selfish motives in connection with your position and service as one under vow to be the Lord's. If true in heart, you are willing to be a debtor to the grace of God for all you require in order to your salvation; and to the doing of the work which the Lord requires at your hand you will make no choice of a sphere or form of service for yourself; you will leave yourself, without any reserve of aught you are or have, in the Lord's hands, and you will desire to set Him always before you as the one source of your strength and the one fountain of your joy. The engagement, involving all this, you are called to renew on a Communion Sabbath, under the all-seeing eye of God, while observed by the "elect angels," watched by the powers of darkness, under supervision of the Church, and while challenging the attention and opposition of the world.[22]

The Lord's Supper is also a *communal* act: the believers have communion with the Lord and with other believers. Fellowship with believers follows on from fellowship with Christ: 'If you enjoy communion with the Lord because He is pleased to manifest Himself to your soul, and to draw you near to Him by the cords of love, in the measure in which this will be your privilege will you desire to enjoy fellowship with all His people.' Kennedy summarises what fellowship with fellow believers involves: 'You will desire to have them all in your heart as embraced in the arms of a guileless love, be disposed to pray for their peace, and be ready to do what is in the power of your hand for their good.'[23]

Preparation for the sacrament involves the following:

> 1. a self-emptying sense of one's weakness and folly;
> 2. carefully let the memory go over one's course of profession and service in the past, and ask light from heaven to discover shortcomings;

3. be not satisfied without conscious integrity in dedicating oneself to the Lord;

4. seek to be fervent in love to the brethren;

5. seek so as to meditate on the Lord's promise of his presence that your heart's desire shall go forth in prayer for his coming;

6. And seek to add to brotherly kindness charity towards all who are not brethren, by forgiving them and praying for them.[24]

In a sermon preached in view of a communion occasion from 2 Corinthians 13:5 on the duty of self-examination—'Examine yourselves whether ye be in the faith; prove your own selves. Know ye not your own selves how that Jesus Christ is in you, except ye be reprobates'—Kennedy argues that self-examination must focus on the question, 'Is Jesus Christ in you?', and then proceeds to mention four areas in which imitating Christ is essential: self-denial, love to the brethren, prayerfulness and purity. Kennedy also gives other reasons for self-examination: the divine injunction to engage in it, the possibility of being reprobates, the danger of professing a lie, the necessity of self-examination in order to discover what to pray for, the dangers of formality and pride, the necessity of watchfulness against the deceitfulness of the old heart, and the attaining of skill in responding to temptations of the devil.[25]

Preaching by gifted ministers

Not many of these communion sermons have been preserved, and of those which have, it is not always stated on which particular day they were preached. Nevertheless, to try and realise something of the contents and intentions of these sermons, I will make comments on sermons by several preachers whose sacramental sermons have survived either in manuscript or note form.

The first preacher is William Forbes who was minister of Tarbat, Easter Ross, from 1800 to 1838.[26] In an action sermon[27] preached on 1 Peter 1:8, on the theme of *Love to an Unseen Saviour*, Forbes first states that believers love Christ for three reasons: (1) because of his actions in his incarnation, his life, and his death; (2) because 'His glorious perfections are manifested in supporting, defending, and comforting the Church which He hath purchased with His own blood'; (3) for Christ's individual dealings with each. The believer loves Christ as a Prophet (who teaches him), as a Priest (who cleanses and strengthens him), and as a King (who defeats his inner and outer enemies, each of which is too strong for him). Secondly, Forbes also mentions *evidences* for this love: a supreme regard to Christ, a regard to his honour, a regard to his disciples, and mourning an absent Christ. Thirdly, Forbes lists some *advantages* of love to Christ: it stimulates obedience to the law and strengthens hatred of sin, it is an evidence of real godliness, and it is an earnest of eternal happiness. But Forbes does not leave believers to apply his comments themselves. He is aware that some of his hearers may have been discouraged by his remarks, so he encourages them to participate by asking a series of questions:

> *1. Let me ask intending communicants, What are your sentiments respecting Christ?* Are you not ready to reply that He is fairer than the sons of men, nay altogether lovely? If, then, you consider this glorious One worthy of your confidence and supreme regard, show this by receiving with cheerfulness the sacrament of the supper in obedience to His command, 'Do this in remembrance of Me.' He who loved your souls unto death should be remembered with the most lively admiration and gratitude. But should you now be inclined to lament your past neglect, as well as the coldness and obduracy of your heart at present, let me ask,
>
> *2. What evidences have you of love to Christ?* Do you admire His person? Do you realise the mysterious union of the divine and human nature constituting in Him such a Saviour as you need? Do you behold in Him One that is touched with a feeling of your infirmities and who was Himself made perfect through sufferings? He came to this world for the special purpose of administering instruction, comfort, and encouragement to such as you…. Do you love His image in His children, and wish well to His Church on earth? Show this by bearing an open testimony to His cause before the world. A reluctant performance of duty gives the world an unfavourable opinion of the service of Christ, and of course retards the prosperity of His Church. 'I am not ashamed of the gospel of Christ,' Rom. i.16. If you have indeed felt its power and efficacy upon your souls; you need not be ashamed to avow before God, angels, and men,

that you glory in the cross of Christ.

3. Do you wish to be prepared for duty? to have your faith strengthened, your love inflamed, and your hope confirmed? Embrace and use the means appointed by the Head of the Church for this purpose.[28]

On another occasion Forbes preached an instructive action sermon on how a believer should approach and participate in the Lord's Supper. Concerning those who should participate, Forbes says the Supper is not only for believers who are strong in the faith but also for those who are weak in the faith. They must take the Supper with knowledge, with faith, with penitence, with love, with thankfulness, with humility. They show the death of Christ to God, to their own conscience, to the world, and to angels.[29]

The second preacher is Charles Calder MacIntosh, who was minister in Tain, Ross-shire, during the middle years of the nineteenth century. Two communion sermons are included in a volume of his sermons.

One sermon is based on Isaiah 47:15: 'For thus saith the high and lofty One that inhabiteth eternity, whose name is Holy; I dwell in the high and holy place, with him also that is of a contrite and humble spirit, to revive the spirit of the humble, and to revive the heart of the contrite ones.' In this sermon, after explaining something of the greatness, eternity and holiness of God and his heavenly dwelling place, MacIntosh describes how the Son of God came down from heaven to Calvary 'in order that God might again have a dwelling place in the hearts of men'. Those in whom he dwells are marked by humility. True humility is the response not only to the greatness of God and to the grace of God, but also to the realisation of sinful tendencies that still remain within believers:

The sense of spiritual need is met by the discovery of the fullness that is in Christ, and the fears of wrath are removed by faith in His atoning blood; but with growth in the knowledge of God and in the experience of His grace, and growth in the knowledge of sin and of the plague of the heart, there is growth in humility. He who says, 'I am less than the least of all saints,' will join the sinner at God's footstool in also saying, 'God be merciful to me a sinner! It is of the Lord's mercies that we are not consumed, because His compassions fail not.' Humility is thus the right disposition of heart in a fallen yet redeemed creature,—a view of God's majesty, holiness, and grace, and a sense of his own emptiness and unworthiness, leading him to exalt God and to glory only in Him.[30]

Humility is not only an attitude towards God: 'And where there is humility in its prime and chief exercise towards God, there will be humility towards fellow-creatures and brethren in the Lord; not only because humility has love as its sister grace—love leading one to honour all men, but especially the brethren—but because every Christian knows his own obligations, shortcomings, and sins, as he cannot know those of others.'[31]

The text MacIntosh is preaching from indicates that humble believers need reviving, and this reviving is promised by the Lord: 'Those who are made humble in spirit need Divine consolation and support, under a sense of their sinfulness, unworthiness, barrenness and spiritual helplessness.' The Lord can and does revive them by powerful application of divine promises. But he also revives them through their partaking of the Lord's Supper:

1. As an ordinance of special fellowship or communion with God. And such it is. It is sitting with Him at His table. As only the contrite in heart can have communion with a bruised Saviour in the gospel, so only they can have communion with Him in the sacrament. The deeper the sense of sin, the more precious is the balm of the covenant; the deeper the humiliation, the more glorious is grace in the soul's view. Besides, the more the Lord humbles Himself in the exercise of His adorable grace—and in no ordinance is this so much to be seen as in the ordinance of the supper—the louder the call to His people to put their shoes from off their feet. If, therefore, you would have nearness to and fellowship with God in His ordinance, seek after contrition and humility of spirit; and seek it in the Lord's way, through the Holy Spirit bringing sin to your remembrance and showing you sin in *the cross.*

2. As an ordinance for special consolation, through the help afforded in it for realising the glory of the one sacrifice for sin and

the unchangeableness of the love which passeth knowledge; an ordinance for consolation, in order to a closer walk with God, and to a hopeful and vigorous following after holiness. If you need deliverance from a doubting of your personal interest in the Saviour, that you may give yourself with a heart freed from killing fear to the great work of purifying yourself; if you need some blessed token for good that to you belongs the promise, 'Sin shall not have dominion over you,' so that in the strength of grace and in the hope of victory you may be engaged in the conflict with the sin that dwelleth in you; if under a painful sense of past unfruitfulness or past declension you seek earnestly to know how you can be kept in time to come, how you can cleave to the Lord and redeem the rest of [your] short life for that work which cannot be done in the grave; or if, under sore personal trial or painful bereavements, you need that peace which Christ gives, that you may be enabled in truth and from experience to speak well of His name and His ways, then hear the Lord's voice, saying, 'Open thy mouth wide, and I will fill it;' and take encouragement to pour out your heart before Him, that He may manifest Himself to you in another way than He does unto the world, and give you so to appropriate the strong consolation which He provided for the 'heirs of promise', as that you shall, to the end, follow them who, through faith and patience, inherit the promises.[32]

MacIntosh's second sermon is from Colossians 3:11: 'Where'— or in which thing—'there is neither Greek nor Jew, circumcision nor uncircumcision, Barbarian, Scythian, bond nor free: but Christ is all, and in all.' He notices from the text firstly that no outward distinctions are of any avail in the matter of a man's salvation, be the distinction one of nationality, observance or non-observance of ordinances, lettered or unlettered, slave or freeman. Secondly, it is only Christ that avails, and he is discovered in the Word by the teaching and work of the Holy Spirit, with the result that Christ is all to every believing sinner. Thirdly, in Christ there is fullness of grace: (i) a fullness in his person as God and man that enabled him 'to obey, suffer, merit, to be the repository of all grace and of all spiritual blessings, to be at once the Keeper and the Friend and the Husband of His people'; (ii) a fullness of justifying merit, in that the merit of his work 'is counted to the believing sinner, so that he is made the righteousness of God in Him'; (iii) a fullness of saving power in Christ 'to illuminate the dark mind, to subdue sin, to change the heart, to renew and sanctify wholly'; (iv) the fullness of divine love and the fullness of human love resides in Christ.[33]

The third preacher is Dr. John Kennedy of Dingwall who, in the second half of the nineteenth century, was given the pre-eminent place among Highland preachers. Some notes have been preserved of communion sermons preached by him in Thurso and Dornoch. In June 1864 he preached at the Thurso communion from 2 Peter 1:10 (it is not stated which day of the Communion season it was preached). In this sermon Kennedy deals with the doctrine of election, in particular the distinction between the general call of God in the gospel to all sinners and his efficacious call to his people. No doubt Kennedy was aware of the problems concerning assurance caused by a wrong use of the doctrine of election. For Kennedy, the remedy is not to ignore election, rather the believer should attempt to get an appreciation of the wonder of election, that God should have given covenant security to insignificant creatures by uniting them to himself. Kennedy wants to help believers concerned by their sin and gives this piece of advice:

> You are in a low case of soul, and you take up your case and begin to consider and examine it, and it doesn't look very encouraging; and what do you do? Perhaps, instead of going to the Lord and confessing your sin, and imploring his mercy, you set your memory to work on some past experiences of His favour, and try if an easy recollection of past attainments will revive and reassure you. Now, it is not good for a soul to forget the Lord's past dealings of mercy towards it; but if you make that a pillow for your head on a bed of sloth, that journey on which you send your memory will be an unsafe and unsanctified one for you. Rather come afresh to the Lord, whatever be your case, that He may anew manifest Himself to you, anew cause the fruits of faith and love to spring up within you to the praise of His grace and for the 'restoring of your soul'.[34]

He also deals with objections unconverted hearers may have to election, particularly the statement that a person would come to Christ if he knew he was elect. Kennedy responds by saying such knowledge would actually make it harder to come to Christ because the knowledge would feed pride. Rather such should come to Christ as sinners.[35]

At the same communion season Kennedy also preached from Luke 22:31-32 on the fall of Peter. Kennedy commented that 'it is usually after seasons of special nearness to their Lord that the adversary lays wait for God's children and seeks their fall'.[36] Because of the intercession of Christ Peter's faith did not fail. Kennedy encouraged 'every tempted, tempest-tossed soul in Caithness or elsewhere…to lay all its weight on this gracious Advocate—this glorious "I"—all its guilty yesterday, all its sinful today, all its unknown tomorrow!'[37]

Notes of a sermon by Kennedy at a communion in Dornoch in 1881, seventeen years after he preached in Thurso, are also available. A sermon on Proverbs 8:30-31 seems to be an action sermon judging by its contents. In the sermon Kennedy deals with the delights of Christ, focusing particularly on his delight in sinners. This delight in sinners was because he delighted in the Father. Kennedy lists several ways in which Christ anticipated this delight: among them were those sinners the Father gave him in eternity; when through his incarnation he became their Brother; when he became their Redeemer; when he would save them in the day of his power; when he would shepherd them throughout their wilderness journey; when they would be in his presence in the eternity to come. Each of these aspects is developed in his sermon.[38]

Kennedy also included in a volume of sermons one preached as an action sermon at a Ferintosh communion. The sermon was based on Psalm 85:10: 'Mercy and truth are met together; righteousness and peace have kissed each other.' He expounded the meeting referred to in the text as wondrous, real and gladsome. It was wondrous because it seemed unlikely that the righteous God and the guilty sinner could meet; it was real because the meeting of righteousness and peace and mercy and truth took place at Calvary; it is a gladsome meeting because the sinner knows that God's righteousness has been satisfied in the death of Christ, that the satisfaction of Christ meets all the needs of the sinner exactly and fully. The sermon closes with an appeal to careless sinners, to anxious sinners, and to believers; the appeal to each group focuses on the necessity of faith in Christ crucified.[39]

The fourth preacher is William McDougall who pastored in Raasay, Appin and Contin in the second half of the nineteenth century. In an action sermon on Zechariah 13:7 ('The Smitten Shepherd'), McDougall deals with the relationship between the Father and the Son, particularly how Christ was the Man (his person) and the Shepherd (his offices of prophet, priest and king). The image of the sword in the hand of Jehovah is used powerfully:

> The sword slept 4,000 years from the fall, and the vengeance demanded by the law was not taken. The avenger of the law saw the church from generation to generation passing from under the curse of the law, into glory, into everlasting life, and still the sword slept in its scabbard; the church's sin was unavenged; justice and righteousness had not yet been satisfied, but in the promise—in the bond of the covenant....Yes, He comes in the fullness of the time. The Ruler sees Him coming. And now hear Him rouse the sword and give it a commission—Awake now and exact the penalty—Here is a sacrifice—one worthy of thine edge—And O! what a sight for the universe is here. The Son of God, Jehovah's Fellow, approaches and lays his humanity upon the altar. The flaming sword awakes in His Father's hand and pierces His soul.[40]

These sermons indicate that preachers at communion seasons presented to their hearers teaching that included difficult doctrines, such as the person and work of Christ, and advice on aspects of Christian living. Difficult doctrines were not presented in a dry and abstract manner, rather the style is devotional and illustrations were given to help grasp the meaning. Practical concerns were not given in a detached and formal style, but were analysed closely in a warm, tender and sympathetic manner, with the aim being the spiritual comfort of believers. The preachers were in no doubt that the Lord's Supper was a means of helping understand doctrine, for developing a spiritual relationship both with God and fellow believers, and for receiving divine comfort.

Fencing of the table

The purpose of this practice was to guard the Lord's Table from unworthy participators, individuals who were not truly converted.

> Every effort was made by ministers and kirk sessions to keep the Communions as 'pure' as possible, and the constant means to this end from the Reformation to the late nineteenth century was the 'fencing of the tables' by the minister. The word 'fencing' may derive from the open space in the body of the church fenced off by the 'travess',[41] but it may come from a legal word 'fence' meaning to proclaim. The fencing was meant to be a final or last-minute challenge to the conscience of the communicant to examine himself.[42]

The timing of the practice was after the action sermon and before the celebration of the Supper. It involved a short discourse in which the minister gave marks, on the one hand, as to who should not participate and, on the other hand, marks as to who should. The practice was a response to the method where all baptised persons were allowed to communicate, and would have been necessary at communion seasons because large numbers of baptised but nominal members were present. There is no doubt that many communicants, particularly those who were lacking a sense of assurance of salvation, found the fencing of the table to be a spiritually helpful feature of a communion service.

Table addresses

The Protestors introduced the practice of lengthy table addresses.[43] Prior to this, the minister would counsel the communicants while they were participating, or else a Scripture passage was read. The General Assembly of 1645 had replaced the reading of the Passion story with a short address or exhortation, but the Protestors did not adhere to this rule.[44]

In the Highlands, when the communicants had seated themselves at the Lord's Table, a minister addressed them both before and after taking the elements, which was a custom in line with Protesting practice. The first address was usually based on a Bible verse and was designed to encourage believers as they waited for the bread and wine. The minister's comments would provide suitable thoughts for meditation.

William McDougall left four sets of table addresses. In the first set, the address before communicating asks the believers to consider where they are—they are at a table in the wilderness, provided by the Lord to feed his people. The food they eat is the benefits of the covenant of grace purchased by Christ's blood. In addition to remembering Christ as he commanded, each believer is there to thank God for his distinguishing grace and to renew their personal covenant with him. In the address after communicating, McDougall mentions several likely questions that believers would have been asking themselves concerning their sins, their spiritual barrenness, their worldliness and their fear of death. He provides answers from Christ in the form of divine promises from the Bible.[45]

In the second set, the address before communicating focuses on how each believer has been brought by the King into his private chambers: to the audience chamber where he hears their petitions; to the guest chamber where they feast with him; to the banqueting chamber where they hear his words of love to them. The believers acknowledge that it was the King's ability, his 'loving violence and power', that removed the obstacles to their entrance to the chambers, despite their unworthiness. In the address after communicating, McDougall reminded the believers that the vows of the Lord were now upon them, they had covenanted anew to be his. He encouraged them by reminding them of the promise that God shall supply all their need, according to his riches in glory, by Christ Jesus. Yet he requires that they walk watchfully, prayerfully and circumspectly.[46]

In the third set, the address before communicating is based on 'God who is rich in mercy'. McDougall notes that unlike human riches God's riches are immeasurable. His mercy is available because Christ in his death met the claims of God's justice. After communicating, McDougall reminds the believers of the exceeding great and precious promises they have been given. Each time a promise comes from Christ to their heart in their time of need, it is a kiss from his lips. The promises are infallible and are concerned with the benefits of the covenant of grace.[47]

In the fourth set, the pre-communicating address is based on the text, 'Thou hast received gifts for men.' McDougall reminds the communicants of some of the gifts given to them by Christ: himself, the Holy Spirit, repentance, forgiveness, peace with the Father, the Bible as a guidebook, a place in the church, and the title to heaven. After they had communicated, McDougall exhorted them to seek fellowship with God and not with the world, and to serve him in the knowledge that he will provide all the strength and grace they would require.[48]

As a means of discipline

Although an orthodox form of Presbyterianism was common throughout the Highlands, this did not mean that an evangelical spiritual life always accompanied the preaching, either in the preacher or in the congregation. In such situations, participation in the Lord's Supper was reduced to mere formality, with no distinction being made between those who should and those who should not share the bread and wine. This practice meant that when an evangelical minister was inducted to a congregation, one of the first things demanding attention was correcting the wrong practices associated with communion seasons.

This was the situation that Thomas Hog faced when he became minister in Kiltearn, Ross-shire; he discovered that the 'ignorance of the people was so great…that it was long ere they were in any readiness to receive it [the Lord's Supper]'.[49] He had then preached for four years before sufficient evidence was given by his parishioners that the Lord was blessing his labours, and this indication led him to decide that the time had arrived to celebrate the sacrament. His decision was honoured by the Lord who 'displayed his saving power on that occasion most comfortably and signally'.[50]

Another such occasion involves the Island of Lewis, where not only is the Presbyterian church regarded as orthodox but during the last two centuries it has experienced several revivals. But it was not always so. Alexander Macleod was inducted to Uig in 1824.[51] The reason why an evangelical minister was inducted to such a parish was the sympathy to evangelical preaching of the Honourable Mrs Stuart Mackenzie, the wife of one of the Lewis landlords, and she used her influence to secure evangelical ministers in chapels and parishes throughout Lewis. Macleod discovered that most of his parishioners, although members of the church, were deficient in spiritual experience. In the first prayer-meeting held by Macleod, one elder 'actually offered a request that a wreck should be cast ashore in the neighbourhood', while another elder, 'referring to the death of our Lord as a misfortune, used strong expressions of deprecation of its having at all occurred'.[52] Yet such assumed it was appropriate for them to take communion.

Macleod decided to postpone observing of the Lord's Supper and instead to preach on the necessity of regeneration and holiness, with an evangelistic thrust to his messages. Within two years a great spiritual movement resulted. The change in the outlook of the parishioners was seen when only six people communicated when the Lord's Supper was re-introduced in the congregation, although Macleod was aware that many others had been truly converted.[53] Douglas MacMillan writes that the Lord's blessing of Macleod's actions 'were the beginnings of a spiritual Awakening in the Island of Lewis which has persisted, in ebbs and flows, until the present day'.[54]

Catalysts for revivals

That communion seasons were an occasion of revivals is not a feature limited to the Highlands. For example, well-documented revivals occurred at communion seasons at Cambuslang and Kilsyth in the Lowlands. It is the case that 'Revivals were certainly no new thing in the nineteenth-century Highlands.'[55] These revivals had occurred in many geographical areas of the Highlands; some of the revivals were widespread, others were local in extent. A major contribution to these revivals was the communion season. 'Larger communal events were particularly suited to the impulses of spiritual awakening. Of fundamental importance to Presbyterians was the great communal gatherings occasioned by the Lord's Supper, a key event in the Presbyterian calendar.... In the Highlands, as in the Lowlands, deep spiritual experiences, productive of revival, were associated primarily with Presbyterian communion services.'[56]

For example, George Wood of Rosemarkie stated in 1743: 'Since the Communion here in July last, the bulk of the congregation seem to have a desire after instruction, and a knowledge of the Gospel, much greater than before. There are now about thirty persons of different ages and sexes, who since that time have come under convictions and awakenings of conscience through the Word.'[57]

As noted above, it was common for the local pastor to invite prominent and gifted preachers to officiate at his communion. One individual who ministered for much of the first half of the nineteenth century was Dr. John MacDonald, minister at Ferintosh, north of Inverness. There are recorded accounts of the effects of his ministry.

One such occasion occurred during a communion season in his own congregation at Ferintosh. The occasion was made more poignant because his wife had died the previous week. His elders, sensitive to his possible feelings, had suggested cancelling the communion but MacDonald refused, and in fact preached the action sermon from Hosea 2:19: 'I will betroth thee unto me for ever.'

According to Allan Sinclair, 'a deep impression was made upon the audience, numbering probably ten thousand.' The ministers who were assisting MacDonald persuaded him to also preach the next sermon that would close the service. He agreed and preached from Psalm 45:10 ('Hearken, O daughter, and consider') and

Genesis 24:58 ('Wilt thou go with this man?'). Sinclair continues:

> The impression already made was greatly deepened. The feelings of
> the audience were overpowering. Urging acceptance of Jesus upon
> them with extraordinary fervour, he put the question once more,
> 'Wilt thou go with this man?' A tall middle-aged woman in the heart
> of the congregation started to her feet, tossed her arms into the air,
> and exclaimed in tones heard over the vast audience — 'Theid, Theid,
> O, Theid!' ('I will, I will, O I will!') The preacher replied, 'God grant
> thee that grace, and to all present here this day!' The great
> congregation broke down. It was a scene never to be forgotten. The
> Burn of Ferintosh was a Bochim indeed that day. Such was the
> weeping, the crying, the commotion among the people, that the
> preacher's voice was drowned. Amid this glorious triumph of the
> King of Zion, the day came to a close, memorable among the many
> memorable days of the ministry of this eminent and dear servant
> of the Lord Jesus.[58]

In September 1816, Robert Findlater, then in Perthshire, invited
MacDonald to come to and preach at an open-air communion
service at Ardeonaig. An attendee at the service describes the
occasion:

> Here a great number of people had assembled to hear the word,
> many of whom had come from a distance. The preaching of Mr.
> McDonald was accompanied by a power such as they had never
> witnessed before. The whole congregation seemed affected by a
> singular movement. I suppose it was something like what the Prophet
> saw in a vision, a shaking among the dry bones in the valley.... The
> impression of that day was carried in many a bosom to distant parts
> of the country, and into remote glens, in which, perhaps, the sound
> of salvation had never before been heard.[59]

I referred above to how Alexander Macleod refused to allow
the Lord's Supper to be celebrated in Uig for two years, until he
was convinced the people understood what they were doing. In
1828, two years after he restored the practice, nine thousand people
from all over the island of Lewis attended his communion season,
an indication that his actions concerning the abuse of the Supper

had, through the Lord's blessing, contributed to revival in the area. By 1833, people were coming from further afield, from Harris and Uist. One writer says of these occasions:

> At these gatherings the Spirit of the Lord was with his servants and people, new cases of awakening ever occurred, believers increased in light and love, and the cause of Christ received, in various forms, new accessions of strength, while Satan's old rule of darkness, superstition, and folly, seemed tottering to an irretrievable overthrow.[60]

Negative aspects of Highland Communion Seasons

Despite these benefits, criticisms of different aspects of Highland communion seasons can be made. One is the *fewness of occasions when the Lord's Supper was held*. It is the case that some parishes only had an annual event and it is difficult to deduce from Scripture the legitimacy of such infrequent communion. The situation was partly remedied by the fact that communions were not held simultaneously in each parish but consecutively, which meant that believers could travel to neighbouring parishes to partake of the Supper as well. But even with this remedy, it still meant that most believers did not partake of the Lord's Supper for ten months of the year, since the sacramental occasions were generally held in August and September.

A second criticism concerns *the lack of emphasis on the concept of a local congregation*. Regarding the lack of an emphasis on the concept of a local church, I do not mean that they did not have this emphasis with other matters, such as regular attendance at parish sermons or for the implementing of church discipline. But there did not seem to be an emphasis on the local church with regard to the Lord's Supper, except with regard to it being the occasion when new members joined the church. I mentioned above the difference between Donald Sage and his elders over his wish to have a local communion without the involvement of Christians from other parishes. The general outlook regarding the Supper seems to take it as an action of several churches, not the action of a local church. They did not see the value for local growth of only local people remembering the Lord. One common effect of this practice was the rarity, if ever, of a pastor administering the Supper to his own congregation.

A third criticism concerns *the lack of assurance found among Highland Christians*. While the two criticisms mentioned above have been rectified in many Highland congregations, the lack of assurance is still a major problem. Therefore I want to assess how the main defender of the Highland practice, Dr John Kennedy of Dingwall, dealt with this third criticism.

True assurance has two unwelcome companions – false assurance and lack of assurance. Jesus taught, for example, in his Sermon on the Mount, that there would be those who imagined that they were his followers, who had thought they were serving him, but to whom he will say at the Day of Judgement, 'I never knew you' (Matt. 7:21-23). What these people had is false assurance. Sinclair Ferguson comments regarding false assurance that it is 'tragically possible to have a kind of faith and assurance that has never opened up the heart to the sweet influences of his [Christ's] grace which enable us to abandon self-reliance. It is not recognised as often as it should be that it is amongst evangelicals rather than liberals, and doctrinal rather than non-doctrinal Christians, that this danger is most subtle. So long as there is a vestige of reliance upon our righteousness, our service, our obedience, our knowledge, our understanding of doctrine, there can be no genuine assurance.'[61] Therefore, it is legitimate for a Christian to examine his assurance.

It was difficult for Lowland Christians, influenced by the revivals of 1839 and subsequent years, 1859 and subsequent years, and by the Moody evangelistic campaigns,[62] to understand the rarity with which a Highland Christian would refer to his own acceptance with God. Kennedy responded with several comments. 'The Highland Christian cannot account for the ease with which a Lowlander, of whose piety he is persuaded, can adopt the language of assurance with which his brother addresses God.'[63] The reason for this was his own personal experience; he based his interaction with God on his subjective experience, and that experience did not always indicate assurance. He would not be honest with himself if he used words of assurance when his feelings contradicted the words. The Highland Christian did not deny assurance was possible; sometimes his critics suggested lack of assurance was not possible. Yet several psalms (and probably Paul's experience in Romans 7) indicate that it is possible for believers to be in the dark about their salvation. Kennedy perceptively comments: 'is there not good reason for affirming that there is as great a tendency to an arid objectiveness on the one side, as to a morbid subjectiveness on the other, to an unlicensed familiarity on the one side, as to a slavish distrust on the other.'[64]

Kennedy also highlights another distinction in assurance: 'Christians in the Highlands had been taught to distinguish between doubting the safety of their state and doubting the truth of the Word.'[65] They were concerned primarily with the trustworthiness of Christ, then secondly with their own state. Once they had been assured of the former, then they would look for evidence of the latter. This is probably a common way among many Christians.

The Highland Christian, however, was more liable to engage in prolonged self-examination and to require more concrete subjective evidence that he was converted than did some of his critics. That this practice may seem unreal to other Christians is granted, but the fact that it produced a healthy spiritual commitment to God cannot be denied. For Kennedy, suspicion about one's faith was healthy when it caused the person to examine his life, and it became hurtful 'only when it degenerated into a slavish fear, under the power of which the soul departs from the Lord'.[66] It seems to me that Kennedy was right to stress the necessity of one possessing evidences before pronouncing that one had assurance of salvation.

Kennedy's thinking was in line with previous Scottish understanding concerning distinctions in assurance. An example of similar teaching arose in the Secession churches in Scotland, where they developed the distinction between what they called the assurance of faith and the assurance of sense. Ebenezer Erskine argued that there were two levels of assurance in the assurance of faith: an intellectual assent based on the truthfulness of God's word concerning Jesus Christ and an assurance of *appropriation* in which the person embraces the promise.[67] The assurance of faith is a direct act whereas the assurance of sense is a reflex act. The former can be very strong when the latter is very weak.

Not only was Kennedy in agreement with his evangelical predecessors, his views are also in agreement with the teaching of the Westminster Confession of Faith concerning assurance. The Confession's chapter contains four short sections and a brief summary of its teaching is as follows.

The first paragraph of this section takes into account the existence of *false assurance*. The existence of this is not a reason to conclude that true assurance is impossible. A set of contrasts are given: those who possess false assurance are called 'hypocrites' and 'unregenerate' whereas those who can possess true assurance are described as those who 'truly believe in Jesus' and who 'love him in sincerity'; those possessing false assurance possess 'false hopes and carnal presumptions' whereas true believers 'endeavour to walk in all good conscience' before Christ and 'may in this life be certainly assured that they are in a state of grace, and may rejoice in the hope of the glory of God'; the hope of the hypocrite 'shall perish' whereas the hope of the righteous 'shall never make them ashamed'. In addition to false assurance, this paragraph allows for the existence of true assurance and the possibility of true faith without this assurance.

The second paragraph describes the nature of the assurance of faith. It is an infallible assurance based on three grounds: the divine truth of the promises of salvation, the inward evidence of the graces to which these promises are made, and the testimony of the Spirit as the Spirit of adoption witnessing with their spirits that they are children of God. The first ground is based on the veracity of the scriptures, the second on the reality of ongoing sanctification, and the third is one of the blessings of adoption.

161

Further, the first is an objective ground, whereas the other two are subjective.

The first ground includes assurance that Christ is a great Saviour based on the descriptions of him in the Bible, that if I come to Jesus I will be saved, that if I repent of my sins and trust in him I will be saved. This aspect of assurance concerns the character and capability of God more than my participation in salvation. Kennedy argued that the first ground was found in the Highland understanding of assurance.

The second ground is concerned with the issue of *self-examination*. This is an important aspect of assurance, because, whereas looking to Jesus will result in the conviction that Christ is a great Saviour, engaging in self-examination will indicate whether or not he has saved *me*. Self-examination is necessary because of the possibility of hypocrisy, of temporary faith, of the process of backsliding. In self-examination, the person is looking for real faith and not strong faith, for weak faith is also true faith. Self-examination should be followed by conviction of salvation leading to growth in assurance, or to repentance because of the discovery of sinful attitudes or practices.

The third ground is *the witness of the Spirit*. The biblical statement is in Romans 8:16, where the word *summartureō* can mean witnesses *to* our spirit or *with* our spirit. The prefix *sun* suggests the intensification of the Spirit's witness to our spirit. The Spirit strengthens and confirms the already existing assurance that the believer has deduced from the divine promises and from self-examination.[68] The paragraph also refers to the possession of the Spirit as the earnest of our inheritance whereby we are sealed to the day of redemption, which suggests that this assurance is a foretaste of the certainty that will mark those who have the full inheritance.

In the third paragraph, the Confession affirms that assurance is not of the essence of faith. This is sometimes taken as a correction of the emphasis of the Reformers that assurance was of the essence of faith.[69] Calvin certainly defined faith as 'a steady and certain knowledge of the divine kindness towards us, which is founded on a gracious promise through Christ, and is revealed to our minds, and sealed on our hearts, by the Holy Spirit'.[70] It is evident that the Reformers personally enjoyed assurance of faith and Cunningham may be correct in his argument that this was due to special grace being given to them to witness for Christ in a difficult situation, although that would not explain why the Reformers deduced that assurance was of the essence of faith.[71] Cunningham's other suggestion, that one's experience of conversion does affect one's sense of what faith is, is a more likely possibility, for the Reformers had experienced spiritual delivery from the bondage brought about by the teachings of the Church of Rome.[72]

It is important to note what Calvin's definition says about faith: it is based on divine revelation, it involves the mind and the heart, and is given to believers by the Holy Spirit. It is also the case that Calvin affirms later in the same chapter in the *Institutes* that he cannot imagine any assurance that is not assailed by some anxiety. He states that while faith ought to be assured, there is not such a thing as a perfect assurance.

The Confession is not here dealing with an assurance that may exist at conversion. Rather the assurance is the kind described in paragraph 2, the assurance that is based on divine promises, personal experience and the witness of the Spirit. It is evident that initial faith cannot be based on the last two aspects since they are the experience of believers. It is absurd to suggest that the Reformers were not aware of this distinction between two kinds of assurance, and Calvin, for example, does acknowledge the reality of believers at times undergoing doubts.

The Confession also allows, by its use of the phrase 'doth not so belong', for the possibility of some believers having assurance from the time of conversion and of others not having it then but attaining to it later. Then the Confession affirms that true assurance can be attained through 'the right use of ordinary means': 'And therefore it is the duty of everyone to give all diligence to make his calling and election sure; that thereby his heart may be enlarged in peace and joy in the Holy Ghost, in love and thankfulness to

God, and in strength and cheerfulness in the duties of obedience, the proper fruits of this assurance: so far is it from inclining men to looseness.'

In its fourth paragraph, the Confession allows that assurance can be shaken, diminished and interrupted. Several reasons are suggested: neglect or a special sin that wounds the conscience and grieves the Spirit; Satanic activity in temptation; God's sovereign decision to withdraw his presence and to allow his people to walk in darkness. Yet the Confession points out that such experiences do not entirely remove basic Christian requirements, such as faith in God, love to Christ and his people, and sincerity of heart and conscience of duty, and from these basic outlooks it is possible for the Spirit to both support them from despair in the present and to restore to them assurance in the future.

The Confession's description of faith enables subsequent generations to distinguish between true and false teachings on assurance and it is difficult to see where Kennedy's teaching differs from the Confessional statements of his church. Kennedy was concerned about the possibility of many church members in the Lowlands having a false assurance which was not based on self-examination and strengthened by the witness of the Spirit in the heart, but instead was the consequence of having gone through a form of commitment in an enquiry room setting where it was possible for wrong assumptions concerning one's salvation to have been made. He may have over-reacted to a change in Scottish church life, but he was witnessing a situation at one level in which personal assurance of salvation was claimed by those advocating rationally critical views of scripture and at another level where religious services were becoming Arminian in theology and where professions of faith were based on belief in an unlimited atonement rather than in a universal offer. Some of his fellow-Calvinists in the Lowlands were able to distinguish between such aspects, but Kennedy did not, and in this he seems to have had the support of Highland Christians who distanced themselves from these changes in the denominational divisions of 1893 and 1900.[73]

Kennedy was aware of the fact that lack of assurance was not a common difficulty in Lowland congregations. He connected this to a distinction between what was required for receiving baptism and what was expected before partaking of the Lord's Supper. The Lowland practice, which demanded the same for both ordinances, resulted in entire congregations sitting at the Lord's Table. The Highland practice, which required a higher degree of evidence for the Lord's Table, resulted in large numbers of baptised individuals not taking the Supper. Kennedy only deals with the two options and does not consider the possibility that both outlooks were wrong. While there were various reasons for true believers not communicating, such as lack of assurance or personal temperaments, it is impossible to justify from Scripture the practice of true Christians, even those lacking assurance, not taking the Lord's Supper. The Larger Catechism allowed for those lacking assurance to sit at the Lord's Table.

> Question 172: May one who doubts of his being in Christ, or of his due preparation, come to the Lord's Supper?
>
> Answer: One who doubts of his being in Christ, or of his due preparation to the sacrament of the Lord's Supper, may have true interest in Christ, though he be not yet assured thereof; and in God's account has it, if he be duly affected with the apprehension of the want of it, and unfeignedly desires to be found in Christ, and to depart from iniquity: in which case (because promises are made, and this sacrament is appointed, for the relief even of weak and doubting Christians) he is to bewail his unbelief, and labour to have his doubts resolved; and, so doing, he may and ought to come to the Lord's Supper, that he may be further strengthened.

Decline of the Significance of Communion Seasons

The evidence presented in this chapter indicates that the large crowds which attended communion services in the past usually came from the surrounding area. Large crowds no longer attend the communion occasions. There are several reasons for this, some social and some religious.

Social changes

One basic cause for the decline is the marked decrease in the numbers of people attending church. In 1851, over 50% of the population in the northern Highlands attended church; in 1984 only between 16% and 18% attended. Whereas in the nineteenth century one out of two attended church, today it is one out of six.[74]

Another factor in the reduction of numbers attending is the loss of males due to two World Wars in the first half of the twentieth century. This factor not only includes those who were killed but also the many, particularly servicemen from rural areas, whose religious convictions were diminished or lost because of the wars.[75]

A third factor in the decline is the dramatic changes in working practices. For example, much of the work in rural localities was connected to agriculture. Some leased smallholdings from landlords, and others worked for farmers. If the community was near the sea, then fishing was an occupation. In the twentieth century, due to inventions connected to farming and fishing, less workers were required, and many families left the Highlands to find employment elsewhere.

A fourth factor is the decrease in the size of families. In the nineteenth century, it was common for the number of children in a family to approach or be above double figures. Large families became less common as the twentieth century progressed. One obvious effect of smaller families is less children being presented for baptism, and thus later taking communion.

Religious changes

An important religious factor in the demise of numbers attending communion seasons was the appearance of denominational loyalties. Prior to 1843 Presbyterians in the Scottish Highlands had belonged in the main to the Church of Scotland, the exceptions being two distinct alternatives. First, there were several Secession churches scattered here and there throughout the Highlands, identified with the Lowland secessions from the Church of Scotland. Second, there were the Separatists, groups of Christians who refused to attend the parish church because of an unevangelical minister. Most of the Separatists refused to form another denomination and continued to regard the Church of Scotland as the only proper denomination; when an evangelical minister was inducted to such a charge the previous Separatists often resumed attending the parish church. Even after 1843, most Presbyterians were within the one denomination since the vast majority of them had identified themselves with the Free Church of Scotland.[76]

The first major division in Highland Presbyterianism occurred with the formation of the Free Presbyterian Church of Scotland in 1893. This separation was a response to the passing of a Declaratory Act by the Free Church, an act that modified ministers' commitment to the contents of the Westminster Confession of Faith. Support for this separation was primarily in the Highlands.[77] Another separation occurred in 1900 when a minority in the Free Church, mainly in the Highlands, refused to follow the majority into a union with the United Presbyterian Church to form the United Free Church.

These divisions meant that in 1900 three different groups competed for the numbers that prior to 1893 met together at communion occasions. Another division occurred in 1929: when the United Free Church merged with the Church of Scotland, a few United Free Churches in the Highlands, as well as many more in the Lowlands, refused to join and continued their denomination. It is inevitable that increasing denominationalism resulted in the disappearance of large crowds.[78] It is now possible in a small Highland community for there to be several separate denominations celebrating the Lord's Supper simultaneously where in the past there would have been only one celebration.

A second religious factor is the lack of religious revivals in Highland communities in the twentieth century. It is of significance that the one area in which travelling to neighbouring communions was the normal practice until recently was the Western Isles (especially Lewis and Harris) and it is the only area in Britain which saw regular revivals through the first half of the twentieth century.[79]

A third religious factor is the appearance of alternative ranges of meetings—conferences such as the Strathpeffer Convention. It is obvious that the themes of the communion seasons and the attendant features of meetings for fellowship and prayer are paralleled in conventions and conferences. With the increased capability of travel, it meant that Highland Christians could attend conferences elsewhere in Britain and receive from these occasions the blessings once available in communion seasons.

This combination of both social and religious phenomena has resulted in the rapid decline of Highland communion seasons. Apart from some churches in the Western Isles, it is rare today to find a communion season that adheres to the practices of the past. In most mainland Highland churches, the length of the communion weekend has been shortened, the number of services decreased, and the prospect of visitors from surrounding parishes has reduced greatly.

The Lord's Supper Today

9

The Lord's Supper and Liturgy

David Larsen, commenting on the current perspective found in many American churches, writes that 'Baptism and the Lord's Supper have fallen on hard times in many a congregation. Strangled by unyielding custom and suffocated by formalism, we do not look forward to these times of sharing as we should.'[1] His assessment is shared by Leonard J. Vander Zee: 'For centuries the main questions asked of the Lord's Supper have been what? and how? Today, especially among evangelicals, the real question is why? Why celebrate the Lord's Supper at all? What good is it? What spiritual benefits does it bring?'[2]

A similar situation exists in churches with inherited practices from Scottish Highland customs which are not valued because believers are not aware of the purposes behind these procedures. Larsen's identification of unyielding custom and formalism as barriers to benefiting from the Lord's Supper points to the necessity of Christians appreciating the purpose of the Supper. Custom and formalism can differ greatly between churches, and not every custom is unhelpful.

The Presbyterian churches in Scotland have used the regulative principle to help distinguish aspects of worship that are essential from those that are not. This principle requires that biblical warrant must exist before any practice can be part of the public worship of God. In Scottish Highland circles, the principle is mentioned usually in connection to whether or not hymns as well as psalms can be used as items of praise and whether or not musical instruments can be used. (Although those arguing the case for exclusive psalmody can give the impression that only they believe in the regulative principle, it is the case that those arguing for an alternative practice can base their claim on biblical statements.)

It is clear, as discussed in Chapter 1, that there is biblical warrant for celebrating the Lord's Supper. But what actions would the regulative principle allow and to what persons should the Lord's Supper be given? The answer to the question concerns the contents of a liturgy.

The Lord's Supper is an occasion when the Lord Jesus feeds the souls of his people, thus making the meal a means of grace. Their eating literal bread and drinking actual wine symbolise that throughout the meal the Lord is providing them with spiritual food. It seems to me that not enough time is given for this to be appreciated at the meal as currently practised, which is to have the meal at the end of the service, after the sermon. The sermon may last an hour but the meal may last fifteen minutes. The order of service suggests that the Lord's Supper is a secondary aspect of the service, sometimes shorter in time than the pastoral prayer. This deficiency is not limited to Highland churches.[3]

At the Reformation, the Mass was central to the worship service. The Reformers, as they adjusted liturgical practices to bring them into line with biblical emphases, developed various liturgies that gave an important place to the preached Word as well as to the Lord's Supper, and that stressed the involvement of the laity as well as the clergy.[4]

Over the centuries since then, a liturgy has developed within Highland churches for the celebration of the Lord's Supper. An order of service usually has these details:

1. Opening praise
2. Prayer
3. Reading of Scripture
4. Praise
5. Sermon
6. Prayer
7. Praise, while all communicants come to the area of the church functioning as a table
8. Reading of 1 Corinthians 11:25ff as warrant for the service
9. Short prayer in which the bread and wine are consecrated

   to God's service and asking his blessing on them

10. Short address to the communicants
11. Communicants are given the bread, then the wine
12. Short address to the communicants
13. Praise
14. Benediction

Some details of the liturgy involve the pastor's public contribution (the prayers, the reading of the scriptures, the sermon and the table addresses), whereas others involve all the congregation of believers (singing, listening to the prayers, sermon and addresses, and sharing in the elements).

In a liturgy, is it necessary to follow the example of Christ and the apostles and include the various features found in the biblical records of the Lord's Supper? The Supper was inaugurated during a liturgical occasion, the Passover. Celebrations of the Passover followed set rituals, depending on the period in which it was held and on the Jewish religious group to which one adhered. The references to the Lord's Supper elsewhere in the New Testament do not indicate what type of liturgy was followed, which may indicate that freedom was given to local churches regarding when and how the Supper was held. Some accompaniments of the Supper such as the love feasts were not regarded as essential, for Paul advised the church in Corinth to cease having it; yet other churches still retained the practice (see Jude 12).

Liturgical practices of the early church have been recorded. Since the early Fathers were nearest in time to the apostolic period, it is likely that their comments on the practice of the Lord's Supper will give insight into how the early Christians implemented apostolic teaching. However, George Dollar, in surveying the contents of the writings of the Fathers on the Lord's Supper, gives a different assessment:

> In no area of early church life among Christians is there greater uncertainty than in the matter of the Lord's Supper. It was not called by its New Testament titles such as the "breaking of bread," "the

giving of thanks," and "the cup of blessing." The most common designation seemed to be the "Eucharist" (from the Greek word for praise or thanksgiving) with the basic connotation of praise to the Lord—and it would have remained a good name if it had not been corrupted by Romish ceremonial. Coleman has concluded that names for the Supper were "chosen out of regard to some peculiar views relating to the doctrine…(with) very few known to the Apostles and primitive Church." The fact is that no church father called it the Supper in a single instance and Pauline names for it ceased.

Much of the language of the Fathers of this era reflects Jewish ideas as seen in the common use of such terms as *altar, priest, ablutions, sacrifices,* and *offerings*. This is evident to such a high decree that the scholarly Neander wrote that we have "the whole system of the Jewish priesthood transferred to the Christian Church." An Anglican scholar has studied this aspect carefully and found that by the end of the second century the "importing of Jewish terms and ideas had increased fearlessly and freely." The American church historian McGiffert believed that this drift had gone so far that there was in embryonic form "the historic Catholic system complete in all its main features." If this is true, and every evidence points that way, then we may have the seeds for such a thing as the "Mass" beginning (Latin, *missa, sent*), arising from the custom of "dismissing" the congregation at the close of a regular service before the Supper was observed.

Other words used in connection with the Supper do not help to clarify the situation at all. One is *sacrifice*. Although originally it may have been used loosely to denote a rendition of praise to the Lord, by 200 it did include some sense of mystical offering beside praise and was a way to enter into spiritual communion with the Lord. Another word is *sacrament* which came from the Latin (*sacramentum*) which meant a "pledge or seal but not the means by which it is received." Another form of it may have been *res sacramenti*, referring to sacred things or the religious articles used in worship. In this connection, it might be helpful to note that second century writers failed to distinguish between the externals and the internals—so much so that by the time of Justin and Irenaeus the two are so confused that little separation is found. Neander had explored this strange mixture and held that there arose a "falsely spiritual external and too much was attached to outward forms." The same thing had happened in baptism which by now (160) had been given the place of a spiritual medium for one's fellowship with the Savior.[5]

What should be deduced from the historical facts that the early church practices gradually deviated from biblical understandings? I would suggest two responses. First, celebrations of the Lord's Supper should include biblical requirements, and second, care should be taken over other features which are introduced to help the occasion run smoothly (these other features will depend on local circumstances). The biblical practices can be identified from the accounts of the inauguration of the Supper in the Gospels, in the Book of Acts, and in 1 Corinthians. Specific details of these records were discussed in Chapter One, so what follows here is a brief comparison between the biblical practices and current practices in some modern churches.

In the Bible the Supper was part of a gathering of Christians from a local community (as in Corinth), to which any visiting Christians were welcome (as in Troas). This feature is true in the current practice, except the believers do not eat a meal together as was the case in biblical times.

The biblical records indicate that the gathering for the Lord's Supper was also an occasion of Christian teaching (as with Jesus in the Upper Room and with Paul in Troas). This is a feature of the current practice through the sermon and then the addresses at the table.

The institution of the Supper was concluded by the singing of a psalm, which would justify the items of praise in the current order of service, and could point to the service finishing with an item of sung worship rather than with a prayer.

Prayer also was included in the early celebrations, and Paul's detailed account in 1 Corinthians 11 stresses that Jesus gave thanks separately for the bread and for the wine, a feature that is not practised in my denomination, for only one prayer is made in connection with both the bread and the wine, although two separate prayers are common in other churches.

The role of the pastor in the current practice is also seen in what he does with the elements, particularly the bread, after he has given thanks for them. Should he break the loaf of bread or should a tray of small portions of bread be prepared beforehand? Traditionally, the action had been regarded as very important:

> The minister is also to take and break the bread. The *breaking* of the bread is an essential part of the ordinance, and, when it is wanting, the sacrament is not celebrated according to the original institution. It is, indeed, so essential, that the Lord's supper is sometimes designated from it alone, the whole being denominated from a part. The 'breaking of bread' is mentioned among the institutions of the gospel (Acts 2: 42); and in Acts 20:7, we are told that, 'upon the first day of the week, the disciples came together to break bread': in both of which passages the celebration of the Lord's supper is doubtless meant by the 'breaking of bread'. The rite is significant, and we are left in no doubt about the meaning of the action. Our Saviour himself explained it when he said, 'This is my body, which is *broken* for you;' intimating that the broken bread is a figure of his body as wounded, bruised, and crucified, to make atonement for our sins. As an unbroken Christ could not profit sinners, so unbroken bread cannot fully represent to faith the food of the soul. Wherefore, to divide the bread into small pieces called wafers, and put a wafer into the mouth of each of the communicants, as is done in the Church of Rome, is grossly to corrupt this ordinance, for it takes away the significant action of breaking the bread.[6]

Robert L. Dabney identified four arguments to support the practice of the pastor breaking the bread. 'The breaking of the bread is plainly one of the sacramental role acts, and should never be done beforehand, by others, nor omitted by the minister.... The proper significancy of the sacrament requires it; for the Christ we commemorate is the Christ lacerated and slain.' Dabney also notes three other reasons: we should do it because Christ did it and commanded us to imitate him; the apostles made it one of the sacramental acts (Paul mentions it in 1 Corinthians 10:16); and the fact that 'breaking of bread' is a name for the Supper indicates the necessity of the action.[7]

On the other hand, Donald Macleod mentions that while he

has followed the practice of 'pausing and quite deliberately breaking the bread', he does so not because he believes it to be a biblical requirement but because it is part of his church's historical tradition. Macleod's difficulty with breaking the bread being an essential practice is because in Jewish meals the breaking of bread was part of the act of thanksgiving, in that the head of the family broke the bread as he gave thanks.[8] Therefore if the breaking of the bread is to be part of the ministerial function, then the pastor should do it during the prayer of thanksgiving.

There are three other problems with Dabney's arguments. First, what did Jesus mean when he instructed his disciples to repeat the feast? Did he mean that the precise order be followed whenever the occasion arose? The celebrations of the Supper in Troas and Corinth were not linked to the Jewish Passover, so it is clear that the early church did not interpret Jesus' words as demanding an exact duplication of the original meal. What is clear is that Jesus commanded his followers to remember him in a meal of which the elements were bread and wine.

Second, it is not clear that Paul is referring to a ministerial act when he says in 1 Corinthians 10:16: 'Is not the cup of thanksgiving for which we give thanks a participation in the blood of Christ? And is not the bread that we break a participation in the body of Christ?' The 'we' in the context refers to all believers, because in the following verse Paul writes: 'Because there is one loaf, we, who are many, are one body, for we all partake of the one loaf.'[9] It is possible that a blessing was said by the congregation rather than by a presiding pastor.

Third, since Paul's comments in 1 Corinthians 10:16 indicate that it is the body of believers who break the loaf, then their actions illustrate the communion that they share with Christ and with one another. Macleod comments on the relevance of this to our liturgy:

> There is a very interesting liturgical point here. In many traditions each individual believer receives the bread or the wafer from a clergyman: a minister, a priest, or sometimes an elder. This requires

more thought than we sometimes give to it. We should seek a form of celebration which provided that each believer receives the bread from his companion and in turn passes it on to his companion, thus maintaining the circularity of giving and receiving. Otherwise we are encouraging priestcraft and superstition.[10]

What is of concern here is the perception of what is going on at the Supper. It may be best for the smooth progress of the service for the pastor to perform the initial breaking of the bread. But it is not the function of church leaders to hand the elements to other believers in a sacramental sense. Believers do not need an intermediary to help them have communion with Christ at the Lord's Supper, and the liturgy should not indicate that they do. Paul's comments also indicate that it is not an exclusive pastoral function to give thanks for the elements, although it may be best for the order of service if the pastor does so. But there is nothing unbiblical taking place if another person, be they elder or member, gives thanks for the elements.

The cup also has symbolic value. Today, in many churches individual cups are used. Two reasons have been given to me for this method. First, it helps avoid the passing on of disease and second it gives the opportunity of each believer drinking the wine simultaneously. It is clear that these reasons are not invalid. In response to the first, I am not aware of evidence that indicates disease is passed on through sharing a cup. The obvious example would be the HIV virus, and where there are believers with this illness special arrangements need to be made. In response to the second, it can be said that the symbol of the taking of the wine becomes an expression of one's relationship to the Saviour because what happens is individual acts performed simultaneously. The practice does not illustrate or symbolise the giving and receiving that a shared cup does, and has the same problem that exists when a pastor or elder hands a piece of bread to each believer. So while the use of individual cups in a liturgy shows gratitude to the Lord, it falls short of illustrating the relationship there is between believers.

An issue that is often discussed is whether or not grape juice should be used instead of wine. Letham says that the issue did not enter the Christian church until the appearance of the temperance movement in the nineteenth century.[11] Two reasons are often given for using grape juice rather than wine: one is that a converted alcoholic might not be able to take wine and the other reason is that it is inappropriate for any Christian to take wine because of its intoxicating nature. Regarding the first, if a converted alcoholic cannot take a sip of wine, then he or she can refrain if he or she is concerned that it will result in a desire for alcohol (or else the congregation can provide him or her with a substitute such as grape juice). The second reason confuses an alcoholic drink with drunkenness and ignores the reality that fermented wine is mentioned in the Bible as being used by believers. The obvious example is the situation in Corinth where believers abused the Supper by getting drunk, which indicates that they were using fermented wine. Yet Paul does not suggest as a remedy for their wrong behaviour that they should change from fermented wine to grape juice.

Having considered aspects of the current practice, I would now make some comments on other issues connected to the Lord's Supper. Perhaps the factor that should be considered alongside the issue of liturgy is the role of the Holy Spirit, for without his presence and activity all liturgy will descend into formalism and mere ritual. But firstly I want to consider the arranging of services that include the Lord's Supper.

Planning a service including the Lord's Supper
If the same liturgy is followed on each occasion, then in a sense little planning is needed apart from ensuring that each person involved knows his particular function. There are advantages to having the same procedure, particularly in that those in attendance know what to expect. Yet the New Testament does not indicate that a fixed order should be followed, rather it reveals the type of activity that should take place. When Jesus instituted the Supper in the Upper Room, not only did he link it to the

Passover, but he washed the disciples' feet (an acted parable indicating their need of daily cleansing from the contamination of sin), gave thanks separately for the bread and the cup, and taught the disciples about various topics. The other New Testament references suggest the Supper was connected to a meal, during which teaching was given. My tradition accepts the necessity of teaching as accompanying the Supper, but does not link the Supper to a meal nor does it include acted parables. What is somewhat unusual, given its adherence to the regulative principle, is the failure to give thanks separately for the bread and the cup, especially as Paul in 1 Corinthians 10 and 11 (breaking the bread and giving thanks for the cup) affirms it was the practice to imitate the method of Jesus.

While a fixed liturgy does inform the participants of what to expect, it also carries the danger of familiarity reducing a sense of expectation. The flexibility seen in the New Testament accounts points to liberty in arranging the Communion service as long as the essential features, such as Bible teaching and the elements of bread and wine, are included.

Exhortation too should be relevant to the occasion. One type of exhortation that is suitable for churches holding a Calvinistic interpretation of the Supper is the *sursam corda* (Latin for 'lift up your hearts), an ancient ritual from the early church[12] in which the congregation, prior to the Eucharist, was exhorted to lift up their hearts to heaven.

Calvin has a version of the *sursum corda* in his tract, *Form for Administering the Sacraments*, where after reading the words of institution from 1 Corinthians 11 and giving suitable advice of how to regard the Supper, he gives this exhortation: 'With this view, let us raise our hearts and minds on high, where Jesus Christ is, in the glory of his Father, and from whence we look for him at our redemption.' His exhortation also includes a warning not to focus on the elements as if they contained the physical body of Christ, which is a refutation of transubstantiation: 'And let us not amuse ourselves with these earthly and corruptible elements which we see with the eye, and touch with the hand, in order to seek him there, as if he were enclosed in the bread or wine.' The *sursum corda* gave expression to Calvin's emphasis that believers ascend to heaven in the Supper: 'Then only will our souls be disposed to be nourished and vivified with his substance, when they are thus raised above all terrestrial objects, and carried as high as heaven, to enter the kingdom of God where he dwells.' The *sursum corda* was followed by 'the Ministers distribut[ing] the bread and cup to the people, having warned them to come forward with reverence and in order. Meanwhile some Psalms are sung, or some passage of Scripture read, suitable to what is signified by the Sacrament.'[13]

Calvin again refers to the ancient custom of *sursum corda* in his Institutes (4.17.36), where he also indicates that he finds the concept useful both for reminding his readers of his belief that believers ascend to Christ in the Supper and for refuting alternative interpretations, particularly transubstantiation.[14]

The custom can also be a tool for pointing out the limitations of mere memorialism and consubstantiation, neither of which contain the idea that believers ascend to Christ in heaven at the Supper. The person leading the worship should remind believers that they are enjoying fellowship in a unique way with the risen Christ as they take part in the Lord's Supper.

Further, attention must be paid to non-Christians who may be present. Tim Keller mentions the likelihood of evangelistic activities resulting in such being present. When that happens, the celebration of the Lord's Supper becomes a possible means of conversion, not in the sense that they need to partake of the elements, but of applying to themselves what they are witnessing. The pastor should be ready to address such, addressing them something like this: 'If you are not in a position to take the bread and cup, then take Christ! It is the best possible time to do business with him, no matter your spiritual condition or position.'[15] Because such are liable to be present, suitable prayers for them to use are included in the order of service. An example of such prayer is this one:

Prayer for Those Searching for Truth. Lord Jesus, you claim to be the Way, the Truth, and the Life. Grant that I might be undaunted by the cost of following you as I consider the reasons for doing so. If what you claim is true, please guide me, teach me, and open me to the reality of who you are. Give me understanding of you that is coherent and convincing, and that leads to the life you promise.[16]

Today, it is common for a congregation to have a weekly bulletin. The pastor should use this as a means to help the congregation prepare for the Supper. It should include the following:

- an explanation, for the benefit of non-Christians who may happen to be present, of what the Supper involves;

- details of the emphases of the sermon so that believers can meditate on these themes;

- assurance that all Christians present are welcome to share in the Supper, with a short description of how the Supper ritual proceeds;

- something for the children to focus on while the Supper takes place;

- guidance on reflecting on the Supper later, perhaps by an appropriate quotation or hymn;

- Sample prayers as the one above for those searching for truth.

The question of liturgy should not only be concerned with outward practice or physical activities seen from the perspective of the human participants. Therefore, the involvement of the Holy Spirit in the Lord's Supper needs to be considered.

10

The Lord's Supper
and the Role of the Holy Spirit

We saw in a previous chapter that Calvin stressed the role of the Holy Spirit in the Lord's Supper in enabling believers on earth to have communion with Christ in heaven. In this chapter, I will not comment on Calvin's argument that through the Spirit believers ascend to heaven to feed on the risen humanity of Christ, apart from noting that there are New Testament passages which indicate that believers have communion with the ascended Christ. For example, Paul wrote to the Colossians (3:1-4):

> Since, then, you have been raised with Christ, set your hearts on things above, where Christ is seated at the right hand of God. Set your minds on things above, not on earthly things. For you died, and your life is now hidden with Christ in God. When Christ, who is your life, appears, then you also will appear with him in glory.

Further the author of the book of Hebrews states:

> But *you have come* to Mount Zion, to the heavenly Jerusalem, the city of the living God. You have come to thousands upon thousands of angels in joyful assembly, to the church of the firstborn, whose names are written in heaven. You have come to God, the judge of all men, to the spirits of righteous men made perfect, *to Jesus* the mediator of a new covenant, and to the sprinkled blood that speaks a better word than the blood of Abel (12:2-24, italics mine).

In his letter to the church in Laodicea, the ascended Christ promised communion to individual believers there if they would respond to him in repentance: 'Here I am! I stand at the door and knock. If anyone hears my voice and opens the door, I will come in and eat with him, and he with me' (Rev. 3:20).

These verses are not primarily connected to the Lord's table but to Christian worship and fellowship in general. They, and other passages, make clear that fellowship in a heavenly sense is the meaning of communion. This communion takes place by the activity of the Holy Spirit.

This relationship between the exalted Christ and the Holy Spirit was described by Jesus when he promised in the Upper Room discourse to send the Spirit as his replacement:

> When the Counselor comes, whom I will send to you from the Father, the Spirit of truth who goes out from the Father, he will testify about me. And you also must testify, for you have been with me from the beginning (John 15:26-27).

> But when he, the Spirit of truth, comes, he will guide you into all truth. He will not speak on his own; he will speak only what he hears, and he will tell you what is yet to come. He will bring glory to me by taking from what is mine and making it known to you. All that belongs to the Father is mine. That is why I said the Spirit will take from what is mine and make it known to you (John 16:13-15).

Regarding the relation between the activity of the ascended Christ and the role of the Holy Spirit, George Smeaton has commented:

> Christ's activity as Lord and Head of the Church seems at first sight to militate against the action of the Holy Ghost the Comforter, and conversely. That these important aspects of truth may not have the appearance of coming into collision, let me refer to their relation. The regulation of the Church's life—sometimes spoken of as if it were retained in Christ's own hand, sometimes described as if it were committed to the Holy Spirit—must be regarded as two announcements of the same great truth, without any difference, two sides of one and the same thing. The Lord Jesus, the Mediator, does all by the Holy Spirit in fostering, quickening, guiding the Church; and so intimately are these two things conjoined,—the Melchizedekian-priesthood on the one hand, and the dispensation of the Spirit on the other,—that they must constantly be seen

together (Acts ii.33). The exalted Christ continuously acts for the Church's good by His Spirit through the Word.

It is possible for Christ to be present in more than one way. Smeaton further comments on the nature of this presence of Christ:

> To put Christ's OMNIPRESENCE in its proper light, it is necessary to remark that it is one of the perfections of His immutable divine nature—a fact belonging to Him as a divine Person, and that cannot be more or less. It is not a matter of promise, but a fact, an inalienable fact. But His GRACIOUS PRESENCE, as the Incarnate One, is matter of promise, and may or may not be according to His relations with His people.[2]

Jesus promised to be wherever his people would meet in his name (Matt. 18:20), so indicating that they should expect his presence on such occasions. What does his presence involve for him, for the Holy Spirit, and for believers? Again, Smeaton describes various activities of each party:

> According to this economy, CHRIST IS PRESENT BY HIS SPIRIT, conducting the communications of God to man, and the worship of man to God, the channel of divine supplies to us, and the medium by which the returns of praise, prayer, service, and obedience are acceptably offered. The Holy Spirit acts in both respects as the Comforter or Deputy in Christ's name, filling His mystic body and presenting their spiritual sacrifices (I Pet. ii.5). This view of worship, to which the action of the High Priest and the aid of the Spirit are absolutely essential, is brought out in a memorable Psalm: 'I will declare Thy name to my brethren; in the midst of the Church will I praise Thee' (Ps. xxii. 22; Heb. ii.12). The Lord Jesus acts from God to us and from us to God; in both instances by the power of the Spirit.[3]

Given that the Holy Spirit is present in every activity of the Church's worship, is his role in the Lord's Supper the same as what he does in other meetings, such as those for prayer or for

Bible teaching, or is there something distinctive? The answer is that it is both similar and distinctive. This twofold contribution is explained by Sinclair Ferguson:

> What, then, is the role of the Spirit in the Supper? It can well be described in the words of John 16:14. The Spirit will take from what is Christ's and 'make it known' to his disciples. He does this fundamentally through apostolic revelation, so that nothing is revealed in the Supper that is not already made known in the Scriptures. But in the Supper there is (1) visual representation, and (2) simple and special focus on the broken flesh and outpoured blood of Christ. This takes us to the heart of the matter, and indeed to the centre of the Spirit's ministry: to illumine the person and work of Christ. No new revelation is given; no other Christ is made known. But as Robert Bruce (1554-1631) well said, while we do not get a different or a better Christ in the Supper from the Christ we get in the Word, we may well get the same Christ better as the Spirit ministers by the testimony of the physical emblems being joined to the Word.[4]

While admitting that the work of the Spirit in the Lord's Supper is incomprehensible, which of course is true of all the works of God, John Yates gives a helpful description of what the Spirit does for believers at the Lord's Supper, and in doing so gives a more detailed account of his role than does the description quoted above from Ferguson:

> It is the role of the Spirit to so concur with the sign, in terms of his operation in the believer, that the sign becomes associated with the thing signified, the death of Christ. The occasion of the presentation of the sign to us is one in which the Spirit is able to stir up a lively faith by which we understand ourselves to be in contemporaneous experience with the reconciling love of the cross, so that we are through faith drawn into its reconciling action. In fact, the believer is in contact with the power by which Jesus was able to offer himself up on his [the believer's] behalf, 'The eternal Spirit' (Heb. 9:14). The Spirit reproduces in the Christian the same character he produced in Christ, and this he does in a particular way within his normal

sanctifying ministration by stimulating a realization of the significance of the central events of salvation.

But Yates affirms that this experience of believers at the Lord's Supper is not merely a subjective one:

> It would be misleading to designate this view 'subjective', for the emphasis lies not upon the believer's power of recall, but upon the initiative of God the Spirit. The description 'personalist' is preferable since by denying any substantial change in the elements the entire emphasis is placed on the work of the personal Spirit in the human person. It may even be claimed that this is the ultimate in objectivity, for nothing can surpass the 'givenness' of the immutable God in his will to save. Likewise, the faith which makes contact with this grace which is the Spirit is itself his gift.[5]

The role of the Holy Spirit enables us to appreciate both the temporal and the personal aspects of the Supper: the temporal being how the Supper involves the past, the present and the future, and the personal involving thankfulness for salvation, awareness of the corporate nature of the Eucharist, and the proclamation that the Supper makes to the world.[6] At the Supper, believers experience in the present an encounter with Christ that has not only its focus on but takes its power from an event in the past.

We noted earlier that the 'remembering' in which communicants engage is not merely recollection. Kibble uses the insight of B. S. Childs regarding biblical acts of remembrance, that while they cannot be identified with a return to a former historical event, they should be interpreted as a real event which occurs 'as the moment of redemptive time from the past initiates a genuine encounter in the present'.[7] The Supper similarly is 'a God-given event in which Christ's redemptive action in the past itself initiates and enables an encounter in the present'.

This encounter between believers and the person and work of Christ is achieved by the Spirit. This experience of encountering an event in the past is not unique to the Lord's Supper. In the Christian life in general, it is by the Spirit that union of believers to Christ is accomplished, a union which involves being crucified with Christ and having fellowship with Christ while receiving life from Christ (Gal. 2:20). In a similar way to preaching, in which the Galatian Christians were said to have seen Jesus Christ as crucified yet were not physically present at Calvary (Gal. 3:1), so in the Lord's Supper the Holy Spirit can bring the effects of Christ's death into the present experience of believers.

But the Eucharist not only looks back, it also looks forward. The kingdom of God has begun already but it has not yet reached its consummation. The Supper expresses this tension of now and not yet. Kibble notes that the Eucharist is both 'a sacrament which we have here and now on this earth in the present time, and yet it is also a sign of the final heavenly banquet'.[8] The Spirit gives to his people longings for the coming kingdom and uses the Supper as a means of stimulating their anticipation of the future state of perfection.

The role of the Holy Spirit in the Lord's Supper is a crucial one. His activity ensures that a liturgical event becomes a dynamic encounter in the present with gracious consequences in the lives of believers as they wait for the return of Christ. The Holy Spirit is present to make the Supper a means of grace for believers.

11

The Lord's Supper and Children

It is sometimes argued that children should be involved in the Lord's Supper. In general, three arguments are used to support their participation: the practice of the early church,[1] the analogy of the Passover and the Lord's Supper, and child membership of the Christian church begun at baptism. The first argument can be used both for and against the practice, so in a sense it does not prove the legitimacy of the practice, only that some early church leaders allowed it. There is no clear evidence of the practice in the first two centuries, although it was the common practice of the Western church between the third and twelfth centuries, and remains the common practice of the Eastern church until the present day. Keidal is of the opinion that the practice ceased in the Western church due to the acceptance of the doctrine of transubstantiation, in that it was feared that children might spill the bread and wine.[2] The Reformers in the main did not return to this ancient practice when they repudiated the claims made for transubstantiation.

The other two arguments support the charge of *inconsistency* on the parts of Reformed and paedobaptist churches regarding the participation of children. Children took part in the Passover[3] and since there is a link between the Passover and the Lord's Supper it is reasonable to assume that the failure to mention that they should not take part means they continued to do so. In case a person should respond by suggesting that this is an argument from silence, it has to be noted that a similar argument is used to allow baptism to children on the analogy between circumcision and baptism. If baptism is the occasion of a child entering the Christian church, in a way parallel to the use of circumcision in the Israelite community, it would suggest that such children would have the right to other privileges of the Christian church in a manner similar to Israelite children having opportunity to participate in the worship and feasts of Old Testament Israel.[4]

These two pieces of evidence initially seem conclusive. But they have been objected to by various writers. Beckwith argues that it is at least an open question, for the reason that it is important for baptised children to complete their baptism and come to faith and repentance before they participate in the Lord's Supper.[5] But he does not say why this should be the case, and the parallel situation in Israel would require that children should not have participated in the Passover until they had completed their circumcision.

Another argument used to refute the automatic participation of children in the Lord's Supper is taken from the similarity between the Passover and the Supper. It was not possible for infants, because of their lack of physical development, to eat the lamb and other items of the Passover meal. Therefore, while every Israelite child had to be circumcised, every child was not expected to eat the Passover.

A more effective objection than the ones mentioned above was given by Calvin[6] and is still appreciated today, which is that a person partaking in the Lord's Supper must understand what he or she is doing, in line with Paul's requirement in 1 Corinthians 11 that intending participants engage in self-examination. Connected to this requirement is the reality that in baptism the recipient is passive whereas in the Lord's Supper the recipient is active, not only in the sense of physically handling the elements but also in the sense of 'remembering' the Lord's death and understanding the meaning of the symbols of the bread and the cup, which young children are not usually able to do. Calvin's objection is a valid one and has to be taken into account.

As far as self-examination is concerned, it should relate to the sins of which the person is aware. A child's sins will be different from those of adults and this has to be borne in mind when assessing the spiritual understanding of children. But self-examination does not require adult abilities.

In this situation, the participation of particular children should be decided on an individual basis. Given that the parents are liable to know best the spiritual condition of their child, it is wise policy for the church rulers to consult them concerning whether or not their children not only show evidence of conversion but also appreciate what is involved in partaking of the Supper. At the same time, church rulers have to be aware of parents assuming too much about their children's evidence of conversion or their understanding of the Lord's Supper. But there has to be care taken that too much is not expected of children.

This modern concern for the involvement of children at the Lord's Table may seem a long way from the practice of the Lord's Supper in the Scottish Highlands. But it does raise an issue with which the Highland church has struggled, as we noted in our previous discussion with regard to baptism. One solution was to create a two-level system of membership, with the requirements for baptism being lower than that for the Lord's Table. But even churches that do not make this distinction with regard to baptism do make it with regard to the Lord's Supper. If we accept that the visible church is made up of believers and their children, can we insist that children should never be at the Lord's Table?

It is the case that an infant before baptism is incapable of expressing faith. But that is not the case with young children. It is obvious that a child can have faith in Christ at a young age and I would suggest that if a child can give a coherent expression of faith, then he or she should be allowed to partake of the Supper. The best position to adopt is neither the view that accepts all children have an automatic right or the view that young children have to wait until they are a certain age, but to have a flexible position in which each child is assessed according to his or her level of discernment.

Having believing children at the Lord's Table means that special attention must be given to them during a communion service. It is the pastor's responsibility to feed them with spiritual food along with the provision he sets before adult believers. This does not mean that he is to trivialise events connected to the Supper by giving a childish talk. Rather he is to focus the hearts and minds of all, both young and adults, on what Christ can give them at the Table.

12

Pastoral Preparation for the Lord's Supper

As with all his activities in a congregation, the pastor should prepare himself for leading God's people in this aspect of worship. An indifferent attitude to his functions opens the preacher to divine chastisement. It is a tragedy for a church to have such a pastor. But if it has a pastor who cares about his own spiritual state as well as the spiritual state of his flock, then that church is blessed. Each pastor should imitate the example of James Durham, of whom it was said that when he preached at communions he

> used at such occasions to endeavour, through grace, to rouse and work himself up to such a divineness of frame as very much suited the spiritual state and majesty of that ordinance, greatly fearing lest he, or any of the people to whom he dispensed the same, should fall under the grievous guilt of the body and blood of the Lord. Then, in a manner, his face shone, as being in the mount of communion and fellowship with God; and at some of those solemn and sweet occasions he spoke some way as a man who had been in heaven, commending Jesus Christ, making a glorious display of the banner of free grace, holding forth the riches of it very clearly and convincingly.[1]

The pastor needs not only to preach suitable sermons but he needs to preach them *suitably*. His emotions as well as his intellect should be in line with the theme of which he is speaking. For example, when speaking about self-examination, he should do so seriously, affirming from personal experience the spiritual benefits that he has known. This does not mean that he has to preach as if he is giving a personal testimony; rather he preaches as one who knows the value of the practice.

The means of pastoral preparation for the Lord's Supper are the same as for other pastoral activities, that is, prayer and meditation on the Scriptures. As far as meditation is concerned, it is not difficult to find appropriate passages for particular themes. For example, Psalm 51 is helpful for making confession of sin, and Isaiah 53 gives insights into the sacrificial death of Christ.

Personal prayer is more difficult to sustain. A pastor knows that if his sermons are well structured and delivered with enthusiasm his lack of prayer may not be noticed by his hearers. The observation of E. M. Bounds is true:

> A ministry may be a very thoughtful ministry without prayer; the preacher may secure fame and popularity without prayer; the whole machinery of the preacher's life and work may be run without the oil of prayer or with scarcely enough to grease one cog; but no ministry can be a spiritual one, securing holiness in the preacher and in his people, without prayer being an evident and controlling force.[2]

A pastor/preacher who does not pray will become the person described by John Piper:

> The aroma of God will not linger on a person who does not linger in the presence of God. Richard Cecil said that 'the leading defect in Christian ministers is the want of devotional habit'. We are called to the ministry of the word *and prayer*, because without prayer the God of our studies will be the unfrightening and uninspiring God of insipid academic gamesmanship.[3]

It is not difficult to prove from Scripture that prayer is a priority for pastors. First, there is the example of the Lord Jesus. Derek Prime summarises how Jesus demonstrated the priority of prayer in pastoral work:

> He prayed when He needed to make decisions, such as the choice of the twelve (Luke 6:12-16). He prayed when He and those around Him were subject to temptation (John 6:15; Matthew 14:23; John 17). He prayed before asking the disciples a key question about their understanding of His identity (Luke 9:18-22). He prayed when people had false views of Him (John 6:15). He prayed for those closest to Him in the light of the dangers He knew them to be in (Luke 22:32).[4]

Second, there is the example of the apostles. In Acts 6:4, they stressed the prior importance, in their callings, of prayer and the ministry of the Word over other church responsibilities. Not only were their personal prayers important, but so were the prayers of other Christians on their behalf. The apostle Paul requested the believers in Colosse to 'pray for us, too, that God may open a door for our message, so that we may proclaim the mystery of Christ, for which I am in chains. Pray that I may proclaim it clearly, as I should' (Col. 4:3-4).

Prayer is essential for pastors because they are engaged in a spiritual battle. They have enemies within, because there is a constant struggle between the flesh and the Spirit. There are enemies without, from the world and from Satan. Prime comments regarding temptations to which pastors are prone: 'As spiritual leaders, some of the temptations we experience will be unique to our tasks, and it is through prayer alone that we find insight to recognise them and power to avoid them. An unrelenting foe demands unrelenting spiritual watchfulness through prayer.' He then adds the solemn reality: 'Satan delights to make casualties of those who have encouraged others to fight the good fight of faith.'[5]

Prayer in connection to a communion season is concerned with a number of different areas.

First, there must be prayer over the sermon(s). Request must be made to God not only for right understanding of the biblical passage and for relevant ways to communicate the message, but also for appropriate feelings. John Piper mentions Cotton Mather's rule, which was 'to stop at the end of every paragraph as he wrote his sermon to pray and examine himself and try to fix on his heart some holy impression of his subject'.[6]

The preacher should also pray for the believers as they approach the occasion of the Lord's Supper. If he is a visiting preacher, then his prayers will be general in nature. But it is different if the preacher is also the pastor of the congregation. In order for his prayers to be meaningful the pastor must know the spiritual condition of his people, and the best way to know this is by pastoral visitation. As he prays for them individually, he will be aware of the particular difficulties or needs of each church member. Some will lack assurance, others will be recovering from backsliding of heart if not of outward behaviour, others will be concerned about health or family problems. In the congregation there will be mature believers and new converts, each of whom is looking for spiritual provision through the preacher at the communion. The pastor needs to pray that his sermons will meet their needy souls.

His prayer for his people should not only focus on the Lord's Supper as it approaches, but should also include ongoing prayer after the communion season has ended. On occasions the Holy Spirit applies the benefit of the Word and the Sacrament immediately, but at other times he works by means of a longer process, and the sensitive pastor should be aware of the continuing need to pray for his flock.

Of course, the pastor should not only engage in private prayer. It is helpful to enlist the prayers of other leaders in the church and to meet to pray together. But this communal form of prayer, because of other commitments such as secular employment and family demands, cannot be held often, and even when it takes place, it is usually for an hour or so. It is probably easier to pray when this type of gathering occurs. But the pastor should not assume that his responsibility to his flock is met by such a gathering. It is only an additional benefit to his pastoral role.

The pastor is also to prepare for praying in public during the services. His public prayers should be a continuation of his private devotions and reflect his role as both pastor and worshipper. The congregation expect him to express their thoughts, and it is important that he is in a suitable spiritual condition. His public prayers should express corporate thanksgiving, confession of sin, desire for instruction, help of the Spirit in enlivening the emotions, and dedication to Christ's service.

The pastor and understanding of his role at the Lord's Table

In most churches, the pastor is the person who publicly leads the various parts of the communion service. It is the case that in some churches he does this because he is regarded as the person appointed by God to do this as an aspect of the pastoral office, and so he is described as 'minister of the Word and Sacraments'. In other churches, he has this role because it is the best method of producing a recognisable order in the service.

The prominence given to the pastor gives opportunity for misunderstanding his role. 'Preachers, because of the nature and function of their office, are exposed to spiritual pride: ministerial pride, intellectual pride, and the pride of acclaim for their eloquence.'[7] Such an attitude is obviously sinful, for humility should mark all servants of Christ.

As the pastor approaches the occasion of the Lord's Supper, an occasion profoundly connected to the humiliation of the Saviour, he should take steps to ensure he conducts his role in as humble a manner as possible.

Paul informs the church in Corinth how they should regard leaders. In that church, sadly most of the believers were identifying themselves with particular leaders. Paul's response to this focus on men was to remind the Christians that these leaders were only servants (1 Cor. 3:5). In 1 Corinthians 4:1 he writes: 'This is how one should regard us, as servants of Christ and stewards of the mysteries of God' (RSV). It is evident that he also perceived himself as fulfilling these roles. The Lord's Supper is an occasion for the pastor to function as a servant of Christ and a steward of the mysteries of God.

The word translated 'servant' in 4:1 is *huperetes*. Some have argued that the term was used of the slave 'who rowed in the lower tier of a war galley',[8] but D. A. Carson claims that there is no evidence for such a meaning in classical Greek,[9] and states that the meaning of the term is similar to *diakonos*, which is the term Paul uses previously in the context. Stott suggests that what Paul has in mind in the context is the idea of power coming from God through those he chooses to be his agents.[10] That a preacher needs divine power should be obvious and a pastor in approaching the celebration of the Lord's Supper should be aware of his need. For Stott, there are three means of divinely-given power: the Word of God, the message of the cross of Christ, and the Holy Spirit.

It is evident that these three means are linked to the occasion of the Lord's Supper. It is in the Word of God that the preacher finds divine wisdom (the heavenly mysteries of which the preacher is also a steward), it is the Word of God that functions as a hammer to break rocks in pieces (Jer. 23:29) and a sword that penetrates to the inner lives of his hearers (Heb. 4:12). The message of the cross of Christ is an essential feature of a communion service.

In a previous chapter, I mentioned aspects of the role of the Holy Spirit at the Lord's Supper. An aspect not mentioned there is the power of the Spirit to help the preacher proclaim God's Word and the message of the cross. Stott identifies two conditions that need to be found in a preacher before he can experience the power of the Spirit, before he can be a channel for living water to flow into the lives of others (John 7:38-39): holiness and humility.[11]

Stott defines these 'mysteries' as 'the self-revelation which God has entrusted to men and which is now preserved in the Scriptures'.[12] In New Testament times, a steward managed the household affairs of a wealthy person, including his property, his accounts and his slaves.[13] The image of a steward indicates that the pastor is responsible to provide appropriate teaching from the Bible that will fit with the biblical purposes of the Lord's Supper. Just as stewards were appointed by superiors to oversee their assets, so pastors have authority from God to pass on to his people what is appropriate for them. This authority is not designed to make a pastor autocratic, rather it should give confidence that what he says is God's truth.

The combined effect of his limitations and the awesomeness of his role in ministering to the people of God as God's agent should make a pastor realise his weakness and cause him to develop an awareness of his dependence on God for all activities connected to God's household, including the Lord's Supper.

The pastor and his preaching

Having discussed aspects of the pastor's personal preparation, I will now detail some features of his preaching that would help ensure the Lord's Supper is a means of grace to the congregation.

Firstly, I would suggest he is careful concerning the terms he uses to describe the meal. In denominational practice several terms are used to describe the meal, e.g. Lord's Supper, ordinance, communion. Some of these titles are biblical (e.g. Lord's Supper, breaking of bread), others are not derived from the Bible (e.g. sacrament). The usual terms used for the meal in Highland Presbyterianism are communion and the Lord's Table, although the term 'communion' is often applied to the series of services that accompany the meal.

Certain descriptions of the meal would not be used because of their religious associations. Donald Macleod suggests we should avoid the use of the term 'sacrament' because it 'has very limited value in helping us understand the Lord's Supper'.[14] The term 'sacrament' is not found in the Scriptures, but is a word of Latin origin, used by the early Christians to designate the confirming ordinances of religion. It was at first applied, in a civil sense, to whatever was consecrated or set apart for a sacred purpose. Money deposited as a pledge by contending parties was so termed, because, in the case of forfeiture, it was handed over to sacred uses. An oath made in the name of some deity was styled a sacrament; and especially the oath of a Roman soldier to his general, in which he bound himself to obey his commands, to follow him in victory or defeat, and never to desert his standard.

It is not till we come to Tertullian that we find *sacramentum* employed by any Christian writer to denote either baptism or the Supper. Tertullian's use of the term was evidently suggested, not by its classical meanings, whether legal or military, but by the fact that in the old Latin versions *sacramentum* had been used as the equivalent of *mustērion*, a word which frequently meets us in the Greek New Testament, though never applied to Baptism or to the Lord's Supper. And if it be asked how it was that the word came to be applied to these practices of the church, the answer is that this was suggested in part by their very nature as symbolic rites with underlying meanings, but also by the fact that in the age of Tertullian the practices had come to be regarded by Christians themselves as having a certain analogy to the mysteries of the

Graeco-Roman world, and had even, in the development of the practice, incorporated within themselves certain of the ritual observances that belonged to the pagan mystery-rites.[15] This connection opened the door for approaching the meal as an event shrouded in mystery, which only the initiated could understand.

A more common understanding is that *sacramentum* was the term that described the oath taken by a Roman soldier. It may be the case that the meal is an occasion for believers to affirm their commitment to Christ. Indeed, a communion season is usually the first occasion for a believer to indicate he or she has become a Christian. The problem with the meaning of commitment or taking an oath is that it does not indicate the uniqueness of the Lord's Supper. Every occasion of Christian activity is an opportunity for re-dedication to Christ. But the meal is not the same as other Christian activities.

I realise that most, if not all, believers will normally use the term 'sacrament' almost without any meaning attached to it. In effect, the term has become meaningless and says nothing about the meal. When we use it we are not communicating our understanding of the meal or our expectations from the meal. It is better to use terminology that does convey meaning.

To do this, I would suggest it is best to use biblical terminology. The terms used in the New Testament are 'breaking of bread' and 'Lord's Supper', with other terms such as communion and eucharist being derived from it. Of course, it is possible to use these terms with extra-biblical input derived from denominational practice. For example, it is common for Anglicans to use Eucharist, and one effect of their use may be that others will imagine that in order for the meal to be a Eucharist it has to include all the Anglican rites. Nevertheless, since the meal should be accompanied by the preaching of the Word, it is obvious that those called to teach should inform the congregation of the meanings of biblical terms.

Eucharist indicates that the meal is linked with thanksgiving. Jesus gave thanks when instituting the meal and Paul reminds the Corinthians that Jesus did this (1 Cor. 11:24). Jesus' original thanksgiving was connected to the Passover that thanked God for the Exodus of the Israelites from bondage in Egypt, but by changing the focus to his own Exodus, Jesus was indicating that from then on thanksgiving should be made to God for the sacrifice of Christ.

The discourse that is preached before the Lord's Supper takes place is often called the 'action' sermon, which is the name given to it in the Westminster Directory of Public Worship. One suggestion concerning this terminology is that it is taken from the Latin phrase *actio gratiarum* (the giving of thanks), and has therefore a similar meaning to eucharist. I suspect this meaning of the term is not realised by most of the participants and also by the ministers, since the sermon does not often contain the theme of thanksgiving. The meal is an occasion of corporate thankfulness.

Communion indicates that there is an active interaction between Christ and his people at the meal. This interaction is achieved through the work of the Holy Spirit who enables Christ and his benefits to be applied to his people. While there is a horizontal aspect to the communion in that believers share the elements with one another, even their sharing points to the fact that the prior aspect to the communion is vertical. The believers have communion together as they share Christ and his benefits.

In addition to explaining that the meal is a eucharist, a communion and a supper, the minister should also inform the participants of the blessings to be received from Christ. The meal not only contains symbols (or signs) of Christ's sacrifice but is also a seal or confirmation of the reality indicated in the symbols. The reality may be summarised by referring to the blessings promised in the new covenant, which covenant was referred to by Christ when he took the cup and gave it to his disciples. The meal is confirmation that the participants will experience a new heart, knowledge of God, and forgiveness by God of their sins. The minister should encourage believers who doubt their interest in Christ to come to the meal in order to obtain assurance through the ministry of the Spirit sealing to them what is indicated by the symbols.

The minister should also warn his congregation *concerning partaking unworthily*. In the Highland situation, there are two reasons for this: (1) wrong understanding of the meaning of 'unworthily' prevents true believers from becoming members of the church and partaking of the Supper – they understand it as meaning 'unworthy'; (2) the expectancy that all professing members will partake makes it difficult for some to stay away, such as believers guilty of secret sin or backsliding which should be corrected before coming to the Lord's Table.

Paul's warning about partaking unworthily was connected to abuses at the Supper. He does not use the adjective 'unworthy', which would describe a person's character; 'unworthily' is an adverb, and is concerned with their actions. The sinful behaviour of some Corinthian believers involved not discerning the Lord's body, an expression Paul uses to describe the congregation of believers as well as the physical body of Jesus. For this behaviour they were chastised, with chastisement involving physical illness and death (1 Cor. 11:29-32).

It is unlikely that similar abuses as happened in Corinth would happen in a Highland Presbyterian church because the liturgy of the Lord's Supper would prevent such outward abuse. But it is impossible to prevent internal unworthy behaviour by a liturgy. It is possible for believers at the meal to be in sharp disagreement with one another, with the disagreement amounting to hostility. Further, it is possible for one or more of the believers to be practising a sinful lifestyle. It is possible also for one or more of the believers to regard the Lord's Supper in an easy-going way and not treat it in a solemn manner.

I would suggest that the minister needs to preach on the unity of the congregation in Christ, on how that unity is expressed at the Lord's Supper, and what may be the possible barriers to that unity. Practised sin of any kind, if it is not confessed to God and, when appropriate, to humans, is always a barrier to unity. Toleration of sin indicates that those who tolerate it have different priorities from the others in the congregation. By allowing sin to be there they are guilty of division. The minister should therefore remind all the church of the need of each member to regularly engage in self-examination to see if he or she is allowing sin that will affect the unity of the local congregation.

The occasion of the Lord's Supper allows the preacher to highlight doctrines that are illustrated by it. For example, the Lord's Supper is an opportunity to remind believers that God is a giving God, who gave his Son for them. It is also an evangelistic occasion, if there are people present who don't participate. There are two doctrines in particular that the Lord's Supper illustrates: firstly, union with Christ and, secondly, adoption into the family of God. Union with Christ is illustrated by the participants feeding on the symbols of his flesh and blood. Adoption is illustrated by the participants being members of the family of God sharing together in the privileges of family membership.

These themes contain wide and rich features that can be addressed in a devotional manner at the Lord's Supper. I stress *devotional* because the Lord's Supper is primarily a meeting of lovers, considered either as Christ and his church (where the Scripture analogy is of a marriage relationship), or as the Father and his people (where the emphasis is on the family relationship). The Lord's Supper is not an occasion for an analytical and perhaps detached presentation of doctrine. Because the Lord's Supper should be a regular feature of church life, the pastor must arrange his preaching programme to cater appropriately for this congregational meeting.

13

Personal Preparation for the Lord's Supper

The connection to the Passover suggests an important attitude for believers to have at the Lord's Supper. The way Israelites remembered the Exodus was not by merely recalling an important event, like the way persons born since 1945 may remember the dead of the two World Wars. Rather, the Israelites were to remember the Exodus *as if they themselves had participated in it*. This is not as difficult as it may sound: it was the events of the Exodus which gave identity and meaning to the Israelites, therefore each Passover was an opportunity for Israelites to remind themselves of who they were and how they came to be who they were. Similarly, Christians get their identity from what happened at Christ's Exodus. It is a common New Testament emphasis that believers died with Christ (e.g. Rom. 6:8; Gal. 2:20; Col. 2:20). Each Lord's Supper is an opportunity for Christians to remind themselves and restate to others who they are.

John Brown, in commenting on Christ's command to remember him, asks two questions: '*what* about Christ are we to remember? and *how* are we to remember him?'[1] Regarding the first question, Brown lists several aspects of Christ's person and work on which a believer should reflect. We are to remember who he is as the eternal Son of God, what he became at his incarnation, what he did in his life, what he said, what he suffered from both human and demonic enemies, how he died, and the important consequences of his death. Further we are to remember what Jesus is doing for believers now and what he will yet do for them. Although he is exalted to the highest position, 'the differences in his circumstances has caused no alteration in his affections; that he loves his people with an unabated and unchangeable attachment; that as he bled for them on earth, so he intercedes for them in heaven; that he is preparing a place for them, and that "he will come again and take them to himself, that where he is, there they may be also".'

Brown also gives helpful comments on how the Saviour is to be remembered. First, he must be remembered with faith, for without faith the Lord's Supper is a mere ceremony. Without faith, 'we cannot understand the truth emblematically represented in it, nor participate in the blessings shadowed forth by the instituted symbols.' Second, Jesus must be remembered lovingly, and in this regard believers need to be aware of their tendencies to lose warm affections for Christ. Third, the Saviour must be remembered with reverence; we cannot forget that he is not only our Saviour, he is also our God. The Lord's Supper is an act of worship. Fourth, he must be remembered with penitence, with an awareness of the sins for which he paid the penalty in his death. Fifth, Jesus is to be remembered joyfully, because the 'death of Jesus ought never to be viewed as disconnected with its consequences – his own glory, and the happiness of his followers. In celebrating the Lord's Supper, we commemorate the victory of the Saviour over the foes of man.'[2]

The Lord's Supper is also an occasion for humbling ourselves. As we recall that Jesus humbled himself to go to the cross, we are reminded that pride and self-importance are inappropriate at the meal. The Gospels record that such a spirit was present among the disciples when Jesus instituted the Supper, in that they were concerned which of them should be regarded as the greatest. The spirit of self-importance is advocated strongly in today's society and the Supper is a place that reminds believers of the sin of this outlook.

The Supper is also a place for denying our self-sufficiency. By eating the bread and drinking the cup, we are evidencing that we are dependant on Christ for spiritual nourishment. Self-sufficiency is another feature of society, and Christians are affected by it. Our society may recognize that some people need help, but often it suggests self-help remedies. Christians, when they come to the meal, confess that their help is Christ.

The Lord's Supper is also a place where the sovereignty of Christ is experienced. This sovereignty can be administered in grace or in judgment (the latter was seen in the temporal judgments that came on the sinning Christians in Corinth). The Supper is an opportunity for believers to again confess their submission to their King of grace and their desire to serve him together as his witnesses.

Self-examination is not to be limited to these two options of what and how, but is also connected to the failure to discern the Lord's body. Question 171 of the Larger Catechism, compiled by the Westminster Assembly of Divines, gives suitable comment on this practice:

> They that are to receive the sacrament of the Lord's Supper are, before they come, to prepare themselves thereunto, by examining themselves of their being in Christ, of their sins and wants; of the truth and measure of their knowledge, faith, repentance, love to God and the brethren, charity to all men, forgiving those that have done them wrong; of their desires after Christ, and of their new obedience; and by renewing the exercise of these graces, by serious meditation, and fervent prayer.

Preparation for participation in the Lord's Supper was of paramount importance for the Puritans and in their writings helpful advice is found regarding self-examination. Richard Vines stated the common Puritan view when he said that even for the godly 'it's either too much blindness or boldnesse to rush upon this Ordinance without preparation'.[3]

The way to come to this understanding was by personal application of pulpit instruction on the matter. In a previous chapter I have already discussed the preacher's methods of instruction. Here I will comment on the participant's response, bearing in mind that the preacher is also a participant who should implement the biblical instruction he gives to his congregation.

The Puritan preacher Henry Smith summarised the aspects necessary to self-examination in this way:

1. First, whether thou hast faith, not only to believe that Christ died, but that he died for thee; for as the Scripture calleth him *Redeemer*, Isa. lix. 20, so Job called him *his* Redeemer, Job xix. 25.

2. The second article is, whether thou be in charity; not whether thou love them which love thee, but whether thou love them that hate thee; for Christ commandeth us to love our enemies, Mat. v. 44.

3. The third article is, whether thou repent, not for thy open and gross sins, but for thy secret and petty sins, because Christ saith, Mat. xii. 36, that 'we must give account of every idle word.'

4. The fourth article is, whether thou resolve not to sin again for any cause, but to amend thy evil life, not when age cometh, or for a spurt, but to begin now, and last till death; for Christ is Alpha and Omega, both the beginning and the end, Rev. xxii. 13; as well in our living as in our being, which hath made no promise to them which begin, but to them which persevere, Rev. ii. 11.

5. The last article is, whether thou canst find in thy heart to die for Christ, as Christ died for thee. We are bid not only to follow him, but to bear his cross; and therefore we are called servants, to shew how we should obey, Luke xii. 38; and we are called soldiers, to shew how we should suffer, 2 Tim. ii. 3.[4]

The necessity of self-examination also indicates that sharing in the Lord's Supper by itself does not immunise the participants from sinful attitudes and actions. At the same time, the consequences of self-examination affirm the freeness of God's grace, for the believer is to take part in the Supper after self-examination.

One method of helping self-examination is the keeping of a regular journal detailing one's spiritual activities, intentions, failures, and helps. Many stalwarts of the faith – such as George Whitefield, Andrew Bonar, Murray McCheyne, George Muller and Jim Elliot

– kept diaries or journals. Recording details about ourselves should result in self-accountability.

Self-examination can also be helped by having a trusted friend give his or her opinion on our progress. This is similar to having a mentor, although usually a mentor is a more experienced person. The role I am suggesting is more that of a close friend who is prepared to speak honestly about how things are with us in their perception.

There are two other helps that can be used in preparation for partaking in the Lord's Supper. One is to develop a focussed prayer life that concentrates on issues connected to the Lord's Supper. Such prayer would include matters like obedience from the heart, love to fellow-Christians, increasing discernment of who Jesus is and what he has done, is doing and will yet do. If the Lord's Supper takes place weekly, it could be appropriate to set aside time each day to pray about the approaching ordinance. If the Supper is less frequent, then it may not be necessary to have daily prayer concerning it, but there should be regular prayer as part of the preparation of meeting the risen Christ in the Supper.

The other help that I would suggest is the regular reading of appropriate devotional books connected to the person and work of Christ. A list of such books should always be used, with titles that have been assimilated being replaced by others. The value of reading devotional literature is that it not only informs, but it also presents its content in a manner that usually affects the emotions as well as the intellect.

William Cunningham wrote concerning partaking in the Supper, that 'the essential thing is that the state of mind and heart of the recipient should correspond with the outward act which, in participating in the sacrament, he performed'.[5] The question for participants should be whether or not they can partake of the Supper in the ways outlined above. Do they want to remember Christ? Can they take part in a thanksgiving for Christ? Do they want to proclaim Christ? Do they want to feed on Christ and so have communion with him?

Conclusion

In this study I have considered the Lord's Supper from the viewpoints of biblical interpretation, historical understanding and current concerns. In this chapter, I will provide, under several headings, conclusions to the evidence that has been presented.

1. Strengths and weaknesses of the Highland practice

One strength of the practice is the important place given to the preaching of the Word. This is seen in the expositions that are central to each of the preparatory services as well as the sermon and devotional addresses given during the communion service.

A second strength is the sense of reverence that marks the occasion. Every believer present is aware of the solemnity of the Supper, and the sense of reverence has been increased by the additional services that precede the meal. While it is possible for this reverential outlook to be only the expression of a morbid character, in the main it is the result of a healthy fear of God. Inappropriate behaviour at the Lord's Supper was a reason for divine judgment in Corinth (1 Cor. 11:30), and it is important to remember that God does not change but will still judge such behaviour. The presence of reverence is an indication of a desire to honour God.

A third strength is the sense of gratitude to Christ expressed by many of the participants. It is common to see such partaking of the elements tearfully. This sense of gratitude is also the consequence of the additional services. The believers have been led, through these discourses, to search their own hearts, to confess their sins, and to marvel at the death of Christ. The Supper is an opportunity for emotions to be expressed, and this too is a healthy response.

Other strengths can be stated briefly. Highland communion seasons stimulated a spirit of Christian union between neighbouring parishes or congregations. They were also marked by the desire of local believers to provide hospitality to visiting Christians. The helpful involvement of lay people in producing a vibrant spiritual corporate experience was seen in the question meeting and in times of fellowship in homes. Occasions of the Lord's Supper were opportunities for dedication by believers to serve Christ as well as an opportunity for evangelising local communities.

Yet there are weaknesses in the practice. Firstly, as noted previously with regard to the communion seasons of the past, it is very difficult to argue that the New Testament indicates the Supper should only take place quarterly or twice a year. While the New Testament does not command how often the meal should occur, Acts 20:7 suggests the common practice in New Testament times was weekly. Sometimes the comment is made that frequent occasions would result in over-familiarity, yet such an attitude is not a comment on the Supper but of the spirituality of the believers. The Lord's Supper should be held more frequently than it is in Highland Presbyterian churches.

It would be impractical for the period of preparatory days to be held every week. This indicates another weakness of the practice, in that the use of a period of days to have a communion season is a practice inherited from the past when it was easier for people to congregate on these days. Today, it is not possible, because of work or family or other legitimate commitments, for believers to set aside four or five days four times a year, far less more frequently. This difficulty will increase as modern life makes more demands on people's time. Inevitably, the church will have to change its practice. This will not be a negative consequence but an opportunity to make the events surrounding the Supper more accessible for all in the congregation.

Another weakness of the current practice is that lay people are denied a realistic contribution to the occasion. Nothing approaching the degree of involvement once associated with the fellowship meeting is now included. Lay people are primarily passive rather than active in the services.

An additional weakness of the practice is the formality that often seems to attend the services. It is possible that the formality is a consequence of the emphasis on solemnity, as it is common for some to imagine that solemnity requires the absence of interaction between believers and the necessity of not appearing joyful. In effect, the way the Supper is celebrated, although by a community, results in the Supper being an individualistic event, in which each person tends to focus on his or her relationship to Christ rather than also appreciating the family relationship of brothers and sisters that should mark the occasion.

2. The Lord's Supper and the contemporary situation

With regard to changes in contemporary life in Scotland, and the church's witness to the modern situation, several comments can be made.

Firstly, the Lord's Supper is a *separating ordinance in an inter-faith culture*. In an earlier chapter, I commented on Paul's teaching in 1 Corinthians 10, where the apostle taught that there is a real fellowship between Christ and his people at the Supper. Paul warned the Corinthians that something similar took place between demons and idol worshippers in pagan temples and therefore Christians were not to take part in pagan festivals.

Paul's instruction to the Corinthians is relevant today. His response is a strong condemnation of Christians who involve themselves in inter-faith activities. It will probably be obvious to most evangelicals that they cannot agree to have any merger with non-Christian religious groups when it comes to the exclusivity of Christ for salvation. But inter-faith activities do not limit themselves to the question of salvation, for it is often the case with ethical issues, such as homosexuality and abortion, that different religions can have similar outlooks. For example, a question that can arise with regard to abortion is whether it is right for Christians to work alongside Muslims who pray to Allah for help. As long as the Muslims do not mention Allah, the Christian can join with them in opposing evil. But once Allah is given credit, the Christian cannot be involved. Christians cannot allow themselves to be in fellowship with alternative understandings of who Jesus is and what he did.

Therefore, the Lord's Supper is a separating ordinance. It not only gives identity to who or what Christians are but it also prevents their identifying themselves with a group that would blur or distort the uniqueness they have in Christ.[1] This is not always a popular deduction in modern evangelicalism. One has to be careful how far one pushes this, because Paul was not suggesting that Christians should never have contact with pagans. But he is saying that there will be occasions when to get involved in a certain practice will be a denial of what the Lord's Supper signifies.

The issue of being a separating ordinance would not have been a situation for Highland churches in the past, for they witnessed within communities that were nominally Christian. But that is not the case today, because it is common to have followers of several religions within our communities. These religions often have their own liturgical practices which help them understand their own faith, and it may be that one of the most effective ways for Christians to communicate the gospel to members of another faith is by their own vivid liturgical practice – the Lord's Supper – which clearly shows their ongoing dependence on Christ. For this to happen, members of other faiths would need to be present at the occasions of the Lord's Supper, although not as participants.

Secondly, the Lord's Supper is *a proclamation to a postmodern culture*. To 'proclaim' could also suggest that the Lord's Supper has an evangelistic aspect. Today we live in a postmodern culture. Society no longer regards intellectual explanation as the primary basis of understanding reality. While the term postmodernity covers a wide range of outlooks and activities, its redefining of truth cannot be accepted by evangelicals since the Bible claims to be inspired truth, and also because Jesus claims to be the truth. Yet there are aspects of postmodernity that evangelicalism can approve of, and two of these are the validity of experience and the value of symbols.[2]

The Lord's Supper is not only Word-focused, it also includes experience and symbol. While the experience and the symbol must be interpreted by the Bible, it is through experience that we discover the reality of what the Bible promises and it is by means of symbols that Christ has commanded his people to remember him. Yet Christ did not leave the choice of symbols as an open issue which would allow believers to choose their own symbols. He stipulated that the symbols should be broken bread and outpoured wine shared communally.

The communal use of the symbols is relevant also to another emphasis of postmodernity, that of group participation. The activity by a community of believers in breaking one loaf and in drinking wine from a common cup is a clear witness to others that the community belongs together only through the sacrifice of Christ. Obviously, there has to be some form of verbal explanation of what the symbols mean. But the necessity of the Word does not diminish the contribution of symbols in Christian communication. The symbols of bread and wine give visible expression to a society, confronted by other symbols, that Jesus died to procure forgiveness and reconciliation.

Thirdly, the Lord's Supper is *a unity in contrast to divisive elements in society*. A further feature in modern society concerning which the Lord's Supper has something to say is social division, whether caused by race, class, or other matters. The situation gives an opportunity of witness to local Christians to show to their community that it is possible for the church to bring people from diverse backgrounds into its fellowship once they believe in Jesus for salvation. By evangelism and then by worshipping together the church shows to the surrounding culture that the gospel can bring people together.

Another common divisive element in society today is that of the generation gap, in which young and old have difficulty in meeting together. This difficulty can be exacerbated by regular, helpful church activities such as youth fellowships or older age groups that limit participation to certain ages. The Lord's Supper gives to a local congregation the opportunity of showing that the church is a unity of people of different ages, that both old and young are dependent on Jesus Christ, and that they benefit from interaction with one another.

A third divisive element can be linked to the variety of social levels found in a congregation. It is a reality that most Christians in the West have a form of middle class lifestyle, although the church also has wealthy members and poor members. The absence of possessions and resources does cause resentment in society among those of the poor level and such resentment can be expressed by poor members of a church. Therefore, when individuals of different classes meet together round the Lord's Table it can be a powerful witness to the community.

Of course, the Lord's Supper is not the only aspect of church life that gives opportunity for the breakdown of barriers to union. But it is an important aspect and a visible one.

3. The Lord's Supper as a means of grace

The Lord Jesus as head of his church has given several means, or channels, of grace to his church. The temptation is there to make one means of grace more important than the others, and this has happened with those who make a sacerdotal interpretation of the Lord's Supper. Alan Richardson gives such a place to the Lord's Supper. For him, the Supper is 'supremely the means by which those who have received the Spirit in their baptism are renewed in the spirit on their pilgrimage through this world'. Because 'the Eucharist is the divinely appointed means of communion with God and with our fellow-members in the body of Christ, it is the indispensable means of salvation'.[3] It is unlikely that an evangelical believer would phrase his understanding of the Supper in such a way, yet it is the case that an almost superstitious attitude towards the Supper can exist. For example, some believers who keep themselves away from the Lord's Supper would never stay away from the preaching of the Word, or from the prayer meeting, or from taking the rite of baptism. This outlook suggests that they perceive the Supper as being superior to the other means of grace. In response to such an outlook several things need to be said.

First, the Lord's Supper is not a converting ordinance. This is not to say that the Supper cannot be part of the process of conversion, in the sense that it is a proclamation of the gospel and onlookers, or even unconverted participants, may be enlightened by the Holy Spirit during such a service. But that is different from regarding the Supper as being a means of salvation, and that the elements have supernatural powers.

Second, the Lord's Supper does not give grace through a mere physical participation. Eating the bread and drinking the wine without faith in Christ is not what is required. The bread and wine are symbols, and participants must have communion with what is symbolised before the Supper becomes a means of grace.

Third, although participating in the Supper is expected of all Christians, we cannot say that without doing so, there cannot be spiritual life. Many a doubting Christian has failed to partake of the Supper, but has received grace from God through other of the means, such as the preaching of the Word and through prayer. This is not to minimise the need of partaking, but to note that spiritual life is not dependent on the means but on Christ.

Fourth, it is important to note that the grace given in the Supper is the same grace as is given through the other means of grace. Donald Macleod comments that the Shorter Catechism answer to Question 36, concerning the benefits which in this life do accompany or flow from justification, adoption and sanctification, gives insight into the grace given at the Supper. He notes that partaking in the Supper is part of the process of sanctification, and therefore must contribute to these benefits, which the Catechism defines as 'assurance of God's love, peace of conscience, joy in the Holy Ghost, increase of grace, and perseverance therein to the end'. The Supper assures us of God's love, displayed when he did not spare his own Son but in love delivered him up to the cross to pay the penalty for our sins. It gives peace of conscience, because it declares that the blood shed by Christ has covered our sins, has paid the redemption price, and results in our having no condemnation. It gives joy, because we rejoice with our fellow believers, we have fellowship with the risen, reigning Saviour, and we look forward in hope to his return. It gives increase of grace: 'By presenting the fundamental Christian facts it quickens faith, hope and love into greater vividness of conception and more active exercise; and thus co-operates with the Word in putting the finishing touches to the work which God has begun (Phil. 1:6).'[4]

The last point refers to an important aspect of the means of grace, that is, they must be accompanied by preaching of the Word of God, to ensure an intelligent response to the elements of the Supper. The Supper 'is an object-lesson, which edifies only as it teaches. But apart from the preaching of the Word, the sacrament remains unintelligible. The significance of the elements can be grasped only in the light of the interpretive words, and the sacramental action as a whole is intelligible only in the light of the Passion, the Resurrection and the Parousia, all of which are known to us only from the kerygma.'[5]

Yet the necessity of the preaching of the Word does not require that it occur without other means of grace. Calvin urged that 'we ought always to provide that no meeting of the Church is held without the word, prayer, the dispensation of the Supper and alms'.[6]

It is important to note also that in the Supper we not only get gifts from Christ, such as a heightened sense of God's love or increased joy or renewed peace, we also get Christ himself. John Nicholls notes:

> By faith, then, the believer receives in the Lord's Supper nothing less than Jesus himself, in all his saving fullness. To put it another way, The Lord's Supper intensifies our union with Christ. No-one has expressed this more eloquently than Robert Bruce: 'By the sacrament my faith is nourished...and so, when I had but a little grip of Christ before, as it were betwixt my finger and thumb, now I get him in my whole hand; for the more my faith grows, the better grip I get on Christ Jesus.[7]

Nicholls goes on to explain: 'the Lord's Supper clarifies the Word, vividly certifies it and makes it easier for our imperfect faith to grasp Christ.'

Learning from the past

There are elements of historical communion seasons that are missing from contemporary practice. Not all these elements can be used today because of changes in society. But there are two features that I think can be reduplicated in one way or another.

First, the Lord's Supper should illustrate the unity of Christians. There are several ways in which this can be done, but here I have in mind the witness that was borne to this unity in the large gatherings of the past. The surfeit of denominations in the Highlands has resulted in the Lord's Supper no longer being an occasion that illustrates the oneness of the body of Christ. This is all the more tragic, given that most Highland denominations are committed to the same core group of Christian doctrines. (Of course, this situation can occur elsewhere as well; every town in the country has evangelical churches, the member of which have never sat at the Lord's Table together.) It should be possible for them to so arrange events that they can meet together for the Lord's Supper, either in a neutral venue or else to attend one another's buildings in rotation. This would require taking into account logistical problems such as transport for those without it, childcare for children too young to attend, and catering if there were to be a shared meal after the service was over.

The process could begin denominationally, with congregations of the same denomination meeting together to remember the Lord's death, perhaps with all the congregations in a presbytery meeting together; once this has been established, the practice can be extended to other denominations. Difficulties because of loyalty to denominational distinctives could be overcome by members of other denominations being invited as guests rather than being expected to give up their distinctives. (Given that members of these denominations take part in celebrations of the Lord's Supper at conferences and conventions where their distinctions are not stressed means that they can do so for local occasions as well.)

In addition to the benefits of fellowship that believers would experience, this practice would also be a witness to unbelievers in the community concerning the love and unity that exists between believers. It may also be possible for such a communion occasion to become an opportunity for an evangelistic meeting; the commemoration of the Lord's Supper in a church building could be followed by an evangelistic occasion to which non-Christians would be invited, with the latter gathering taking place in a neutral venue such as a sports stadium or local authority property.

This type of occasion would need to be repeated for several years before it would show its effects. But the communion seasons of the past also had a slow development originally. In a few years it would not be difficult to have a fixed week for such an occasion, with the features of it being common knowledge for both Christians and non-Christians. There are evangelistic events taking place, but as far as I know they are not connected to the Lord's Supper. There is no scriptural requirement that they should be, but past historical evidence is there to show that evangelistic services connected to the remembrance of the Saviour's death were an effective means of evangelism.

Secondly, we need to adopt methods that provide ways and opportunities for lay people to contribute to the communion weekend. Having testimony meetings is one method, although they usually focus on the occasion of a person's conversion rather than on the Lord's Supper itself. It seems to me that the original purpose of the fellowship meeting is still relevant, and the method of implementing it still has value. It would be possible to divide the large congregation into smaller groups in order to discuss aspects connected to the observance of the Supper. Each of these groups could be guided by an elder. Such groups already exist in congregations in the forms of Bible study groups, and it would not be difficult for the organisers of the larger event to suggest a topic for discussion that would be connected to the Lord's Supper.

The Lord's Supper is an essential aspect of church life. It is a means of binding believers together as a community, and so enabling them to display the spiritual union they have with one another. In the Lord's Supper, biblical history becomes alive in the current experience of believers. By the use of bread and wine they not only recall what their Lord did but they also re-enact his death. At the same time, believers receive and develop a biblical future orientation because the Supper is a foretaste of the heavenly banquet, of the eternal celebration depicted as the marriage supper of the Lamb. The Lord's Supper is a reminder to believers on earth that they live in two worlds simultaneously, that they have an earthly life perceived by their five senses and a spiritual life in union with Christ revealed to them by the Spirit.

References

1. The Lord's Supper in the Gospels

[1]J. C. Lambert (1903), *The Sacraments in the New Testament*, T. and T. Clark, 396ff., notes that supporters of this interpretation are of two different theological outlooks. One group he classifies as 'High Churchmen of all shades and kinds, Roman Catholic, Neo-Lutheran, and Anglican' who maintain 'that the Lord was here giving a definite prophecy of the future institution, and describing its nature so particularly that His acts and words on the night of His betrayal many months afterwards are precisely explained by what he said at Capernaum'. The other group are advanced critical scholars who argue that the words in the text are not those of Jesus, but were put into his mouth by the author of the Gospel and indicated the beliefs of the early church regarding the Lord's Supper. Donald Guthrie's assessment of the variety of interpretations is that 'There is a difference of opinion over whether these words refer in a prophetic sense to the Lord's Supper, or whether they originally belonged to the passion story and have been misplaced' (Donald Guthrie, [1981], *New Testament Theology*, IVP, p. 729).

[2]Leon Morris (1971), *The Gospel According to John*, Eerdmans, pp. 311-12. Morris is an evangelical interpreter of the passage. No doubt writers with other Christian persuasions would disagree with him.

[3]Morris' comment can be criticised; 'eating' and 'drinking' can be regarded as 'pictures' of faith as well as being its 'consequences'.

[4]Herman N. Ridderbos (1997), *The Gospel of John, A Theological Commentary*, Eerdmans, p. 243.

[5]Guthrie, p. 729.

[6]Hugh Anderson (1976), *Commentary on Mark*, New Century Bible, Oliphants, pp. 308-9.

[7]Details are from Steve Motyer (1995), *Remember Jesus*, Christian Focus, pp. 63-65. See also R.T. France (1985), *Matthew*, TNTC, IVP, pp. 364-66.

[8]John Hamilton (1992), 'The Chronology of the Crucifixion and the Passover,' *Churchman*, Vol. 106, No. 4, p. 324.

[9]Mentioned in D. A. Carson (1984), Matthew, *The Expositor's Bible Commentary*, Zondervan, p. 529.

[10]Leon Morris (1974, rpt. 1986), *Luke*, TNTC, IVP, p. 302.

[11]France, p. 365.

[12]Motyer, p. 66. Plummer also comments: 'The question has been raised whether Peter and John prepared the lamb, or whether this was left to the master of the house. Almost certainly, there was no lamb. The killing of this ought to be done in the Temple on Friday afternoon in the presence of the whole company. Two disciples would not suffice for this (Exod. xii. 4) and it could not be done two days before the Passover. Moreover, Peter and John were probably not aware that the Supper was to take place on the Thursday, but believed they were getting the room ready for the Friday' (Alfred Plummer [1909, rpt. 1920], *An Exegetical Commentary on the Gospel of Matthew*, Robert Scott, pp. 357-58).

[13]Graham N. Stanton (1989), *The Gospels and Jesus*, Oxford University Press, p. 256.

[14]Hamilton, p. 335.

[15]Carson, *Matthew*, p. 531.

[16]Carson, pp. 531-32.

[17]Carson, p. 532

[18]I. Howard Marshall (1980, rpt. 1993), *Last Supper and Lord's Supper*, Paternoster, p. 38

[19]Carson, *Matthew*, p. 535

[20]Stanton, p. 257.

[21]Stanton, p. 257.

[22]The technical term for this action of remembrance is *anamnesis*, from the Greek word **anamnēsi**.

[23]Paul Barnett suggests that 'remembering' involves watching the elements and listening to the words before eating the elements (Barnett [2000], *1 Corinthians*, Christian Focus, pp. 216-17).

[24]Eugene Merrill (2002), 'Remembering/Memory and the Theology of Worship,' *Journal of the Evangelical Theological Society*, Vol. 43, p. 35.

[25]Merrill, pp. 35-36.

[26]Kevan (1966), *The Lord's Supper*, Evangelical Press, pp. 31-32.

[27]A. M. Stibbs (1962), *Sacrament, Sacrifice and Eucharist*, The Tyndale Press, p. 42.

[2]William L. Lane (1974), *The Gospel of Mark*, NICNT, Eerdmans, p. 507.

[29]S. Lewis Johnston, Jr. (1997), 'The Last Passover, The First Lord's Supper, and the New Covenant,' *Reformation and Revival Journal*, Vol. 6, pp. 130-32.

[30]Lane, p. 507

[31]Johnson, p. 129.

2. The Lord's Supper in Acts

[1]James D. G. Dunn (1996), *The Acts of the Apostles*, Epworth Press, p. 35.

[2]Ben Witherington, III, *The Acts of the Apostles*, Eerdmans, pp. 160-61.

[3]Simon J. Kistemaker (1990), *Exposition of the Acts of the Apostles*, Baker Book House, p. 111.

[4]I. Howard Marshall (1980, rpt. 1993), *Last Supper and Lord's Supper*, pp. 127, 132.

[5]William J. Larkin (1995), *Acts*, IVP, p. 62.

[6]Luke is not using the Jewish reckoning of a day (from evening to evening). Paul left the following morning, which Luke says was the next day. If he had been using Jewish time, it would have been the same day.

[7]F. F. Bruce (1988), *The Book of the Acts*, Eerdmans, p. 384.

[8]John R. W. Stott (1990), *Acts*, IVP, p. 321.

[9]Everett F. Harrison (1975), *Acts*, Moody Press, p. 311.

3. The Lord's Supper in the Epistles

[1]John Polhil (1999), *Paul and His Letters*, Broadman and Holman, p. 245.

[2]Gordon Fee (1987), *I Corinthians*, Eerdmans, p. 443.

[3]Ralph P. Martin (1964), *Worship in the Early Church*, Eerdmans, p. 124.

[4]Richard Pratt (2000), *1 and 2 Corinthians*, Broadman and Holman, p. 167.

[5]Pratt, p. 197

[6] There is textual variant in 11:24 between 'this is my body, broken for you' (KJV) and 'this is my body which is for you' (ESV). The KJV rendering is unlikely, given that Christ's body was not broken. In the accounts of Matthew and Mark of the Last Supper, Jesus does not add anything to his statement about the bread. Luke's account adds, 'which is given for you.' Given that there are close similarities between Luke's and Paul's accounts, why did one include 'given' (*didōmi*) and the other omit it? Perhaps Marshall's suggested answer is the best solution. Both Luke's and Paul's renderings are valid translations from the original Aramaic spoken by Jesus (I. H. Marshall [1980, rpt. 1993], *Last Supper and Lord's Supper*, Paternoster, 46-47, 49).

[7]Gordon D. Fee (1987), *I Corinthians*, p. 469.

[8]Paul Barnett (2000), *1 Corinthians*, pp. 213-14.

[9]Donald Macleod (1998), *A Faith to Live By*, Christian Focus, p.242.

[10] Fee, p. 557.

[11] Stibbs, p. 46.

[12]Fee comments, concerning Jesus' breaking the bread, that 'for Jesus himself this is almost certainly a prophetic symbolic action, by which he anticipated his death and interpreted it in light of Isa. 53 as in behalf of others' (p. 551).

[13]Steve Motyer, *Remember Jesus*, p. 101.

[14] Robert Halley (1851), *The Sacraments*, Vol. 2, London: Jackson and Walford, p. 189.

[15]Donald Macleod, 'Qualifications for Communion,' *Banner of Truth*, No. 65, p. 14.

[16]Pratt, p. 202.

[17]Craig Bloomberg (1994), *1 Corinthians*, Zondervan, p. 231.

[18]Fee, p. 563.

[19]Fee, p. 564.

[20]Macleod, 'Qualifications for Communion,' p. 17.

[21]Motyer, p. 93

4. Reformed Understanding of the Lord's Supper

[1]Alexander Macrae (n.d.), *The Life of Gustavus Aird, Creich*, p. 239.

[2]Timothy George (1989), *Theology of the Reformers*, IVP, pp. 145-47.

[3]'Moreover, there is one universal Church of the faithful, outside of which no one whatever can be saved, in which Jesus is at the one time Priest and Sacrifice. His body and blood are truly contained in the sacrifice of the altar under the appearance of bread and wine, the bread being transubstantiated into the body, and the wine into the blood by human power, so that for the effecting of the mystery of unity, we receive of His what He received of ours. This Sacrament especially no one can administer but the priest who has been ordained according to the Church authority, which Jesus Christ gave to the Apostles and their successors' (Alexander Barclay [1927], *The Protestant Doctrine of the Lord's Supper*, Jackson, Wylie and Co., pp. 19-20).

[4]'The Real Presence of Christ in the Eucharist,' *Catholic Encyclopedia*, www.new advent.org.

[5]It is the case that objections to the notion of transubstantiation were also made prior to the Reformation. For example, Broughton Knox, in his *The Lord's Supper from Wycliffe to Cranmer*, claims that the main arguments used against transubstantiation by the Reformers had already been made by John Wycliffe in the fourteenth century. Wycliffe had argued that transubstantiation was not based on a legitimate interpretation of scripture, that it was an irrational concept, and that it led to idolatry. Wycliffe's work on the Eucharist, translated by Ford Lewis Battles, is found in 'Advocates of Reform,' *The Library of Christian Classics*, Vol. XIV, SCM Press, 1953. Broughton Knox is of the opinion that it was the influence of Wycliffe's teaching that led to the Church of England, at the Reformation, adopting the Calvinistic rather than the Lutheran view of the presence of Christ in the Supper.

[6]Robert Letham (2001), *The Lord's Supper*, Presbyterian and Reformed, pp. 20-21.

[7]Letham, p. 22.

[8]Keith A. Mathison (2002), *Given For You*, Presbyterian and Reformed, pp. 241-42.

[9]Mathison, p. 242.

[10]Letham, p. 21.

[11]Mathison, pp. 250-51

[12]Luther wrote several treatises in connection with the Lord's Supper. In this section, I have considered three of these treatises. *The Babylonian Captivity of the Church* (1520) details his rejection of Roman Catholic practices, *The Sacrament of the Body and Blood of Christ—Against the Fanatics* (1526) was written against Swiss theologians, including the Anabaptists, who adhered to a form of memorialism, and his *Confession Concerning Christ's Supper* (1528).

[13]Wayne Grudem, *Systematic Theology*, IVP, 1994, p. 994.

[14]Martin Luther, 'The Babylonian Captivity of the Church,' *Luther's Works*, Vol. 36, Fortress Press (1959), pp.19-28.

[15]Ibid., p. 31.

[16]Ibid., p. 33

[17]Ibid, p. 34

[18]Ibid., p. 35

[19]Ibid., pp. 35-36

[20]Ibid., p. 38

[21]Ibid., p. 44

[22]Ibid., p. 51

[23]Martin Luther, 'The Sacrament of the Body and Blood of Christ—Against the Fanatics,' *Luther's Works* (1959), Vol. 36, Fortress Press, p. 335.

[24]Ibid, pp. 339-41

[25]Ibid, pp. 343-45.

[26]Ibid, pp. 347-51.

[27]Ibid, p. 351-52.

[28]Ibid. p. 352.

[29]Ibid. pp. 354-60.

[30]Paul Althaus (1966), *The Theology of Martin Luther*, Fortress Press, p. 179.

[31]David Wells (1984), *The Person of Christ*, Crossway, p. 122.

[3]Martin Luther, 'Confession Concerning Christ's Supper,' *Luther's Works*, Vol. 37, pp. 222-23.

[33]Wells, p. 123. This teaching had two consequences: 'This in

turn flowed later either into a pantheistic view (that all human nature receives and is transformed by the divine), or into one which posited that Christ's humanity, precisely because of its capacity for the divine, is unlike that possessed by any human being.'

[34]Letham, pp. 24-25.

[35]Geoffrey W. Bromiley (1953), *Zwingli and Bullinger*, The Westminster Press, p. 176.

[36]Bromiley, pp. 185-86.

[37]W. P. Stephens, *The Theology of Huldrych Zwingli*, Clarendon Press, 1984, p. 231.

[38]Bromiley, pp. 262-65.

[39]Bromiley, p. 187.

[40]Bromiley, p. 188.

[41]Bromiley, p. 190.

[42]Bromiley, p. 191.

[43]Bromiley, pp. 213-14.

[44]Bromiley, p. 211.

[45]*Select Writings of Huldrych Zwingli*, Vol. 2, translated by H. Wayne Pipkin, Pickwick Publications, 1984, pp. 138-39.

[46]Bromiley, p. 199

[47]Pipkin, Vol. 2, p. 133.

[48]Pipkin, Vol. 2, p. 134.

[49]Pipkin, Vol. 2, p.220.

[50]Pipkin, Vol. 2, p. 139.

[51]Pipkin, Vol. 2, p. 141.

[52]Bromiley, p. 259

[53]Stephens, p. 253

[54]Bromiley, pp. 181-82.

[55]The comment of Gregory Dix, cited by Derek Moore Crispi, (1975), 'The Real Absence: Ulrich Zwingli's View,' *Union and Communion*, Westminster Conference Report, p. 22.

[56]Calvin's teaching on the Lord's Supper is also found in other writings concerned with it, including *Short Treatise on the Lord's Supper, Mutual Consent as to the Sacraments, Second Defence of the Sacraments, Last Admonition to Joachim Westphal, True Partaking of the*

Flesh and Blood of Christ, Best Method of Concord on the Sacraments, found in John Calvin (rpt. 2002), *Treatises on the Sacraments*, Christian Focus, which is a reprint of Beveridge's translations of these tracts.

[57]References to Calvin's *Institutes* are book, chapter and section.

[58]John Calvin, *Tracts*, Calvin Translation Society, Edinburgh, 1849.Vol. 2, p. 172.

[59]Calvin, *Tracts*, p. 502.

[60]Calvin, *Institutes*, 4.17.33.

[61]Calvin, *Tracts*, p. 578.

[62]Calvin, *Institutes*, 4.17.10.

[63]Calvin's views have been summarised under the term *virtualism*, taken from the Latin *vis, vires*, which refers to the power of the Holy Spirit to draw believers to heaven where he gives them Christ and his blessings.

[64]Calvin, *Institutes*, 4.17.32.

[65]Calvin stressed a further requirement for the proper observation of the Lord's Supper – it is essential that the Supper be accompanied by the preaching of the Word (Calvin, *Tracts*, p. 190).

[66]William Cunningham (1862), *The Reformers and the Theology of the Reformation*, T. and T. Clark, p. 240.

[67]Robert L. Dabney, *Systematic Theology* (1871, rpt. 1985), Banner of Truth Trust, pp. 810-13.

[68]Sinclair B. Ferguson (1996), *The Holy Spirit*, IVP, p. 203.

[69]Robert L. Reymond, *A New Theology of the Christian Faith*, Thomas Nelson, 1998, p. 962.

[70]Reymond, pp. 963ff.

[71]John Calvin, Comments on John 6:53, *John Calvin Collection*, Ages Digital Library Series.

[72]John Calvin, Comments on John 6:54, *John Calvin Collection*, Ages Digital Library Series.

[73]Ronald Wallace (1953), *Calvin on the Word and Sacrament*, Oliver and Boyd, pp. 217-18.

[74]Wallace, pp. 219-21.

[75]Wallace, pp. 221-23

[76]Wallace, pp. 223-25.

[77]Wallace, pp. 225-26

[78]Ferguson, *The Holy Spirit*, pp. 203-04.

[79]Alexander Barclay (1927), *The Protestant Doctrine of the Lord's Supper*, James Wylie, pp. 226-27.

[80]R. Scott Clark, 'The Means of Grace: The Lord's Supper,' in Armstrong, *The Compromised Church*, p. 134.

[81]Timothy George, pp. 319-20.

[82]For example, John Calvin said that the Supper could have been administered most becomingly if it were set before the church very often, and at least once a week (*Institutes*, 4.17.43).

[83]George, p. 320.

[84]James Kirk (1989), *Patterns of Reform*, T. & T. Clark, p. 71.

5. Communion Seasons in the Scottish Lowlands

[1]Robert M. Adamson (1905), *The Christian Doctrine of the Lord's Supper*, T. & T. Clark, p. 79.

[2]Adamson, pp. 79-80.

[3]James Kirk (1989), *Patterns of Reform*, p. 74.

[4]The suggested dates were the first Sunday of March, the first Sunday of June, the first Sunday of September and the first Sunday of December. It was recognised, however, that individual congregations could have the Supper more frequently if they desired (James K. Cameron [1972], *The First Book of Discipline*, Saint Andrew Press, p. 184).

[5]King James I later introduced liturgical practices from England. One of these, in 1615, was that parish ministers celebrate the communion annually, at Passover or Easter. It took a while for the practice to become common, with broad acceptance occurring in the north as well as the south of Scotland (Foster, *The Church Before the Covenants*, Scottish Academic Press, pp. 182-84).

[6]Cameron, pp. 91-92.

[7]Cameron, p. 184.

[8]A. M. Hunter, 'The Celebration of Communion in Scotland Since the Reformation,' *Scottish Church History Society*, 1929, Vol. 3, p. 162.

[9]G.W. Sprott (1901), *The Book of Common Order of the Church of Scotland*, Blackwood and Sons, p. xv.

[10]The first article enjoined kneeling at the communion; the second, private communion in cases of sickness; the third, private baptism, 'upon a great and reasonable cause'; the fourth, Episcopal confirmation; the fifth, permitting the observance of five festival days.

[11]Sprott, pp. xvi-xvii. Sprott refers to the confusion that the introduction of these articles caused in congregations that included them; he also refers to Calderwood's assertion that two-thirds of the congregations in Scotland had not accepted them, and to Spottiswoode's statement that kneeling for the communion was given up in many parts where it had been introduced and that private communion had not been introduced (pp. xlii-xliii).

[12]A description of a Scottish communion was given by the historian Calderwood in 1623: 'Among us, the Minister, when the sermon is finished, reads the words of institution, gives a short exhortation and admonition, then blesses. The blessing or thanksgiving ended, he says, "Our Lord, on that night on which He was betrayed, took bread, and gave thanks, as we have already done, and brake, as I also now break, and gave to His Disciples, saying (then he hands it to those nearest on the right and on the left), This is my body," &c. He adds nothing to the words of Christ, changes nothing, omits nothing. Then those next break a particle off the larger fragment or part, and hand what is left to those sitting nearest, so long as there is any portion of the fragment over. Then those who serve the tables, when one fragment is done, offer the paten [the communion bread plate], from which another in like manner takes a similar larger fragment or *klasma*, and breaking, hands to the next, and so on. In like manner the Minister delivers the cup to those nearest, repeating the words of Christ, without addition, mixture, change, or omission, and they hand it to those sitting beside them; and when the wine is done, those who serve fill it anew. As soon as he has delivered both elements to those sitting nearest him, using only the words of Christ, whilst they distribute amongst themselves the bread and the cup, the Minister, as long as the action of eating and drinking lasts, addresses those at the table....

'Whilst they are rising from the table, and others are taking their place, the Minister is silent, and those leaving and those approaching the table, together with the whole Congregation, either sing, or the Reader reads the history of the Passion. But when the Minister is speaking, and when the communicants hand to one another the elements, neither is the history of the Passion read nor Psalms sung, as it is not expedient....

'If the whole communicants could sit at one time at the tables, it would be more agreeable and advantageous, as they could thus all together eat, drink, meditate, sing, and hear the Minister's address. In this form our Church has now for sixty years celebrated the Holy Supper' (G.W. Sprott [1901], *The Book of Common Order of the Church of Scotland*, William Blackwood and Sons, pp. xxxviii-xxxix).

[13]A. Mitchell Hunter, 'The Celebration of Communion in Scotland Since the Reformation,' p. 162.

[14]Hunter, pp. 162-67.

[15]Hunter, pp. 165-66.

[16]Hunter, p. 166. He also notes that many churches connected to the Secession did not use white cloths, a practice that may have developed from the custom of the Praying Societies to meet for the Lord's Supper in private houses where a white cloth would not have been used.

[17]Hunter, pp. 50-53.

[18]'Bread and a cup of wine are brought to the President of Bishop, which he takes' (cited in Burnet [1960],*The Holy Communion in the Reformed Church of Scotland*, Oliver and Boyd Ltd., p. 57).

[19]I will explain this term later.

[20]Burnet, *The Holy Communion in the Reformed Church of Scotland*, pp. 58-59.

[21]Todd, *The Culture of Protestantism in Early Modern Scotland*, pp.91-92.

[22]Todd, pp. 92-93

[23]Henry Grey Graham (1906), *The Social Life in the Eighteenth Century*, Adam and Charles Black.

[24]These details of how the Reformed Church in Scotland

celebrated the sacrament in the sixteenth century are taken from Burnet, *The Holy Communion in the Reformed Church of Scotland*, pp. 44–63. Sprott mentions that in Glasgow in 1586 and 1587, the time of convening on communion Sundays was at four in the morning and eight in the morning (Sprott, p. xxxviii). At a communion in St. Andrews on Sunday, October 21st, 1638, the preparatory sermon was preached on the previous day by George Hamilton; on the Sunday, the morning sermon was preached by Andrew Auchinlek, the forenoon sermon by Alexander Henderson, and the thanksgiving sermon by David Forrest (Alexander Henderson, *Sermons, Prayers and Pulpit Addresses* [edited by R. Thomson Martin in 1867], John Maclaren, 55).

[25]One such gathering, from 1678, is described by John Blackader: 'The place where we convened was every way commodious, and seemed to have been formed on purpose. It was a green and pleasant haugh, fast by the waterside.... The communion tables were spread on the green by the water, and around them the people had arranged themselves in decent order. But the far greater multitude sat on the brae-face, which was crowded from top to bottom – full as pleasant a sight as ever was seen of that sort. The tables were served by some gentlemen and persons of the gravest deportment. None were admitted without tokens as usual, which were distributed on the Saturday, but only to such as were known to some of the ministers or persons of trust to be free of public scandals. All the regular forms were gone through. The communicants entered at one end and retired at the other, a way being kept clear for them to take their seats again on the hillside. Mr. Welsh preached the action sermon, and served the first two tables, as he was ordinarily put to do on such occasions. The other four ministers...exhorted the rest in turn; the table service was closed by Mr Welsh with solemn thanksgiving; and solemn it was and sweet and edifying to see the gravity and composure of all present, as well as of all parts of the service. The communion was peaceably concluded, all the people heartily offering up their gratitude, and singing with a joyful noise to the Rock of their salvation' (Thomas M'Crie [rpt. 1988], *The Story of*

the Scottish Church, pp. 308-10).

[26]Burnet, *The Holy Communion in the Reformed Church of Scotland*, pp. 119, 120, 122.

[27]Andsell (1998), *The People of the Great Faith*, Acair, pp. 12-14.

[28]Leigh Eric Schmidt (1989), *Holy Fairs*, Princeton University Press, pp. 21-50.

[29]John MacInnes (1951), *The Evangelical Movement in the Highlands of Scotland*, The University Press, Aberdeen, p. 99. Also, Macmillan (1931), *Worship of Scottish Reformed Church*, pp. 222f.

[30]A. R. MacEwan, *The Erskines*, Famous Scots Series, Oliphant, Anderson and Ferrier, 1900.

[31]'The fervency of the preaching of the leading men among the Protesters, which more or less characterized the work of all the members of that party, was shown conspicuously on the occasion of the dispensation of the sacrament of the Lord's Supper. It was this party which first took advantage of communion seasons for great gatherings of the people to hear sermons before and after the administration of the ordinance. However great the abuses may have been which crept in as years went on, so as to make such gatherings fit subjects for the scourge of the satirist's tongue, it cannot be denied that in those days of trouble and confusion, those great preachers at communion gatherings did more than any other agency to keep alive the flame of genuine religion among the people, and to prevent the universal spread of cold indifference which the godlessness of ambitious and worldly men in church and state so strongly fostered' (John MacPherson [1901], *History of the Church in Scotland*, Alexander Gardner, 214).

[32]Somerset, 'A History of the Communion Season,' *The Free Presbyterian Magazine*, Vol. 109, p. 12.

[33]Burnet, p. 126.

[34]Burnet, p. 126.

[35]Burnet, p. 127

[36]Burnet, p. 128.

[37]Hunter, pp. 59-60.

[38]Hunter, p. 61.

[39]Hunter, p. 61.

[40]Hunter, p. 60. Not every minister approved of the common programme and associated practices of the communion season. For example, John Brown, minister of the Associate Burger congregation in Haddington – the author of many books including *The Self-Interpreting Bible* and a *Dictionary of the Bible*, and later Professor of Divinity of the Associate Burger Synod – in 1756 added another communion occasion to the previous annual celebration. He not only disapproved of the infrequency of the then current practice, he even suggested that it had potential overtones of a form of Popery.

In a letter to a ministerial friend, he wrote the following: '...I fear it will be no easy task to prove that our way of administering the Supper is agreeable to the Word of God....That its infrequency tends to make it solemn I do not see, for if it so why not administer baptism but once a year also, as it, in its own nature, is as solemn as the Supper? Why not pray seldom, preach seldom, read God's Word seldom, that they may become more solemn too?...Can even human appendages of a fast, or two or three sermons on Saturday and Monday, make up for the unfrequency of it? Can what is of human institution, though of itself very good, make up for the want of what is of divine institution?'

In an article written about that time, but not published until twenty years after his death, Brown explained his concerns: 'I am not averse to the custom of a fast preparation, and a thanksgiving day, if the exercises on these days are considered as means for encouraging strangers to attend, as they have it so seldom at home; and when they are considered as means for deepening the solemnity of the approach to God in this ordinance, which in our present case is quite, or next to quite, worn off in the long intervals between ordinances of this nature. But is it not plain, that in case the Church were returned to the primitive custom, there would be no need to encourage strangers to attend, because they would have weekly opportunities for partaking at home? And there could be less need to use means of this nature to fix or deepen those impressions; the conscientious approach to God in this solemn ordinance, the Sabbath before, and the Sabbath after, would more effectually prepare the soul for receiving and rivetting divine impressions than all the work of these three days.

'When these days' exercises are considered as well-meant human helps, during the present unfrequency of administration, nobody regards them more than I do; but if anybody considers them, as too many ignorant people do, as essential parts of this ordinance, and plead the absolute necessity of them, as a reason against the more frequent administration of the Supper, can I, in consistency with our *Confession of Faith*, chap. xxi. sect. 1, refrain from detesting that view of them, and the usage proceeding therefrom as refined Popery? Are they not of human invention? Was not the invention of them merely occasional? Are they not still unknown in many Protestant Churches? Were they not unknown in the Church of Scotland for about seventy years after the Reformation? Do we not find one of our best Assemblies, namely, that of 1645, prohibiting to have any more than one sermon upon Saturday and another upon Monday? Did not Mr. Livingston, as long as he lived, refuse to allow any more sermons on the Saturday and Monday at his sacramental occasions? Now, is it not plainly Popish to count human inventions and occasional additions, essential parts of this great ordinance?...

'In fine, whether is it grace or corruption that most affects to add human devices to God's worship, in order to make it more splendid than Christ has left it? May not persons be as really guilty of Popery by doting on the splendid pomp of divine ordinances that consists in the variety of days, sermons, and ministers, as by doting on the variety of fantastic ceremonies used in the Popish Mass? Ought we not to beware of adding to God's ordinances, as well as of taking from them? Is God content to barter with us in this point, by giving up with the frequent administration of the Supper, if we will annex a few days' sermons, ministers, and people to it, when seldom administered? Where does he either make or declare his acceptance of this proposal?' (Robert Mackenzie [1918, rpt. 1964], *John Brown of Haddington*, Banner of Truth, 99-103).

[41]John Brown (1853), *Discourses Suited to the Administration of the Lord's Supper*, William Oliphant and Sons, pp. 50-52. This John

Brown was the grandson of John Brown of Haddington, mentioned in the previous reference. He was the minister of Broughton United Presbyterian Church in Edinburgh and Professor of Theology in the United Presbyterian College in the same city. His views will also be discussed in the following chapter.

[42]Hunter, pp. 53, 63.

[43]Adamson, pp. 124-25.

[44]Adamson, pp. 125-27.

[45]John Brown (1853), *Discourses Suited to the Administration of the Lord's Supper*, William Oliphant and Sons, pp. vii and viii.

[46]D. Douglas Bannerman (1889), *Fast Days and Christian Festivals*, Andrew Elliot, p. 1.

[47]A. Sinclair (1885), *Reminiscences of the Life and Labours of Duguld Buchanan*, MacLachlan and Stewart, pp. 25-39.

6. Theology of the Lord's Supper in the Scottish Lowlands

[1]The Scots Confession was one of several Reformed Confessions which agreed with the teaching of Calvin. Mathison (pp. 73-91) provides details from the First Helvetic Confession (1536), The Colloquy of Worms (1557), The Gallican Confession (1559), the Belgic Confession (1561), and the Heidelberg Catechism (1563).

[2]D.C. MacNicol (1907), *Master Robert Bruce*, Oliphant, Anderson and Ferrier, 231ff.

[3] I. R. Torrance, in an article on Robert Bruce in *The Dictionary of Scottish Church History and Theology*, says that Bruce's sermons on the Lord's Supper brought together Reformed doctrine and evangelical application in a way that helped to shape and became characteristic of the Scottish Reformed tradition (p. 104). They were first preached in 1589 and published the following year.

[4]Robert Bruce, *Sermons on the Sacraments*, p. 46.

[5]Bruce, p. 46.

[6]Bruce, pp. 46-47.

[7]Bruce, p. 47.

[8]Bruce, p. 49.

[9]Bruce, p. 53.

[10]Bruce, p. 55.

[11]Bruce, pp. 63-65.

[12]Bruce, pp. 73-80.

[13]'I. Our Lord Jesus, in the night wherein he was betrayed, instituted the sacrament of his body and blood, called the Lord's Supper, to be observed in his Church unto the end of the world; for the perpetual remembrance of the sacrifice of himself in his death, the sealing all benefits thereof unto true believers, their spiritual nourishment and growth in him, their further engagement in and to all duties which they owe unto him; and to be a bond and pledge of their communion with him, and with each other, as members of his mystical body.'

[14]'II. In this sacrament Christ is not offered up to his Father, nor any real sacrifice made at all for remission of sins of the quick or dead, but a commemoration of that one offering up of himself, by himself, upon the cross, once for all, and a spiritual oblation of all possible praise unto God for the same; so that the Popish sacrifice of the mass, as they call it, is most abominably injurious to Christ's one only sacrifice, the alone propitiation for all the sins of the elect.'

[15]'The Lord Jesus hath, in this ordinance, appointed his ministers to declare his word of institution to the people, to pray, and bless the elements of bread and wine, and thereby to set them apart from a common to an holy use; and to take and break the bread, to take the cup, and (they communicating also themselves) to give both to the communicants; but to none who are not then present in the congregation.'

[16]'IV. Private masses, or receiving this sacrament by a priest, or any other, alone; as likewise the denial of the cup to the people; worshipping the elements, the lifting them up, or carrying them about for adoration, and the reserving them for any pretended religious use, are all contrary to the nature of this sacrament, and to the institution of Christ.'

[17]'V. The outward elements in this sacrament, duly set apart to the uses ordained by Christ, have such relation to him crucified, as that truly, yet sacramentally only, they are sometimes called by the name of the things they represent, to wit, the body and blood

of Christ; albeit, in substance and nature, they still remain truly, and only, bread and wine, as they were before.'

[18]'VI. That doctrine which maintains a change of the substance of bread and wine, into the substance of Christ's body and blood (commonly called transubstantiation) by consecration of a priest, or by any other way, is repugnant, not to Scripture alone, but even to common-sense and reason; overthroweth the nature of the sacrament; and hath been, and is, the cause of manifold superstitions, yea, of gross idolatries.'

[19]'VII. Worthy receivers, outwardly partaking of the visible elements in this sacrament, do then also inwardly by faith, really and indeed, yet not carnally and corporally, but spiritually, receive and feed upon Christ crucified, and all benefits of his death: the body and blood of Christ being then not corporally or carnally in, with, or under the bread and wine; yet as really, but spiritually, present to the faith of believers in that ordinance, as the elements themselves are to their outward senses.'

[20]'VIII. Although ignorant and wicked men receive the outward elements in this sacrament, yet they receive not the thing signified thereby; but by their unworthy coming thereunto are guilty of the body and blood of the Lord, to their own damnation. Wherefore all ignorant and ungodly persons, as they are unfit to enjoy communion with him, so are they unworthy of the Lord's table, and can not, without great sin against Christ, while they remain such, partake of these holy mysteries, or be admitted thereunto.'

[21]Robert Baillie wrote concerning the practice of the Independents: 'The Independents way of celebration, seems to be very irreverent: They have the communion every Sabbath, without any preparation before or thanksgiving after; little examination of people; their very prayers and doctrine before the sacrament uses not to be directed to the use of the sacrament. They have, after the blessing, a short discourse, and two short graces over the elements, which are distribute and participate in silence, without exhortation, reading, or singing, and all is ended with a psalme, without prayer' (Robert Paul (1985), *The Assembly of the Lord*, T. & T. Clark, p. 362).

[22]Paul, pp. 367-73.

[23]'The communion, or supper of the Lord, is frequently to be celebrated; but how often, may be considered and determined by the ministers, and other church-governors of each congregation, as they shall find most convenient for the comfort and edification of the people committed to their charge. And, when it shall be administered, we judge it convenient to be done after the morning sermon.'

[24]'Where this sacrament cannot with convenience be frequently administered, it is requisite that publick warning be given the sabbath-day before the administration thereof: and that either then, or on some day of that week, something concerning that ordinance, and the due preparation thereunto, and participation thereof, be taught; that, by the diligent use of all means sanctified of God to that end, both in publick and private, all may come better prepared to that heavenly feast.'

[25]'When the day is come for administration, the minister, having ended his sermon and prayer, shall make a short exhortation: "Expressing the inestimable benefit we have by this sacrament, together with the ends and use thereof: setting forth the great necessity of having our comforts and strength renewed thereby in this our pilgrimage and warfare: how necessary it is that we come unto it with knowledge, faith, repentance, love, and with hungering and thirsting souls after Christ and his benefits: how great the danger to eat and drink unworthily. Next, he is, in the name of Christ, on the one part, to warn all such as are ignorant, scandalous, profane, or that live in any sin or offence against their knowledge or conscience, that they presume not to come to that holy table; shewing them, that he that eateth and drinketh unworthily, eateth and drinketh judgment unto himself: and, on the other part, he is in an especial manner to invite and encourage all that labour under the sense of the burden of their sins, and fear of wrath, and desire to reach out unto a greater progress in grace than yet they can attain unto, to come to the Lord's table; assuring them, in the same name, of ease, refreshing, and strength to their weak and wearied souls."'

[26]'After this exhortation, warning, and invitation, the table being before decently covered, and so conveniently placed, that the communicants may orderly sit about it, or at it, the minister is to begin the action with sanctifying and blessing the elements of bread and wine set before him, (the bread in comely and convenient vessels, so prepared, that, being broken by him, and given, it may be distributed amongst the communicants; the wine also in large cups,) having first, in a few words, shewed that those elements, otherwise common, are now set apart and sanctified to this holy use, by the word of institution and prayer.'

[27]'Let the words of institution be read out of the Evangelists, or out of the first Epistle of the Apostle Paul to the Corinthians, Chap. 11:23. *I have received of the Lord, &c.* to the 27th Verse, which the minister may, when he seeth requisite, explain and apply.'

[28]'Let the prayer, thanksgiving, or blessing of the bread and wine, be to this effect: 'With humble and hearty acknowledgment of the greatness of our misery, from which neither man nor angel was able to deliver us, and of our great unworthiness of the least of all God's mercies; to give thanks to God for all his benefits, and especially for that great benefit of our redemption, the love of God the Father, the sufferings and merits of the Lord Jesus Christ the Son of God, by which we are delivered; and for all means of grace, the word and sacraments; and for this sacrament in particular, by which Christ, and all his benefits, are applied and sealed up unto us, which, notwithstanding the denial of them unto others, are in great mercy continued unto us, after so much and long abuse of them all.

'To profess that there is no other name under heaven by which we can be saved, but the name of Jesus Christ, by whom alone we receive liberty and life, have access to the throne of grace, are admitted to eat and drink at his own table, and are sealed up by his Spirit to an assurance of happiness and everlasting life.

'Earnestly to pray to God, the Father of all mercies, and God of all consolation, to vouchsafe his gracious presence, and the effectual working of his Spirit in us; and so to sanctify these elements both of bread and wine, and to bless his own ordinance, that we may receive by faith the body and blood of Jesus Christ, crucified for us, and so to feed upon him, that he may be one with us, and we one with him; that he may live in us, and we in him, and to him who hath loved us, and given himself for us.'

[29]'All which he is to endeavour to perform with suitable affections, answerable to such an holy action, and to stir up the like in the people.'

[30]'The elements being now sanctified by the word and prayer, the minister, being at the table, is to take the bread in his hand, and say, in these expressions, (or other the like, used by Christ or his apostle upon this occasion:) 'According to the holy institution, command, and example of our blessed Saviour Jesus Christ, I take this bread, and, having given thanks, break it, and give it unto you; (there the minister, who is also himself to communicate, is to break the bread, and give it to the communicants;) *Take ye, eat ye; this is the body of Christ which is broken for you: do this in remembrance of him."* 'In like manner the minister is to take the cup, and say, in these expressions, (or other the like, used by Christ or the apostle upon the same occasion:) 'According to the institution, command, and example of our Lord Jesus Christ, I take this cup, and give it unto you; (here he giveth it to the communicants;) *This cup is the new testament in the blood of Christ, which is shed for the remission of the sins of many: drink ye all of it.'* 'After all have communicated, the minister may, in a few words, put them in mind, "Of the grace of God in Jesus Christ, held forth in this sacrament; and exhort them to walk worthy of it."'

[31]'The minister is to give solemn thanks to God, 'For his rich mercy, and invaluable goodness, vouchsafed to them in that sacrament; and to entreat for pardon for the defects of the whole service, and for the gracious assistance of his good Spirit, whereby they may be enabled to walk in the strength of that grace, as becometh those who have received so great pledges of salvation.'

[32]'The collection for the poor is so to be ordered, that no part of the publick worship be thereby hindered.'

[33]James Durham (1764, rpt. 2002), *The Unsearchable Riches of Christ*, Soli Deo Gloria.

[34]Durham, p.5.

[35]Durham, p. 341.

[36]Durham, pp. 27-28.

[37]Durham, pp. 28-29.

[38]Durham, pp. 29-31.

[39]Durham, pp. 31-32.

[40]Durham, p. 275.

[41]Durham, p. 280.

[42]Durham, pp. 281-82.

[43]Durham, pp. 338-39.

[44]Durham, p. 356.

[45]Thomas Boston, 'The Nature of the Lord's Supper,' *Collected Works of Thomas Boston* (1853), Vol. II, William Tegg, pp. 481-88.

[46]Boston, 'The Nature of the Lord's Supper,' p. 483.

[47]Boston, pp. 183-84.

[48]Boston, p. 485.

[49]Boston, pp. 485-86.

[50]Boston, p. 486.

[51]Boston, p. 487.

[52]Boston, 'Of the Worthy Receiving of the Lord's Supper,' *Works*(1853), Vol. II, pp. 489-97.

[53] *The Practical Works of John Willison* (1844), Blackie and Son.

[54] The Directory was first published in 1716 and an enlarged edition was published in 1726.

[55]Willison, pp. 127-33.

[56]Willison, pp. 154-200

[57]Willison, pp. 200-28.

[58]Willison, pp. 229-41.

[59]Willison, 'A Sacramental Catechism,' *Works*, pp. 467-72

[60]Willison, p. 473

[61]Although Hill was a Moderate in ecclesiastical outlook, his *Lectures in Divinity* was the textbook of Thomas Chalmers, the leader of the Evangelicals, when he taught in New College after the Disruption (H.R. Sefton, 'George Hill', *Dictionary of Scottish Church History and Theology*, IVP, 408).

[62]George Hill (1825), *Lectures in Divinity*, Vol. 3, Waugh and

Innes, pp. 331-32

[63]Hill, p. 341.

[64]Hill, p. 341.

[65]Hill, p. 344.

[66]John Brown, p. 56.

[67]John Brown, pp. 56-64.

[68]John Brown, p. 66.

[69]John Brown, p. 69.

[70]John Brown, pp. 74-88.

[71]Archibald Alexander of Princeton commended it as the best systematics in English (*Dictionary of Scottish Church History and Theology*, p. 242).

[72]John Dick (1834), *Lectures in Theology*, Volume 4, William Oliphant, p. 187.

[73]Dick, pp. 184-202.

[74]Dick, pp. 203-13.

[75]Dick, pp. 213-16.

[76]Dick, pp. 216-29. He comments that Bucer's explanation of the presence of Christ as being 'not naturally, and after the manner of this world' would also have been said by both 'Papists and Lutherans'.

[77]Dick, pp. 220-21.

[78]Dick quotes from the *Confession of Faith of the Reformed Churches in France*, which affirms: 'We confess that, in the Holy Supper, Jesus Christ feeds and nourishes us truly with his flesh and blood, that we may be one with him, and that his life may be communicated to us. For, although he is in heaven till he come to judge the world, yet we believe that, by the secret and incomprehensible virtue of his Spirit, he nourishes and quickens us with the substance of his body and blood. We hold that this is done spiritually, not to put imaginations and thoughts in the place of the effect and the truth, but inasmuch as this mystery surmounts, by its height, the measure of our senses, and the whole order of nature' (Dick, p. 224).

[79]Dick, pp. 224-40.

[80]Daniel Dewar was a Haldane preacher who became a Church

of Scotland minister. Later he became Principal of Marischal College in Aberdeen (1832) and Professor of Church History (1833). He remained in the Church of Scotland at the Disruption (*Dictionary of Scottish Church History and Theology*, p. 240).

[81]Daniel Dewar (1866), *Elements of Systematic Divinity*, 3 volumes, Thomas Murray.

[82]Dewar, pp. 306-7.

[83]Dewar, p. 308.

[84]William Cunningham (1862), *The Reformers and the Theology of the Reformation*, T and T Clark, p. 230.

[85]Cunningham, p. 240.

[86]Cunningham, pp. 235-36.

[87]Cunningham, p. 254.

[88]Cunningham, p. 256.

[89]Cunningham, p. 259.

[90]Cunningham approves of the decision of the Westminster Assembly not to regard the Lord's Supper as a converting ordinance (p. 267).

[91]Cunningham, p. 263.

[92]Cunningham, pp. 273ff.

[93]Mathison, p. 105, notes a similar development in English Puritanism at that time, and this may indicate that the development was widespread among Calvinists.

7. The Lord's Supper in the Scottish Highlands

[1]In this chapter I will give an historical survey of the growth and subsequent decline of the communion season in the Highlands. Because of length, I will leave discussing various features of the Highland communion season until the next chapter.

[2]James E. Kirk, 'The Kirk and the Highlands at the Reformation,' in *Patterns of Reform*, p. 305.

[3]Kirk, p. 305.

[4]Ian B. Cowan (1982), *The Scottish Reformation*, Weidenfeld and Nicolson, p. 169.

[5]Kirk, p. 333.

[6]Kirk, pp. 332-33.

[7]Kirk, 'The Jacobean Church in the Highlands,' in *Patterns of Reform*, pp. 477-78. Kirk mentions that in 1623 the Synod of Moray insisted that any non-communicants should be given adequate warning, in the presence of two witnesses, twenty days before the next celebration. In 1627, it was noted that the minister in Kingussie had failed to have a communion that year and he was told to notify his people of the date of the next celebration.

[8]Douglas Andsell (1998), *The People of the Great Faith*, Acair, pp. 9, 27.

[9]Burnet, *The Holy Communion in the Reformed Church of Scotland*, pp. 124-25. John Mackay records that 'the Sacrament of the Supper was seldom administered in Highland country parishes under the Episcopal regime. The necessary vessels and linen cloths were often lacking, and when needed had to be borrowed. In the parish of Loch Broom, the Lord's Supper was only administered once in seven years; at Fodderty, once in twelve; and at Glenurquhart not once in twenty-four' (John Mackay [1914], *The Church in the Highlands*, Hodder and Stoughton, p. 151).

[10]William Ferguson, 'The Problems of the Established Church in the West Highlands and Islands in the Eighteenth Century,' in *Records of the Scottish Church History Society*, Vol. 17, p. 16.

[11]Donald Maclean, 'Presbytery of Ross and Sutherland,' in *Records of the Scottish Church History Society*, Vol. 5, pp. 251-61.

[12]John Kennedy (rpt. 1927), *The Days of the Fathers in Ross-shire*, Northern Chronicle, p. 11.

[13]Ibid., pp. 1-12

[14]M. Macdonald (1892), *The Covenanters in Moray and Ross*, Melven Brothers, p. 91

[15]M. Macdonald, *The Covenanters in Moray and Ross*, pp. 100-11.

[16]John Kennedy (rpt. 1979), *The Days of the Fathers in Ross-shire*, Christian Focus, p. 37.

[17]Cited in 'The Religion of the Highlands,' *The Original Secession Magazine*, Vol. XVIII, p. 539.

[18]J. Douglas MacMillan (1997), *The God of All Grace*, Christian Focus, pp. 305-6.

[19]MacInnes, p. 99.

[20]MacInnes, p. 99.

[21]Donald Sage (rpt. 1899), *Parish Life in the North of Scotland*, John Menzies, p. 97.

[22]Sage, p. 98.

[23]John Macleod (1979), *Bypaths of Highland Church History*, Knox Press, p. 82.

[24]Kennedy, 'The Minister of Killearnan', *The Days of the Fathers in Ross-shire*, Christian Focus, pp. 185-86. Kennedy also relates how the opposition of an elder, Simon Bisset, to the introduction of private communions was overcome by the spiritual blessing he and others received during the service. 'The Sabbath service over, honest Simon could not rest till he had confessed his fault to the minister. Coming to the manse, he requested an interview, during which he confessed, with tears, how greatly he had erred in opposing the private communion, acknowledged how his soul had been feasted during the day, and declared his resolution never to oppose what the Lord had so manifestly blessed' (pp. 161-62).

[25]Kennedy (1979), *The Days of the Fathers in Ross-shire*, Christian Focus, p. 183.

[26]Dr. John Macdonald of Ferintosh, north of Inverness, was a prominent Highland preacher and evangelist. A biography, entitled *The Apostle of the North*, was written about him by Dr. John Kenendy of Dingwall. Aspects of Macdonald's ministry will be discussed in the following chapter.

[27]Murdoch Campbell (1989), *Gleanings of Highland Harvest*, Christian Focus, pp. 11-12.

[28]Campbell, pp. 13-14.

[29]'John M'Rae,' *Disruption Worthies of the Northern Highlands*, John Grant, 1866, pp. 117-18.

[30]'Peter M'Bride,' *Disruption Worthies of the Northern Highlands*, John Grant, 1866, p. 163.

[31]Kennedy, *Days of the Fathers in Ross-shire*, Christian Focus, pp. 100-01.

[32]*Memorials of the Life and Ministry of Charles Calder Macintosh* (1870), Edmonston and Douglas, pp. 24-25.

[33]J. Douglas MacMillan, *The God of All Grace*, Christian Focus, pp. 315-16.

[34]MacMillan, p. 317.

8. Features of Highland Communion Seasons

[1]Donald Macleod (1998), 'The Highland Churches Today,' in James Kirk (ed), *The Church in the Highlands*, The Scottish Church History Society, 1998, p. 161.

[2]Macleod, p. 163.

[3]The Act states: 'That because the communicants in each Presbytery in our bounds are by the blessing of God become so numerous that their meeting all in one Parish to partake in the Sacrament of the Lord's Supper is attended with several inconveniences, particularly that the communicants are often straightened for want of room in the churches, and that the work is rendered tedious, therefore, the Synod should appoint that, at least in the Presbyteries of Caithness and Dornoch where a sufficient number of assistants can be got, the foresaid ordinance shall for hereafter be as often as may be administered in two parishes on the same Lord's Day' (Somerset, *The Free Presbyterian Magazine*, Vol. 109, No. 1, pp. 16-17).

[4] 'Communion Days in Creich,' *Monthly Record of the Free Church of Scotland*, December, 1927.

[5] 'Alexander Macdonald,' *Disruption Worthies of the Northern Highlands*, John Grant, 1866, p. 120.

[6] George B. Burnet (1960), *The Holy Communion in the Reformed Church of Scotland 1560-1960*, p. 224.

[7]'Alexander Macleod,' *Disruption Worthies of the Northern Highlands*, John Grant, 1866, p. 228.

[8]Macrae, *The Life of Gustavus Aird*, p. 139.

[9] J. P. MacQueen, 'The Friday Fellowship Meeting,' *Free Presbyterian Magazine*, Vol. 63, pp. 304-5.

[10] David Stephenson, Conventicles in the Kirk, 1619-37, *Scottish Church History Records*, Vol. VIII, Part 2, p. 107.

[11]Murdo Macaulay, *Aspects of the Religious History of Lewis*, Eccles.

[12]This was the same Act that expressed concern about the large

crowds that attended communion seasons in the area. Concerning the Friday Fellowship meeting it said: 'As also, that because the meetings ordinarily kept on Fridays before the administration of the Sacrament are often inconvenient to the ministers who join in the ministration by diverting them from what they should be principally employed about, and to the communicants in insomuch as their coming from their apartments and attending these meetings takes up a good part of that day, which ought to be rather spent as much as may be in meditation and other private devotions, and that the main design of these meetings may be obtained without those inconveniencies by the people's communicating their cases of conscience to their ministers at home. Therefore, that the Synod appoint that these meetings on Friday before the Sacrament to be forborne for the future in all the bounds of this Synod; and appoint the ministers before they come from home to assist at that ordinance to give the communicants of their respective parishes opportunities of consulting them about such questions of cases of conscience relative to that work as may happen to be straitening to them. But that these conferences be as private as may be' (cited by Somerset, p. 17).

[13]John Macleod, *Bypaths of Highland Church History*, Knox Press, 1965, p. 79.

[14]Gustavus Aird, minister of Creich Free Church for most of the second half of the nineteenth century, recorded the following details in a letter: 'As to the origin of the Monday monthly meeting and then of the Communion Friday meeting, I really am not sure. I thought, from a paragraph in Mr. Stevenson's Life of Mr. Hog of Kiltearn, that I saw there the origin of the monthly question meeting, and that it originated in a revival of true religion, and that where true religion manifested itself in other parishes that the minister set on foot the question meeting, just as Mr. Hog did in Kiltearn. Then during the time of the [Covenanting] persecution, such as would not hear the curates assembled in meetings on the Sabbath, and this was to some extent the case until the Revolution. Then, after the Revolution, as Presbyterian ministers were got and settled, this practice was followed on Mondays once a month. It was some thirty to

forty years after the Revolution ere Presbyterian ministers were got over the whole of Ross and Sutherland. Then a revival took place to a considerable extent along the coast of Sutherland and the Reay country, and most part of the Synod of Ross, and then, I suppose, the question meeting on the Communion Fridays was set on foot' (Macrae, *Aird,* pp. 143-44).

[15]Macrae, *Aird*, p. 144.

[16]Macrae, *Aird*, p. 145.

[17]He must mean in addition to Sutherland and Caithness, for he had explained the practice in these counties.

[18]Macrae, *Aird*, p. 146.

[19]Alexander Macdonald, *Disruption Worthies of the Northern Highlands,* John Grant, 1866, p. 110.

[20]J. P. MacQueen, 'The Friday Fellowship Meeting,' *The Free Presbyterian Magazine*, Vol. 63, pp. 304-5.

[21]Kennedy, *The Days of the Fathers in Ross-shire*, Christian Focus, p. 83

[22]Auld, p. 261.

[23]Auld, pp. 261-62.

[24]Auld, pp. 253-65.

[25]John Kennedy, 'The Duty of Self-examination,' *Sermons*, pp. 119-29

[26]William Forbes (1767-1838). A volume of his sermons was published, edited initially by John Kennedy of Dingwall and completed after Kennedy's death by Malcolm MacGregor, Free Church minister of Ferintosh, called *Communion and other Sermons*, Gemmill, 1887. 'His services were very much sought after to assist at Communion seasons in all the parishes around' (xi-xii).

[27]Action sermons were the sermons delivered immediately before the Lord's Supper was celebrated. These sermons were usually focused on aspects of the person and work of Christ and were designed to help communicants participate in the Supper.

[28]William Forbes, 'Love to an Unseen Saviour,' *Communion and other Sermons*, pp. 170-71.

[29]Forbes, 'The Lord's Supper,' in *Communion and other Sermons*, pp. 46-61.

[30]*Memorials of Charles Calder Macintosh* (1870), Edmonston and Douglas, p. 297.

[31]*MacIntosh*, p. 297.

[32]*MacIntosh*, pp. 301-03.

[33]*MacIntosh*, pp. 370-84.

[34]Alexander Auld, *The Life of John Kennedy*, pp. 270-71.

[35]Auld, pp. 272-73.

[36]Auld, p. 274.

[37]Auld, p. 278.

[38]Auld, pp. 280-91

[39]John Kennedy, 'A Wondrous, Real and Gladsome Meeting,' *Sermons*, 1884, pp. 251-62.

[40] William McDougall, *Memorial Sermons*, Melven Brothers, 1897.

[41]'The whole space containing tables and forms was railed off by a kind of paling or "travess" resembling a sheep pen "for holding furth of ye non-communicants." But the travess was made low enough for the observers to witness the celebration. Sometimes the floor of the enclosed area was strewn with rushes, for many were earthen. In the Edinburgh Dean of Guilds accounts for 1561-2 there is an entry of payment for "4 warkmen at ye helpin oupe of ye said travess" ' (George B. Burnet (1960), *The Holy Communion in the Reformed Church of Scotland 1560-1960*, p. 27).

[42]Burnet, p. 39.

[43]Burnet, p. 130.

[44]Burnet, p. 130.

[45]William McDougall (1897), *Memorial Sermons*, Melven Brothers, pp. 239-41.

[46]McDougall, pp. 242-44.

[47]McDougall, pp. 245-47.

[48]McDougall, pp. 248-49.

[49]*Memoirs of Thomas Hog*, published by the General Assembly of the Free Church of Scotland, 1846, p.95.

[50]Hog, p. 96.

[51]Alexander Macleod,' *Disruption Worthies of the Northern Highlands*, John Grant, 1866, p. 222.

[52]'Alexander Macleod,' *Disruption Worthies of the Northern Highlands*, John Grant, 1866, p. 223.

[53]Macleod recorded in his diary on June 25th, 1827: 'Yesterday the Sacrament of the Lord's Supper was administered in this place, and much of the presence of the Lord appeared in the congregation. There were from 800 to 1000 communicants formerly in the parish, there being a habit of indiscriminate communion. This is the first occasion we had the communion here in my time, and only six individuals have come forward to the Lord's Table. There were no more than twenty communicants in all. The whole of the unworthy communicants kept back, and a great many of our young converts did not take upon them to come forward. The congregation was much impressed through the whole day....' (Donald Beaton [1925], *Memoirs and Sermons of the Rev. Alexander Macleod*, pp. 8-9).

[54]J. Douglas MacMillan, 'Evangelical Religion in the Scottish Highlands,' *The God of All Grace*, 1997, pp. 317-18.

[55]Donald Meek, 'Gaelic Bible, Revival and Mission,' in James Kirk (ed), *The Church in the Highlands*, The Scottish Church History Society, 1998.

[56]Meek, p. 123.

[57]Cited in John Mackay (1914), *The Church in the Highlands*, Hodder and Stoughton, p. 187.

[58]'John Macdonald,' *Disruption Worthies of the Northern Highlands*, John Grant, 1866, pp. 23-24.

[59]Meek, pp. 124-25.

[60]'Alexander Macleod,' *Disruption Worthies of the Northern Highlands*, John Grant, 1866, p. 228.

[61]Sinclair Ferguson, 'The Assurance of Salvation,' *Banner of Truth Magazine*, March 1979, p. 4.

[62]The Moody missions were the background to the disagreement between Kennedy and Lowland ministers such as Horatius Bonar over the emphases the missions brought into Scottish Calvinistic experience.

[63]Kennedy, p. 104.

[64]Kennedy, p. 104.

[65]Kennedy, p. 104.

[66]Kennedy, p. 105.

[67]A.T.B. MacGowan (1993), 'Assurance,' *Dictionary of Scottish Church History and Theology*, IVP, p. 38.

[68]Sinclair Ferguson (1996), *The Holy Spirit*, IVP, 184-86.

[69]The discussion by William Cunningham (1862, rpt. 1967), 'The Reformers and the Doctrine of Assurance,' *The Reformers and the Reformation*, Banner of Truth, pp. 111-48.

[70]John Calvin, *The Calvin Collection*, CD Rom, The Ages Digital Library Series.

[71]William Cunningham, p. 113.

[72]William Cunningham, p. 114.

[73]In 1893, the Free Presbyterian Church of Scotland was formed by ministers and elders who left the Free Church of Scotland. In 1900, the majority of the Free Church of Scotland united with the United Presbyterian Church of Scotland to form the United Free Church of Scotland. The minority of the Free Church who did not enter this union continued as the Free Church of Scotland. Both the Free Presbyterian Church and the minority Free Church claim to follow the opinions of Kennedy.

[74]Callum Brown (1987), *The Social History of Religion in Scotland Since 1750*, Methuen and Co. Ltd. pp. 78-79. The decline was more obvious in Inverness, the main town in the Highlands, during the latter part of the nineteenth century, with 80% of the population attending church in 1851 but only 20% in 1881 (Brown, pp. 82-83). Brown points out that the 1851 figure is a combination of attendance at morning, afternoon and evening services, which means that it is likely that many attendees were counted at least twice. The figure for 1881 is probably the number attending the morning service. 35.4% of the population attended the morning service in 1851, so if the comparison is between the two morning attendance, there was a decrease of almost 50% in thirty years..

It is possible that the decrease in attendance was caused by individuals from Inverness worshipping in country congregations around the town, of which there were many. They could have done this in order to listen to particular ministers. It is not that there were no rural churches prior to 1851; but by the 1880s travel to them was much easier.

One factor in the reduction of numbers attending communion seasons was rural depopulation ('Communion Days in Creich,' *Monthly Record of the Free Church of Scotland*, December, 1927, p.292.).[76] This was due in the main to two factors: people moving to urban communities in the south and forced emigration to foreign lands. Concerning the connection between the spiritual life of Ross-shire and the appearance of forced evictions, John Kennedy commented:

> It is worthy of remark that it was at the climax of its spiritual prosperity [1780s] the cruel work of eviction began to lay waste the hill-sides and plains of the north. Swayed by the example of the godly among them, and away from the influences by which less sequestered localities were corrupted, the body of the people in the Highlands became distinguished as the most peaceable and virtuous peasantry in Britain. It was just then that they began to be driven off by ungodly oppressors, to clear their native soil for strangers, red deer, and sheep. With few exceptions, the owners of the soil began to act as if they were also owners of the people, and, disposed to regard them as the vilest part of their estate, they treated them without respect to the requirements of righteousness or to the dictates of mercy. Without the inducement of gain, in the very recklessness of cruelty, families by hundreds were driven across the sea, or were gathered, as the sweepings of the hill-sides, into wretched hamlets on the shore (John Kennedy [rpt. 1927], *The Days of the Fathers in Ross-shire*, pp. 17-18).

The population of the Highlands continued to rise until 1851; since then it has reduced in most places (Eric Richards [2000], *The Highland Clearances*, Edinburgh: Birlinn, p. 313). Available statistics bear this out. In 1801, 233,694 out of a national population of 1,608,420 lived in the Highlands, that is 14.5%; in 1841 [its peak] the figure was 298,637 out of 2,620,184, that is 11.4%; in 1891 the figure was 264,026 out of 4,025,647, that is

6.6%. Over a century in which the standards of living rose and which Scotland as a whole had a population increase of almost 2,500,000, the Highland population increased by under 31,000 (Statistics from Charles W. J. Withers [1998], *Urban Highlanders*, Tuckwell Press, p. 26). What the statistics do not reveal is two main factors in the depopulation of the Highlands. One is emigration to foreign countries and the other is migration to the cities of southern Scotland and England.

[75]Callum Brown, pp. 211-12.

[76]Seventy-two Highland ministers joined the Free Church and seventy-nine remained in the Church of Scotland. It was different with the people, with a clear majority opting for the Free Church (Andsell, pp. 62-65).

[77]The Free Presbyterian leader, Donald MacFarlane, estimated that 20,000 people joined the new denomination. The official Free Church figure, given four years later, was 6,756 (James Lachlan Macleod, *The Second Disruption*, Tuckwell Press, 2000, p. 234).

[78]Another two denominations, both relatively small, appeared as the century drew to a close, mainly in the Highlands: one was the Associated Presbyterian Churches who seceded from the Free Presbyterian Church in 1989; the other was the Free Church (Continuing) who left the Free Church in 2000.

[79]For example: Norman Macleod (nd), *Lewis Revivals of the 20th Century*, Hebridean Press Service; Murdo Macaulay (1984), *The Burning Bush in Carloway*, Carloway Free Church; Duncan Campbell (1954), *The Lewis Awakening 1949-1953*, The Faith Mission; Colin and Mary Peckham (2004), *Sounds From Heaven*, Christian Focus.

9. The Lord's Supper and Liturgy

[1]David L. Larsen (1991), *Caring for the Flock*, Crossway, p. 70.

[2]Leonard J. Vander Zee (2004), *Christ, Baptism, and the Lord's Supper*, IVP, p. 188.

[3]For example, Robert Anderson, an American pastor, writes: 'For me, the timing of a Communion service is important. For instance, I do not like to see Communion tacked on to the morning service. When that happens, there is little time for meditation

on the meaning of the Lord's Supper. The observance becomes a race with the clock' (Robert C. Anderson, [1985], *The Effective Pastor*, Moody Press, p. 216).

[4]Examples of liturgies followed by Zwingli, Bucer, Calvin, Knox, Cranmer and the Puritans are found in Bard Thompson (1961), *Liturgies of the Western Church*, Fortress.

[5]George W. Dollar, 'The Lord's Supper in the Early Church—Part I: The Lord's Supper in the Second Century,' *Bibliotheca Sacra*, 117:466, April 1960, p. 144.

[6]Robert Shaw (rpt. 1998), *Exposition of the Confession of Faith*, Christian Focus, pp. 355-56.

[7]Robert L. Dabney (1878, rpt. 1985), *Systematic Theology*, Banner of Truth, p. 802.

[8]Donald Macleod (1998), *A Faith To Live By*, Christian Focus, p. 241.

[9]Simon Kistemaker (1993), *1 Corinthians*, Baker Books, p. 342.

[10]Macleod, *A Faith To Live By*, p. 243.

[11]Robert Letham (2001), *The Lord's Supper*, Presbyterian and Reformed, p. 52.

[12]The ritual was also mentioned by the Puritans. For example, Matthew Henry, in his comments on John 17:1, where Jesus lifted up his eyes to heaven, says: 'The outward expression of fervent desire which he used in this prayer: He *lifted up his eyes to heaven*, as before (John 11:41); not that Christ needed thus to engage his own attention, but he was pleased thus to sanctify this gesture to those that use it, and justify it against those that ridicule it. It is significant of the lifting up of the soul to God in prayer, Ps. 25:1. *Sursum corda* was anciently used as a call to prayer, *Up with your hearts*, up to heaven; thither we must direct our desires in prayer, and thence we must expect to receive the good things we pray for.' John Flavel, in commenting on the incident between the risen Christ and Mary Magdalene in John 20, says, 'Christians, you ascended with him, virtually, when he ascended; you shall ascend to him, personally, hereafter; Oh that you would ascend to him, spiritually, in acts of faith, love, and desires daily. *Sursum corda*, up with your hearts, was the form used by the ancient church at the

sacrament. How good were it, if we could say with the apostle, Philippians 3:20. "Our conversation is in heaven, from whence we look for the Savior." An heart ascendant, is the best evidence of your interest in Christ's ascension' (Flavel, *The Fountain of Life* (Discourse 40), www.housechurch.org).

[13]John Calvin (rpt. 2002), *Treatises on the Sacraments*, Christian Focus, 121-22.

[14]'And for no other reason was it formerly the custom, previous to consecration, to call aloud upon the people to raise their hearts, *sursum corda*. Scripture itself, also, besides carefully narrating the ascension of Christ, by which he withdrew his bodily presence from our eye and company, that it might make us abandon all carnal thoughts of him, whenever it makes mention of him, enjoins us to raise our minds upwards and seek him in heaven, seated at the right hand of the Father (Colossians 3:2). According to this rule, we should rather have adored him spiritually in the heavenly glory, than devised that perilous species of adoration replete with gross and carnal ideas of God. Those, therefore, who devised the adoration of the sacrament, not only dreamed it of themselves, without any authority from Scripture, where no mention of it can be shown (it would not have been omitted, had it been agreeable to God); but, disregarding Scripture, forsook the living God, and fabricated a God for themselves after the lust of their own hearts...' (*Institutes* 4.17.36).

[15]Timothy J. Keller (2002), 'Reformed Worship in the Global City,' in *Worship by the Book* (ed. D.A. Carson), Zondervan, p. 234

[16]Keller, p. 249.

10. The Lord's Supper and the Role of the Holy Spirit

[1]George Smeaton (1882, rpt, 1958), *The Holy Spirit*, Banner of Truth, p. 237.

[2]Smeaton, *The Holy Spirit*, p. 238.

[3]Smeaton, *The Holy Spirit*, p. 239. He regarded Zwinglianism as one of two alternative concepts that vitiated this understanding of worship, the other being Ritualism (pp. 239-41).

[4]Sinclair B. Ferguson (1996), *The Holy Spirit*, IVP, p. 204.

[5]John Yates (1991), 'Role of the Holy Spirit in the Lord's Supper,' *Churchman*, Vol. 105, No. 4.

[6]The two distinctions of temporal and personal, and their various aspects, are taken from David G. Kibble (1980), 'The Reformation and the Eucharist,' *Churchman*, Vol. 94, No. 1.

[7]Kibble, p. 49.

[8]Kibble, p. 50.

11. The Lord's Supper and Children

[1]Keidal mentions that the first known witness to the practice is Cyprian in 251. Augustine of Hippo referred to the practice, and it was approved by the Council of Macon in 585 and the Council of Toledo in 675 (Keidel [1975], 'Is the Lord's Supper for Children?' *Westminster Theological Journal*, Vol. 37, No. 3, p. 303).

[2]Keidal, p. 303.

[3]Keidal, pp. 309-17.

[4]E.g., Deuteronomy 16:11, 14.

[5]Roger T. Beckwith (1976), 'The Age of Admission to the Lord's Supper,' *Westminster Theological Journal*, Vol. 38, No. 2, pp. 130-31.

[6]'The ancients fell into a gross error by supposing that little children were deprived of eternal *life*, if they did not dispense to them the eucharist, that is, the Lord's Supper; for this discourse does not relate to the Lord's Supper, but to the uninterrupted communication *of the flesh of Chris*t, which we obtain apart from the use of the Lord's Supper. Nor were the Bohemians in the right, when they adduced this passage to prove that all without exception ought to be admitted to the use of the cup. With respect to young children, the ordinance of Christ forbids them to partake of the Lord's Supper; because they are not yet able to know or to celebrate the remembrance of the death of Christ. The same ordinance makes *the cup* common to all, for it commands us *all to drink of it* (Matthew 26:27)' (John Calvin, Comments on John 6:53, *John Calvin Collection*, Ages Digital Library Series [CD Rom]).

12. Pastoral Preparation for the Lord's Supper

[1]John Carstairs, 'The Epistle Dedicatory,' in James Durham, *The*

Unsearchable Riches of Christ (1764, rpt. 2000), Soli Deo Gloria.

[2] Cited by Michael Fabarez (2002), *Preaching that Changes Lives*, Thomas Nelson, p. 70.

[3] John Piper (1990), *The Supremacy of God in Preaching*, Baker Books, p. 60.

[4] Derek Prime (1989, rpt. 1995), *Pastors and Teachers*, Highland, p. 54.

[5] Prime, p. 53.

[6] Piper, pp. 60-61.

[7] Errol Hulse (1986), 'The Preacher and Piety', *Preaching* (ed. S. T. Logan Jr.), Evangelical Press, p. 76.

[8] John R. W. Stott (1961), *The Preacher's Portrait*, The Tyndale Press, p. 92.

[9] D. A. Carson (1984), *Exegetical Fallacies*, Baker Book House, pp. 27-28. Carson traces the translation 'under rower' to scholars who assumed that *hupēretēs* was derived from the verb *eressō* (to row), which combined with *hupo*, gave the idea of a lowly servant.

[10] Stott, pp. 94-97.

[11] Stott, p.107.

[12] Stott, p. 15.

[13] Stott, p. 15.

[14] Donald Macleod (1998), *A Faith to Live By*, p. 240.

[15] John C. Lambert (1903), *The Sacraments in the New Testament*, T. & T. Clark, pp. 7-8.

13. Personal Preparation for the Supper

[1] John Brown (1853), *Discourses Suited to the Administration of the Lord's Supper*, William Oliphant and Sons, pp. 37-39.

[2] Brown, pp. 40-42.

[3] Cited by Jon D. Payne in 'John Owen (1616-1683) and The Sacraments,' unpublished dissertation, New College, 2002. The quotation is from Richard Vines, *A Treatise of the Institution, Right Administration, and Receiving of the Sacrament of the Lords-Supper*, (London, 1660), p. 305.

[4] 'A Treatise on the Lord's Supper,' in *Henry Smith's Sermons*,

Vol. 1, James Nichol, 1866, p. 82.

[5]William Cunningham, *The Reformers and the Theology of the Reformation*, Banner of Truth, p. 229.

Conclusion

[1]Witherington notes that 'both baptism and the Lord's Supper are seen as establishing or reaffirming an exclusive unity and relationship that precludes other ones' (*Paul's Narrative Thought World*, Westminster, 1994, p. 306).

[2]Robert Webber, *Ancient–Future Faith*, Baker Books, 1999, pp. 100-01, 110-12, 134.

[3]Alan Richardson (1958), *An Introduction to the Theology of the New Testament*, SCM Press, p. 373.

[4]Donald Macleod, 'The Lord's Supper as a Means of Grace,' *Banner of Truth Magazine* (no. 64), pp. 21-22.

[5]Donald Macleod, 'The Lord's Supper as a Means of Grace,' p. 18.

[6]John Calvin, *Institutes*, 4.18.44.

[7]John D. Nicholls, 'The Lord's Supper in Christian Experience,' *Banner of Truth Magazine* (no. 232), p. 27.

Bibliography

Robert M. Adamson (1905), *The Christian Doctrine of the Lord's Supper*, T. & T. Clark.

Paul Althaus (1966), *The Theology of Martin Luther*, Fortress Press.

Hugh Anderson (1976), *Commentary on Mark*, New Century Bible, Oliphants.

Robert C. Anderson, [1985], *The Effective Pastor*, Moody Press.

Douglas Ansdell (1998), *The People of the Great Faith*, Acair.

Alexander Auld (1887), *The Life of John Kennedy*, Thomas Nelson.

D. Douglas Bannerman (1889), *Fast Days and Christian Festivals*, Andrew Elliot.

Alexander Barclay (1927), *The Protestant Doctrine of the Lord's Supper*, James Wylie.

Paul Barnett (2000), *1 Corinthians*, Christian Focus Publications.

Donald Beaton [1925], *Memoirs and Sermons of the Rev. Alexander Macleod*.

Roger T. Beckwith (1976), 'The Age of Admission to the Lord's Supper,' *Westminster Theological Journal*, Vol. 38, No. 2.

Craig Blomberg (1994), *1 Corinthians*, NIV Application Commentary, Zondervan.

Thomas Boston, 'Of the Worthy Receiving of the Lord's Supper,' *Collected Works of Thomas Boston* (1853), Vol. II, William Tegg.

Thomas Boston, 'The Nature of the Lord's Supper,' *Collected Works of Thomas Boston* (1853), Vol. II, William Tegg.

Geoffrey W. Bromiley (1953), *Zwingli and Bullinger*, The Westminster Press.

Callum Brown (1987), *The Social History of Religion in Scotland Since 1750*, Methuen and Co. Ltd.

John Brown (1816, rpt. 1853), *Discourses Suited to the Administration of the Lord's Supper*, William Oliphant and Sons.

F. F. Bruce (1988), *The Book of the Acts*, Eerdmans.

Robert Bruce (1958, trs by Thomas F. Torrance), *The Mystery of the Lord's Supper*, James Clarke & Co.

George B. Burnet (1960), *The Holy Communion in the Reformed Church of Scotland 1560-1960*, Oliver and Boyd Ltd.

John Calvin, *Institutes*, 2. Vols. Beveridge edition, James Clarke.

John Calvin (1849), *Tracts*, Calvin Translation Society, Vol. 2.

John Calvin, *John Calvin Collection*, Ages Digital Library Series.

James K. Cameron (1972), *The First Book of Discipline*, Saint Andrew Press.

Nigel M. de S. Cameron (1993), *Dictionary of Scottish Church History and Theology*, IVP.

Murdoch Campbell (rpt. 1989), *Gleanings of Highland Harvest*, Christian Focus Publications.

D. A. Carson (1984), *Exegetical Fallacies*, Baker Book House.

D. A. Carson (1984), 'Matthew,' *The Expositor's Bible Commentary*, Zondervan.

R. Scott Clark (1994), 'The Means of Grace: The Lord's Supper,' in John Armstrong (ed), *The Compromised Church*, Crossway Books.

Ian B. Cowan (1982), *The Scottish Reformation*, Weidenfeld and Nicolson.

Derek Moore Crispi (1975), 'The Real Absence: Ulrich Zwingli's View,' *Union and Communion*, Westminster Conference Report.

Daniel Dewer (1866), *Elements of Systematic Divinity*, 3 volumes, Thomas Murray.

John Dick (1834), *Lectures in Theology*, Volume 4, William Oliphant.

George W. Dollar, 'The Lord's Supper in the Early Church—Part I: The Lord's Supper in the Second Century,' *Bibliotheca Sacra*, 117:466, April 1960.

William Cunningham (1862), *The Reformers and the Theology of the Reformation*, T and T Clark.

'Communion Days in Creich,' *Monthly Record of the Free Church of Scotland*, December, 1927.

Robert L. Dabney (1871, rpt. 1985), *Systematic Theology*, Banner of Truth Trust.

Disruption Worthies of the Northern Highlands (1866), John Grant.

James D. G. Dunn (1996), *The Acts of the Apostles*, Epworth Press.

James Durham (1764, rpt. 2002), *The Unsearchable Riches of Christ*, Soli Deo Gloria.

Walter Elwell (1984), *Evangelical Dictionary of Theology*, Marshall Pickering.

Michael Fabarez (2002), *Preaching that Changes Lives*, Thomas Nelson.

Gordon D. Fee (1987), *I Corinthians*, Eerdmans.

William Ferguson, 'The Problems of the Established Church in the

West Highlands and Islands in the Eighteenth Century,' in *Records of the Scottish Church History Society*, Vol. 17.

Sinclair B. Ferguson (1996), *The Holy Spirit*, IVP.

William Forbes (1887), *Communion and other Sermons*, Gemmill.

Walter Roland Foster (1975), *The Church Before the Covenants*, Scottish Academic Press.

R.T. France (1985), *Matthew*, TNTC.

Timothy George (1989), *Theology of the Reformers*, IVP.

Henry Grey Graham (1906), *The Social Life in the Eighteenth Century*, Adam and Charles Black.

Michael Green (1993), *Acts For Today*, Hodder and Stoughton, 1993.

Wayne Grudem (1994), *Systematic Theology*, IVP.

Robert Halley (1851), *The Sacraments*, Vol. 2, Jackson and Walford.

John Hamilton (1992), 'The Chronology of the Crucifixion and the Passover,' *Churchman*, Vol. 106, No. 4.

Everett F. Harrison (1975), *Acts*, Moody Press.

Alexander Henderson, *Sermons, Prayers and Pulpit Addresses* (ed ited by R. Thomson Martin in 1867), John Maclaren.

William Hendrickson (1978), *Gospel of Luke*, Banner of Truth.

George Hill (1825), *Lectures in Divinity*, Vol. 3, Waugh and Innes.

Memoirs of Thomas Hog (1846), published by the General Assembly of the Free Church of Scotland.

Thomas Houston (1878), *The Lord's Supper*, James Gemmel.

Errol Hulse (1992), 'The Passover and Reformation of the Communion Service,' *Reformation Today*, No. 127.

Errol Hulse (1986), 'The Preacher and Piety', in *Preaching* (ed. Samuel T. Logan Jr.), Evangelical Press.

A. Mitchell Hunter, The Celebration of Communion in Scotland Since the Reformation, *Records of the Scottish Church History Society*, 1929, Vol. III.

A. Mitchell Hunter, The Celebration of Communion in Scotland Since the Reformation, *Records of the Scottish Church History Society*, 1932, Vol. IV.

S. Lewis Johnson, Jr. (1997), 'The Last Passover, The First Lord's Supper, and the New Covenant,' *Reformation and Revival Journal*, Vol. 6.

Timothy J. Keller (2002), 'Reformed Worship in the Global City,' in *Worship by the Book* (ed. D.A. Carson, Zondervan.

Christian Keidel (1975), 'Is the Lord's Supper for Children?' *Westminster Theological Journal*, Vol. 37, No. 3.

John Kennedy (rpt. 1927), *The Days of the Fathers in Ross-shire*, Northern Chronicle.

John Kennedy (rpt. 1979), *The Days of the Fathers in Ross-shire*, Christian Focus Publications

Ernest Kevan (1966), *The Lord's Supper*, Evangelical Press.

David G. Kibble (1980), 'The Reformation and the Eucharist,' *Churchman*, Vol. 94, No. 1.

James Kirk (1989), *Patterns of Reform*, T. & T. Clark.

Simon J. Kistemaker (1990), *Exposition of the Acts of the Apostles*, Baker.

Simon J. Kistemaker (1993), *1 Corinthians*, Baker Books.

D. Broughton Knox (1983), *The Lord's Supper from Wycliffe to Cranmer*, The Paternoster Press.

Hans-Joachim Kraus (1993), *Psalms 60–150*, Fortress.

John C. Lambert (1903), *The Sacraments in the New Testament*, Edinburgh, T. & T. Clark.

William L. Lane (1974), *The Gospel of Mark*, NICNT, Eerdmans, p. 507.

William J. Larkin (1995), *Acts*, IVP.

David L. Larsen (1991), *Caring for the Flock*, Crossway.

Robert Letham (2001), *The Lord's Supper*, Presbyterian and Reformed.

Martin Luther, 'Confession Concerning Christ's Supper,' *Luther's Works*, Vol. 37, Fortress Press (1961).

Martin Luther, 'The Babylonian Captivity of the Church,' *Luther's Works*, Vol. 36, Fortress Press (1959).

Martin Luther, 'The Sacrament of the Body and Blood of Christ—Against the Fanatics,' *Luther's Works*, Vol. 36, Fortress Press (1959).

Murdo Macaulay, *Aspects of the Religious History of Lewis*, Eccles.

M. Macdonald (1892), *The Covenanters in Moray and Ross*, Melven Brothers.

William McDougall (1897), *Memorial Sermons*, Melven Brothers.

A. R. MacEwan (1900), *The Erskines*, Famous Scots Series, Oliphant, Anderson and Ferrier.

Memorials of the Life and Ministry of Charles Calder Macintosh (1870), Edmonston and Douglas.

John MacInnes (1951), *The Evangelical Movement in the Highlands of Scotland*, The University Press, Aberdeen.

John Mackay (1914), *The Church in the Highlands*, Hodder and Stoughton

Robert Mackenzie (1918, rpt. 1964), *John Brown of Haddington*, Banner of Truth.

Donald Maclean, 'Presbytery of Ross and Sutherland,' in *Records of the Scottish Church History Society*, Vol. 5.

Donald Macleod (1998), *A Faith to Live By*, Christian Focus.

Donald Macleod, 'Qualifications for Communion,' *Banner of Truth*, No. 65.

Donald Macleod (1998), 'The Highland Churches Today,' in James Kirk (ed), *The Church in the Highlands*, The Scottish Church History Society.

Donald Macleod, 'The Lord's Supper as a Means of Grace,' *Banner of Truth Magazine*, no. 64

James Lachlan Macleod (2000), *The Second Disruption*, Tuckwell Press.

John Macleod, *Bypaths of Highland Church History*, Knox Press.

J. Douglas MacMillan (1997), 'Evangelical Religion in the Scottish Highlands,' in *The God of All Grace*, Christian Focus.

W. MacMillan (1931), *Worship of Scottish Reformed Church 1550-1638*, The Lassodie Press.

John MacPherson (1901), *History of the Church in Scotland*, Alexander Gardner.

J. P. MacQueen, 'The Friday Fellowship Meeting,' *The Free Presbyterian Magazine and Monthly Record*, Vol. LXIII

Alexander Macrae (nd), *The Life of Gustavus Aird, A.M., D.D, Creich*, Stirling.

Thomas M'Crie (1988), *The Story of the Scottish Church*.

I. Howard Marshall (1978), *The Gospel of Luke*, NIGTC; Eerdmans.

I. Howard Marshall (1980, rpt. 1993), *Last Supper and Lord's Supper*, Paternoster Press.

Ralph P. Martin (1964), *Worship in the Early Church*, Eerdmans.

Keith A. Mathison (2002), *Given For You*, Presbyterian and Reformed.

Donald Meek (1998), 'Gaelic Bible, Revival and Mission,' in James Kirk (ed), *The Church in the Highlands*, The Scottish Church History Society.

Eugene Merrill (2002), 'Remembering/Memory and the Theology of Worship,' *Journal of the Evangelical Theological Society*, Vol. 43.

Leon Morris (1974, rpt. 1986), *Luke*, TNTC.

Leon Morris (1971), *The Gospel of John*, NICNT, Marshal, Morgan and Scott.

Steve Motyer (1995), *Remember Jesus*, Christian Focus.

John D. Nicholls, 'The Lord's Supper in Christian Experience,' *Banner of Truth*, No. 232.

Robert Paul (1985), *The Assembly of the Lord*, T. & T. Clark.

Jon D. Payne (2002), 'John Owen (1616-1683) and The Sacraments,' unpublished dissertation, New College.

Colin and Mary Peckham (2004), *Sounds From Heaven*, Christian Focus Publications.

John Piper (1990), *The Supremacy of God in Preaching*, Baker Books.

Select Writings of Huldrych Zwingli (1984), Vol. 2, translated by H. Wayne Pipkin, Pickwick Publications, Pennsylvania, 1984.

Alfred Plummer (1909), *An Exegetical Commentary on the Gospel of Matthew*, Robert Scott.

John Polhil (1999), *Paul and His Letters*, Broadman and Holman.

Richard Pratt (2000), *1 and 2 Corinthians*, Broadman and Holman.

Derek Prime (1989, rpt. 1995), *Pastors and Teachers*, Highland.

Tim Ralston (2002), 'Remember and Worship: the Mandate and Means,' *Reformation and Revival*, Vol. 9.

'The Religion of the Highlands,' *The Original Secession Magazine*, Vol. XVIII.

Robert L. Reymond (1998), *A New Theology of the Christian Faith*, Thomas Nelson.

Eric Richards (2000), *The Highland Clearances*, Birlinn.

Alan Richardson (1958), *An Introduction to the Theology of the New Testament*, SCM Press.

Hermann N. Ridderbos (1997), *The Gospel of John, A Theological Commentary*, Eerdmans.

Donald Sage (1899), *Parish Life in the North of Scotland*, John Menzies.

Leigh Eric Schmidt (1989), *Holy Fairs*, Princeton University Press.

Robert Shaw (1845, rpt. 1998), *Exposition of the Confession of Faith*, Christian Focus.

A. Sinclair (1885), *Reminiscences of the Life and Labours of Duguld Buchanan*, MacLachlan and Stewart.

George Smeaton (1882, rpt, 1958), *The Holy Spirit*, Banner of Truth.

Henry Smith (1866), 'A Treatise on the Lord's Supper,' in *Sermons*, Vol. 1, James Nichol.

Douglas Somerset, 'A History of the Communion Season,' *The Free Presbyterian Magazine*, Vol. 109, No. 1.

G.W. Sprott (1901), *The Book of Common Order of the Church of Scotland*, William Blackwood and Sons.

W. P. Stephens, T*he Theology of Huldrych Zwingli*, Clarendon Press, 1984.

Graham N. Stanton (1989), *The Gospels and Jesus*, Oxford University Press.

David Stephenson, Conventicles in the Kirk, 1619-37, *Scottish Church History Records*, Vol. VIII, Part 2.

Alan Stibbs (1962), *Sacrament, Sacrifice and Eucharist*, The Tyndale Press.

John R. W. Stott (1990), *Acts*, IVP.

John R. W. Stott (1961), *The Preacher's Portrait*, The Tyndale Press.

'The Real Presence of Christ in the Eucharist,' *Catholic Encyclopedia*, www.new advent.org.

Bard Thompson (1961), *Liturgies of the Western Church*, Fortress.

Margo Todd (2002), *The Culture of Protestantism in Early Modern Scotland*, Yale University Press.

Union and Communion, Collections of Papers from the Westminster Conference, 1979.

Leonard J. Vander Zee (2004), *Christ, Baptism, and the Lord's Supper*, IVP.

Richard Vines, 'The Passover,' in *The Puritans on the Lord's Supper* (1997), Soli Deo Gloria Publications.

Ronald Wallace (1953), *Calvin on the Word and Sacrament*, Oliver and Boyd.

Robert Webber (1999), *Ancient–Future Faith*, Baker Books.

David Wells (1984), *The Person of Christ*, Crossway Books.

John Willison, *The Practical Works of John Willison* (1844), Blackie and Son.

Ben Witherington III (1994), *Paul's Narrative Thought World*, Westminster.

Ben Witherington III (1998), *The Acts of the Apostles*, Eerdmans.

Charles W. J. Withers (1998), *Urban Highlanders*, Tuckwell Press.

John Yates (1991), 'Role of the Holy Spirit in the Lord's Supper,' *Churchman*, Vol. 105, No. 4.

Persons Index

Subject Index